Second Edition

The Change

Previously Published By The Author:

The Miracle of Speech (1976)
Creating the Future (1994)

Second Edition

The
Change

DYNAMICS FOR CREATING YOUR PERSONAL AND BUSINESS FUTURE IN UNCERTAIN TIMES

Robert C. Grupe, Ph.D.

THE CHANGE, First Edition, Copyright © 1993, Robert C. Grupe

ISBN 0-963-2495-6-8

THE CHANGE, Second Edition, Copyright © 1994 by Robert C. Grupe. All rights reserved. Published in the United States of America by Koinonia Press. Printed by Whitehall Printing Co. No part of this book may be reproduced in any manner whatsoever without written permission except in the case of brief quotations embodied in critical articles or reviews. For information, address: Quality Productions, 4230 NW 36th, Oklahoma City, OK 73112.

Acknowledgments:

Sylvester, Kathleen, "The 2.4 Billion Dollar Suggestion Box." from *Governing Magazine,* May, 1992. Reprinted with permission *Governing Magazine.* Copyright © 1992.

Lawton, LaJoyce Chatwell, "Integrating Ethnic Cultures Into the Team Environment." Lawton International, 5838 Arabian Run, Indianapolis, IN 46208 Reprinted with permission. Copyright © 1993.

Art work, Pages 31, 65, 96, 137, 151, 157, 184, 268, and 273 reproduced from *Humorous Office Spot Illustrations* by Bob Censoni, Dover Publications, Copyright © 1987.

To my wife, Dusti, my best friend ever.

Contents

Chapter One   21
How We Got Here

Part I -- Our Business Roots   21
    Directive-Driven Industry   21
    Need For Quality   22
    The Historical View of Work   23
    The Typical Structure   24
    A New Look at The Structure   25
    Roles and Responsibilities   26
    "It's the Company Rule."   28
    It's About Time   30

Part II -- Our School Roots   33
    The Factory Roots of our Schools   34
    A Too True Real Life Story   36
    The Messages   37
    The Workplace/The Schoolroom   53

Chapter Two   55
Responding To The Challenge

    Old and New Views of Employees   59
    Someone Listened   61
    The Thermostat Syndrome   62
    The Envelope of Fear   63
    Work - A "Mushroom" Job?   65
    Empowering Your Staff   67
    The Front Line   70
    The Super Computer   71
    Make Haste Slowly   73
    Positive Learning   77

Chapter Two (Cont.)

Left Brain/Right Brain	79
Company Visioning	83
The Vision "Narration"	85
Vision and Emotion	89
New Information	91
The Power of Focus	98
Restructuring Habits	101
Personal Commitment	103
Depth of Communication	104
Breadth of Communication	105
Time Table for Change	106

Chapter Three — 111
Personal Dynamics for The Change

The Challenge	111

LifeChangers — 115

Program One: LifeValue — 115

A Look in the Mirror	115
The Past Can Be a Poor Future	118
The Value of Time	119
A New Perspective	120
Waiting for Happiness	120
Steps to Personal Growth	122
The Price of Personal Growth	125
The Value of Discipline	127
We All Reach "Crossroads"	128
A Journey to Our Potential	129

Program Two: LifePerceptions — 133

The Van Story	133
The Wrong Key	134
The Assumption Monster	136

Program Three: LifeFeelings   140
    The Teddy Bear Solution   140
    The Weird Sales Call   142
    Lessons Learned   143
    The "If Onlys"   144
    Happy Time Recipe   144

Program Four: LifeStress   147
    Modern Day Stress   147
    The Days of Og   148
    The Jogger Experience   149
    The Paradigm   149
    The Grocery Store From Hell   151
    The Seminar That Wasn't   154

Chapter Four   161
Creating The Change in Your Company
    Empowerment and Your Staff   163
    A New Dimension   164

Module One - Management   166
    Communication as Lifeblood   167
    Overview of Habits   170
    "Triggers"   171
    The Fear of Failure   175
    Use of Questionnaires   177
    "That's Not My Department"   179
    Steps to Visioning New Responses   180
    Setting Priorities   181
    The Company Meeting   183
    Committed to the Company Vision?   185
    Our Focus of Interest?   185
    The Issue of Separateness   186
    Organizing   186

Module Two - Management — 188
- Communicating the Company Vision — 188
- Departmental Competition — 189
- Vertical Chimneys — 191
- Personal Motivation — 192
- Fear-Based vs Joy of Creating — 192
- Three Phase Emotional Control — 194
- The Power of Ownership — 196
- Old Man Story — 197
- Handling Conflict — 197
- Sharing Power — 198
- Comfort Zone Listening — 199
- Breaking Down Generalizations — 201
- The Role of Representational Systems — 208
- The Creative "What if" Technique — 211
- Viewing Staff As Customers — 212
- Personality Profiles — 214
- The Unintentional Insult — 220
- Honoring Different Solutions — 221
- The Bicameral Brain — 222
- Our "Left-Brain Society" — 223
- Using the Separate Hemisperes — 230
- Whole Brain Synergy — 231
- Creating a Unity — 232
- "Hemispheric" Addicts — 233
- Utilizing Both Hemispheres — 235
- Qualities Of An Effective Manager — 252

Module Three - Staff — 255
- What is Communication? — 255
- Communication - The Lifeblood — 257
- Overview of Habits — 259
- What Are The "Triggers?" — 260
- "Trigger" Responses — 261
- Fear of Failure — 264

Module Three (Cont.)
    "That's Not My Department" — 266
    Visioning New Responses — 267
    Setting Priorities — 269
    The Company Meeting — 271
    How Committed Are You? — 272
    Attitude — 273
    Timetable — 274
    Creating Your Own "Job Security" — 275

Module Four - Staff — 279
    Communication Skills Training

Module Five - Management and Staff — 285
    Intergroup Communication Skills Training

Chapter Five — 291
Integrating Ethnic Cultures Into the Team Environment
    When English Is Second — 291
    Spelling and Word Meanings — 292
    Rank And Status — 293
    Ethics — 294
    Non-Verbal Communication — 294
    Concept Of Time — 295
    Space — 296
    Businesswomen — 296
    Yes, No, And Silence — 297
    Religion — 297
    What Will You Do? — 298
    Oops! — 298
    The Home Front — 299

Chapter Six — **301**
Technology With An Attitude
- The Power of Technology — 302
- The Dumbness Of Downsizing — 303
- Surviving Global Challenges — 305
- U.S. Economic Renewal — 307
- Higher Technology Or Lower Wages — 308
- What's Holding Technology Back — 309
- Technology And "The Knowledge Barrier" — 311
- "Shelf-Sitting" Technologies — 314
- The Demise of U. S. Technical Innovation — 314
- A Solution — 316

Chapter Seven — **321**
Overview of Right/Left Brain Research
- Historical Hemispheric Transition — 323
- Contemporary Reliance — 326

Appendix — **333**
Additional Training Materials
60 Pages of Stories and Illustrations of Empowerment Concepts

FOREWORD

The first step in implementing quality is to change the culture. Dr. Robert Grupe very ably addresses the inhibitors of change and provides many concepts and examples for changing paradigms and managing the process of organizational change. *The Change* should be read by anyone who wants to be part of a winning team and who realizes that work, at whatever level, should be satisfying and successful.

The Change is easily read as the writing style allows the reader to see the pitfalls which effect the implementation of concepts related to continuous improvement.

Dr. Grupe's message is very appropriate for anyone managing and working in these turbulent times. He emphasizes the habit patterns, beliefs and perceptions which are so prevalent in American business and the actions which must be taken for all employees to be involved in a productive and satisfying culture.

Managers, especially, need to read and understand the implications for leadership style presented in this book. When readers accept and use the approaches to establishing a vision and its implementation which are presented in *The Change* - the benefits for the user and the organization will be enormous.

William J. Nelson, Ph.D.
Associate Vice-Provost
Center for Organizational Improvement
Oklahoma State University - Oklahoma City Campus

ACKNOWLEDGEMENTS

It would, of course, be impossible to list everyone who has influenced the formation of the information contained in this book. Ideas, germinated over a period of time, are molded by coming into contact with many circumstances and people.

In addition to providing extensive formatting and editing, Dr. Peter S. Pierro, Professor of Education at Oklahoma University, has contributed significantly to the text of this work, especially in Chapter One. As in the past, he continues to challenge the author to think in new pastures and greater depths relating to the important issues covered in this writing. He and I will collaborate again in the near future on what will surely be a major work linking the shortcomings of our educational system to the deficient learning strategies that make American business too often top heavy and process oriented.

The five module quality cultural change program presented in this book has been extensively field-tested through Oklahoma State University-Oklahoma City. Through the invaluable cooperation of Dr. William J. Nelson, Associate Vice-Provost, Center for Organizational Improvement at OSU-OKC, many groups of CEO's., Business owners and employees have gone through this cultural change process - providing essential feedback along the way.

To Dr. James Hooper, Provost; OSU-OKC, a debt of gratitude for his visionary leadership in the building of a wonderful bridge between OSU-OKC and the business community. Such powerful bridges are also being built by Oklahoma City University President Dr. Jerald Walker, University of Central Oklahoma President George Nigh, and University of Oklahoma President David Boren. Without such priceless interconnections being formed nationwide, *The Change* as outlined in this book would be much more difficult to achieve.

Theory must be tempered with much pragmatism. Life is a story to be sure, but unless it is really lived and lessons learned - the story is never true. My dear friend, Charles Stalsworth, a "Ph.D." in the deepest sense of the word through life experience, has helped me see that behavior and vision must work together. The best laid plans with no action - are no plans at all. And action with no meaning soon becomes ritual with no inner change of heart. Let us have a reason to do what we are to accomplish. Then, let us "faith" the new habits and actions for awhile if necessary. Those new actions will truly become us if there is a deep enough reason for *The Change* to happen.

I must make a special mention of my marketing director, Jim Keating. Jim has made the word "blessing" real in my professional life. Having an excellent product without effective marketing is a totally incomplete cycle. How often does someone read a newspaper article about a book (the first edition of *The Change* published in the fall of 1993), purchase the book, and then after reading it, respond by offering his full-time dedicated service to the author? Jim left his upper management position with a successful business and joined me in a mission to bring *The Change* to the business world. It takes a uniquely talented and perceptive individual to market and educate clients relative to the attitudinal and behavioral implications of business growth.

Robert C. Grupe, Ph.D.
Oklahoma City, OK
November, 1994

INTRODUCTION

Human relationship changes are not just intellectual maneuvering. They involve transformation at a deeper level. They can be promoted by a shift in the system that encourages behavioral change - but for long term shifting there must be a guiding vision, a reason for the change and a clear freedom for the employee to be an active participant in the change process. REAL COMPANY CHANGE CAN ONLY BE DONE FROM THE TOP DOWN THROUGH A MODELING PROCESS.

The process, in the best of worlds, is a challenge as Anthony Carnevale emphasizes in *America and the New Economy*. "Words fail to communicate the depth and difficulty inherent in the normative aspects of quality. Deep-seated changes in human perspectives and commitments and a willingness to take responsibility are easily advocated but not easily done."

"70 per cent of all Total Quality Management initiatives fail," laments Jim Clemmer in *Firing on All Cylinders*.

Quality initiatives often fail because intellectually the company wants the change leading to more employee participation and responsibility but it becomes defensive and nervous when eventually confronted with the need to change radically their personal perception of the role and potential of the worker.

Even in successful programs there are belief system "plateaus" that management faces "but the majority of efforts are blocked before they reach this point (encroaching on domains that have been defined as 'Management Prerogatives.' - after an initial round of successes they reach a 'plateau' discouraged at every turn from proceeding to more ambitious projects." Charles Heckscher, author of *The New Unionism* explains.

I wanted to produce a book that would answer the questions I had as a company employee: Why, in our society, does work become so draining? Is this the way it has to be? As an employee, I often thought, Why is it that my hobbies and outside activities seem to become so interesting as opposed to job activities? A seemingly moot question. But is the answer really as obvious as it might seem? What are the dynamics or "mind-mechanics" involved in our perspective of work?

Chapter One paints a simple background of how we got to the work environment in which we now exist. Dr. Peter S. Pierro joins me in this chapter as he describes some of the influences of our public school system in this environment.

Chapter Two explains the role of visioning and emotional commitment to creating enjoyable focus in whatever we do. Once we understand how our mind works we face a choice; to fall in love with what we are currently doing or go find an area of work that matches our desires and talents. Otherwise we will continue to live with the vast emotional separation between "work" and "desired" activities.

NO COMPANY CAN CHANGE UNLESS THE PEOPLE IN IT CHANGE INDIVIDUALLY

Chapter Three is a four-part (Workbook style) program taking the participant through a series of challenges to determine what they want out of life, what they expect of themselves, and what they expect of others. The primary focus is on each person's freedom and power to see their habit patterns and then to change what they don't like - to cease being victims of their habits and begin taking control over their personal growth.

Chapter Four then allows management to take the company through a five module training series based upon bringing long-standing Staff/Management attitudes to the table for open and honest dialogue - moving the "grapevine" into the official line of communication for perhaps the first time.

Chapter Five, contributed by LaJoyce Lawton, addresses some of the basic challenges faced by companies involved in integrating other cultures into a team environment.

Chapter Six, contributed by Dr. Steven Paley, extends the challenge to integrate appropriate technical expertise and risk-taking so as to move the United States ahead in the global marketplace.

Chapter Seven offers an overview of background research on brain hemispheric attributes in relation to "mind-mechanics."

Additional Training Materials provides trainers and managers stories and illustrations they can use in inviting everyone in the company to explore their growth potential and to understand better the processes of change and how the stress of change can be managed.

REFERENCES

Carnevale, Anthony P. *America and the New Economy,* Josey-Bass, San Francisco, CA, 1991.

Clemmer, Jim. *Firing on All Cylinders,* Business One Irwin, Homewood, IL, 1992.

Heckscher, Charles C. *The New Unionism - Employee Involvement in the Changing Corporation,* Basic Books, Inc., New York, NY, 1988.

―― Second Edition ――

The Change

A Right Time For Everything

When we come to a time of success in our life, why do we so often regret the past?

When we achieve a success, why do we so often interrogate ourselves with questions like "Why didn't I figure this out sooner?" or " Why didn't I start doing this earlier?" We will never know. That's the answer. We will never know.

For us at a time of success to dwell on why it didn't happen sooner - is like asking how big is the universe. It's anybody's guess. Maybe we didn't achieve this success earlier because it just wasn't time. Maybe we were not ready. Maybe our skills were not quite sufficient. Maybe we would not have handled the success as well before.

Maybe there is indeed a right time for everything to happen. Usually that right time is when ability meets opportunity. The key to enjoying the successes that we achieve is to have the wisdom to continue to appreciate and respond to opportunities when they are brought into our view.

1 How We Got Here
Part I - Our Business Roots

> *I think and think for months and years.*
> *Ninety-nine times the conclusion is false.*
> *The hundredth time I am right.*
> Albert Einstein

Historically, right after World War II, business and industry had it made in the United States. The Three Stooges could have been running our factories and we still would have sold everything we made because we had virtually no competition. Those were the boom years. It was during that time that management by directive seemed to work so well.

Even while W. Edwards Deming was teaching a quality team approach during WWII to mobilize the ingenuity and efforts necessary to produce the war machinery to meet the challenge in record time, quality was not an imperative in the typical workplace. Years later, Dr. Deming commented that his major error during the war was in teaching quality to American professionals while leaving the company owners and decision makers out of the training loop.

Directive-Driven Industry

Frederick Winslow Taylor, who published *Principles of Scientific Management* in 1911, would have been elated to see the mammoth

The Change

factories and the industrial base that was built in the United States between 1942 and mid 1960's. While Taylor's prescription for the workplace replaced craftsmanship with machine efficiency, it brought wealth to the nation. In many cases, after the Allied Victory, business owners said, in so many words, "Quality? We have quality inspection. What we really need is to put out every item we can as quickly as we can because we can't make them fast enough to meet demand. If something's bad, we'll fix it later."

In a word, Frederick Taylor won that round. Mass production - Park your brain at the door - Give us your warm body - Do what we tell you and nothing else. This served us well in many ways as long as we were the only game in town. Then the world started to change. The sun began to set in the East. Between 1970 and 1990, the wages of the typical American worker declined in real dollars and the wage erosion continues. According to the Economic Policy Institute, wages for blue-collar males fell 5.9 percent in the four years since 1989. Income losses for white-collar males, though not as severe, were 2.4 percent.

Need For Quality

Quality is becoming the imperative because buyers are gaining more power. They can now shop world wide to get goods and services - they are not restricted to one manufacturer or one country. As the buyer is given more choices, he becomes more demanding and quality becomes more essential. But quality is not the finished product. Quality control never controlled quality, unless there is really a Santa Claus and reindeer can fly. Quality is our *Attitude*, along with *Effectively Focused Internal Communication* and *Knowledge* of consumer needs and expectations and methods for satisfying, exceeding, those needs. In that order. *Quality* is holistic. It's a smoothly functioning system analogous to the human body. More, much more, about that in Chapter Two.

How We Got Here

The Historical View of Work

Do you know what Frederick Taylor did to my father? When I was four years old (1952), I can remember my dad arriving home from work on a Friday evening. "Well, Son," the big burly man would say "I've put in my time. Now, let's go to the park and have fun." We went to the park and we had fun.

Over the years of hearing "I've put in my hours, done my time," I began to wonder if perhaps work wasn't the closest thing to hell a person could experience before death. My father did his time. Once I asked him if he had been in jail. He said " No, Son. Just at work" but he didn't smile.

Many baby boomers, like myself, ages 30 to 45 have such memories. Work is a drain, a drudge, something to be put off if possible. It's something to be avoided. It's monotonous. It is no fun, at all.

If I were to walk up to you and say that work can indeed be as exciting, invigorating and rewarding as play - you might laugh me out of the room. We have been programmed with a certain set of beliefs as to how we should act or react as both employees or as management in a business setting. We easily become creatures of habit.

Most of us are victims of the biggest lie to ever affect our life. We have wordlessly been told that work cannot be enjoyed - this activity that affects our lives eight hours a day, five days a week. A lie that touches that much of our life is Big Time. Serious. Let's analyze then evaluate some of our belief systems relating to business so that we can seek some new options that may open new horizons to this thing called WORK.

The Change

The Typical Structure

Let's look for a moment at the typical structure of an organization; the kind of organization that produces the work and the worker of the Past and Present:

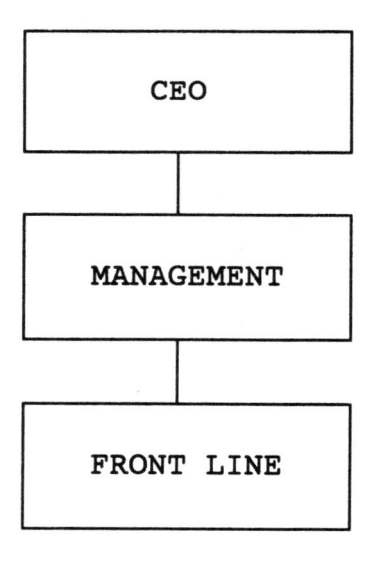

```
┌─────────────────┐
│      CEO        │
└────────┬────────┘
         │
┌────────┴────────┐
│   MANAGEMENT    │
└────────┬────────┘
         │
┌────────┴────────┐
│   FRONT LINE    │
└─────────────────┘
```

We start with the CEO/owner, and then we usually see several levels of management and, finally, the front line individuals - the people who are making it happen. Those who are producing the goods and services.

How We Got Here

A New Look at The Structure

Now let's look at this same structure in a new and dynamic way. If we strip the veneer from the system, we can identify the ultimate and unique purposes of each of the levels:

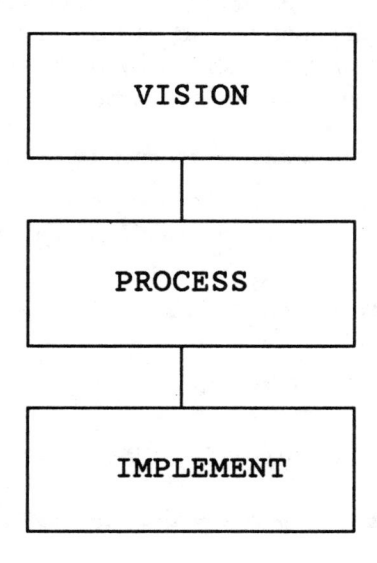

```
┌─────────────────┐
│     VISION      │
└────────┬────────┘
         │
┌────────┴────────┐
│     PROCESS     │
└────────┬────────┘
         │
┌────────┴────────┐
│    IMPLEMENT    │
└─────────────────┘
```

We must have company vision...

Who is the person or the people responsible for the vision of that company? - Who creates it?

What's going to happen five years, ten years from now in the business?

The Change

Roles and Responsibilities

Obviously the ownership: the CEO and upper management are instrumental in looking at the economic, business climate in the country and around the world in order to formulate the vision.
Then, typically, it has been the middle management taking the responsibility for developing the specific departmental processes. How do we reach, actualize the vision? How, specifically, do we make it our objective for a year from now, three years or five years down the road? Management has historically developed the processes that are then implemented by those on the front line who are directed to make the processes work.

Characteristics of a Directive-Driven Culture

- *Little Upward Feedback*

- *Feedback is Altered*

- *If The Process is Not Working - Work Harder*

Typically there has been little upward feedback. After all, what is the job of the front line person? It's to do. White collar think - blue collar do. It's management by directive from "above." As one employee bluntly told me, "They asked me many times to park my brain at the door and get to work."

Also, in many cases upward feedback is altered through politics and desire to please the next upper echelon with whatever information is being presented. If the process is not working many times the

How We Got Here

signal to those on the front line is "We designed the processes correctly. Just work harder."

When I show this next headline as a graphic slide to groups and organizations, I often get chuckles:

Too Many Rules Create Madness!!

When we talk about cultural change, we're dealing with an entire system within a company -an ecology. For an employee to change a concept or an attitude, there is a concurrent demand for reciprocal action by management to begin to reflect differently on the process and to perceive the employee differently.

Whether we have viewed it this way in the past or not - a company is like a family. If it is a dysfunctional family, just one person who is "out of whack" can affect the entire unit. The system, the unit, may need to change in order to allow a greater number of options and ownership of activities for everyone involved.

The employee is not at fault. Management is not at fault. It's really nobody's "fault" because all of us are living and dwelling and working the best we can within a system that may need to be rejuvenated - that may need to be retooled to make it a more effective system into which we can channel our energies.

> *LAW: It's not the amount of energy that we expend in trying to do any particular thing, it's the direction of the energy and the effectiveness of the system in which the energy is being utilized.*

The Change

"It's the Company Rule."

Let me recount a personal story about customer service that illustrates how too many rules create madness. I went into a small shop on a Saturday with two of my children. It was a little thrift shop filled with all kinds of toys. One of my children came up to me with a cute little creature - the elastic type that allows you to bend their arms and legs and create all kinds of little monster shapes. It was called a Gorple or something like that. The little fellow wanted the toy in the worst way. I went up to the front desk and told the clerk I wanted to buy the Gorple. The person at the counter looked at me, looked at the toy and said "I'm sorry, I can't sell that to you."

Well, I thought to myself - this is interesting. What's the purpose of having a shop if you don't sell things to customers? Hmm! This is worth pursuing. "Why can't you sell me this Gorple?" I quizzed. He replied "Wasn't that in a plastic bag with a bunch of other little figurines?" "Yes, It was," I replied, "The bag had broken and several had fallen out. I just picked this one up and my child wants it."

"Well" he intoned, "Our policy here is that if the bags are ever broken" and he emphasized *broken* while giving me a hard stare. Did you break it, sir? I think you did, sir. His stare said. "Then none of these can be sold until they are all properly rebagged."

Well, it's a Saturday. I'm happy. My kids are with me, so I locked eyes with the clerk and said with a smile, "What did the whole bag cost?" He instantly replied " $3.50 for the bag." So I said "I'll tell you what I'll do. I'll pay you $3.50 for this one Gorple, this one little rubber figurine, and you can do whatever you want with the others in the broken bag. How about that?"

With strained tolerance he replied "I just explained to you that we can't sell any of those until they are rebagged. That's the policy of the company." Before I had a chance to voice any other ideas or, perhaps, ask what the shop was in business for - the young man stood a little straighter and announced, "By the way, you don't need to talk to anyone else in the store - because I'm the manager."

As I walked out, I thought to myself, I'm going to use that illustration and take the risk of offending management for a very important reason. So many times a company begins with a vision. Later, as certain rules and regulations are laid down that were maybe reflective of that initial vision, a paralysis of policy occurs (in scientific terms: Processus Petrificationus). Rules begin to generate a life of their own and become divorced from the real needs of that company or the real mission to serve customers and thereby make a profit. It certainly would have been more advantageous for that clerk to have sold me that one figurine for the price of that whole sack and then do whatever was needed with the broken sack. But remember - Rules are Rules. Too many rules in an organization when it becomes divorced from it's real vision, from it's mission, create madness.

Insanity Is Doing The Same Thing Expecting Different Results

Psychologists who work with rats and motivation are struck with their persistence on the one hand and their pragmatism on the other. If a rat goes through a maze and reaches his goal, perhaps a piece of cheese, he will be all set to go again. After a number of successful, rewarding trials, the experimenter may cease putting food at the end of the maze. The rat will run the maze and be a bit put out that no cheese is present. If he is run through again, he will make another attempt and the cheese had better be there. If it isn't, the rat will terminate his maze running and it will be very difficult, possibly impossible, for the experimenter to get him back in the mood.

The Change

Contrast that to people who have the stamina and desire to keep after a goal, even when they never reach it with their present methods of operation. As humans, however, we have the ability to change our processes, our methods, to make choices.

If you are interested in sports, you probably will understand this football fan, the hero of this story. Most colleges have that special rivalry that leads to a major game each year. In this case: Oklahoma University and Texas University. The evening before the big game, our hero who had a little too much to drink exited from a Dallas lounge. As he staggered out, he walked directly into a street lamp pole and the impact knocked him over. He lay there for a moment gathering his wits and then got up again to walk away. He walked directly into the lamp post again. For the second time he lay on the ground, immobilized. Finally, up again on shaky legs with a little cut on his forehead from his two collisions, he tried again to walk away. You guessed it - into the pole once more he went, flattening him again. As some of the bystanders walked away, they heard him mumbling a few words, kind of sobbing, over and over again. "It's no use" he was heard saying "they've got me surrounded."

I've worked and counseled with so many companies that keep going in the same direction and hitting the same roadblocks because they are experiencing a paralysis of process. They have developed certain ways of implementing certain things. Certain processes have been developed at a distance from the actual functioning of the production of some goods or the giving of a service. What is the solution? Hold on to your hat when we get to Chapter Two.

It's About Time

Have we inherited our concept of time from our parents? After several years of extensive research, I've come up with a most

How We Got Here

exciting discovery -perhaps the most monumental development in the understanding of time since Einstein enunciated the Theory of Relativity. I have determined that the amount of time between 4:00 p.m. and 5:00 p.m. on Friday is actually 2 hours and 12 minutes. Many workers have secretly guessed that for most of their working life, right?

What happens at 4:45 p.m. on Friday? The body lingers, doesn't it? - But the mind is gone. That is, in vision, we are already where we want to be that evening or noon on Saturday. We're not focused on our job as well, are we? What do we really want? What we want is recreation time. We want to go out and do something we can fall in love with or have already fallen in love with: a hobby, a pastime, some activity that is ours - that we own. 8:00 a.m. on Monday morning will arrive soon enough and until that time, we are going to live.

One researcher in the Behavioral Science field commented that while working with companies, he has seen employees leave after eight hours of work and then play basketball, football, baseball - some game or sport - for three or four hours that evening. They would use ten times the amount of energy as expended during the workday and were having what seemed like a hundred times more fun. American educators Eleanor Clancy and Richard Diggs write, "Our nation's productivity could easily double if 70 percent of our workers enjoyed going to work each day."

The Change

What are the elements that cause the absence of desire or interest in what's happening within the typical organization? Who is really being shortchanged? Are the sources of our problems entirely within our work/corporate structures or shall we explore some of our roots, including the first experiences we have with an institutional structure?

Attitude Pays

Regardless how often you receive a paycheck from your employer, you pay yourself every day with the most important currency in the world.

The currency with which we pay ourselves every day is the attitude we choose that day. That attitude will determine how other people react to us all day because they will mirror our attitude. Our attitude will determine how willing we are to learn, how willing we are to step out-make mistakes and try new things. Our attitude will determine how persistent we will be in whatever we are doing. It will determine how we cope with stress and setbacks which happen to all of us. It is the X factor that will determine how we interpret the world.

Some pay themselves daily with a miserly currency that sees the world as a cold, deadly place where no one can be trusted, or as a sticker on a beatup car read, "Life is hell and then you die." Others pay themselves with the rich attitude currency in which the world is a cornucopia of opportunities, inhabited by people ready to offer encouragement - an atmosphere filled with learning experiences and fun.

How We Got Here

Part II -- Our School Roots

Recently, Robert Fulghum wrote a marvelous book, entitled *All I Really Need to Know I Learned in Kindergarten.* In the opening narrative he described the good stuff he learned; being on time, doing his best, and being honest. These messages are great for all areas of our lives including our work with Total Quality Management.

However, there are other things that we learned as children in school that may not be so helpful and fulfilling. I guess you could describe this section as the reverse side of the coin, *What I Learned in School That Has Hindered My Growth in the Adult World.* This section is intended to help give us insight into the experiences that children have in our schools - it is far from an indictment of our public school system - the greatest educational system the world has ever known. There are enough critics of this unique and great system - most of them being quite ignorant of what classroom teachers do and how children learn.

Rather, I intend to suggest how we might put the lessons of our classrooms and the messages that they have left with us into some kind of perspective, especially in terms of the effects they may have on our adult lives. And, most important in terms of the theme of this book, the effects they have on our operations relative to TQM.

You will recognize that many of these messages may have also been transmitted from other sources; your home, church, clubs, sports teams, and unfortunately from some of your past and present work-places. The team "Teacher" can be broadened to include anyone who has been influential in your personal and professional growth.

Part II was written by Dr. Peter S. Pierro, Professor of Education, Oklahoma University

The Change

We were given these messages by our teachers to keep us safe, to direct us in our learning, or simply to keep "order" in the classroom. These same messages in our adult life can cause us real problems if we don't interpret them in a new light and then deal with them proactively and positively.

An additional problem arises in that these same messages are repeated and reinforced in the workplace by supervisors, bosses, and co-workers. As we list and discuss them you will recognize them being delivered daily in your office or shop. They, in fact, are given new life and new appearances of truth by sheer repetitition and by the fact that they are given new emphasis and strength by new superordinates as one is introduced into the workplace.

The Factory Roots of our Schools

How did we get here? Perhaps one important factor in the origin is the historical fact that our present public school system was patterned after the factory system. During the Industrial Revolution, most of the rural schools were replaced by city schools as workers moved into the city to take jobs in the factories. The rural school, the country one-room and two-room schools, demanded that the children be independent, self-disciplining, self-sufficient learners - they were trained to eventually supervise and develop their family farms; each child had to be a leader.

The task of the city school on the other hand was to prepare people to work in the factories so it developed a model that was hierarchical in nature with the Superintendent, the Principal, the Teacher, and the Child set up in the same order as the factory setup diagrammed by Dr. Grupe earlier in this chapter. The school buildings, themselves, were modeled after the factories and to this day our schools generally retain that architectural design. The curriculum, likewise, moved more and more toward the preparation of children to get and keep a job.

How We Got Here

The evolution and development of our schools has continued up to this time and what we now have is a convoluted, confused system which is increasingly unable to create Vision, determine Process, and effect Implementation. The common school organization in simple form looks like this:

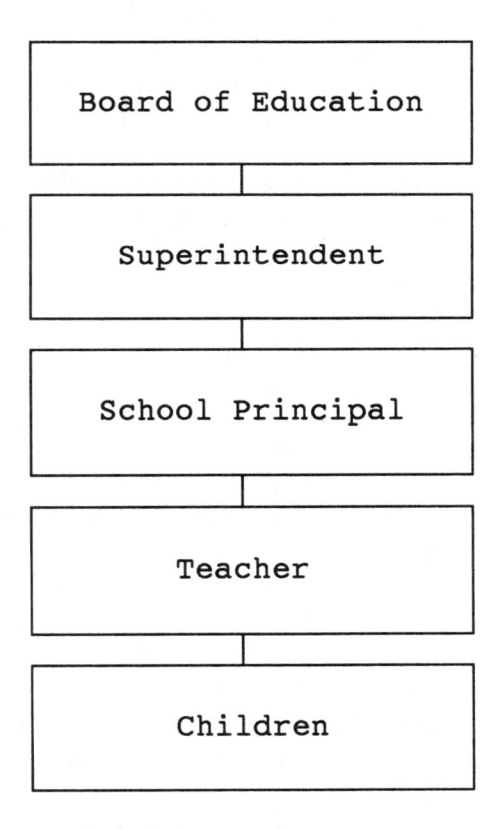

```
┌─────────────────────────┐
│   Board of Education    │
└─────────────────────────┘
            │
┌─────────────────────────┐
│     Superintendent      │
└─────────────────────────┘
            │
┌─────────────────────────┐
│    School Principal     │
└─────────────────────────┘
            │
┌─────────────────────────┐
│        Teacher          │
└─────────────────────────┘
            │
┌─────────────────────────┐
│       Children          │
└─────────────────────────┘
```

Note that in this case the Consumer and the Product (the children) are the same. Note also that there are many other power elements that are involved in all decision-making areas; these elements include parents, State and National Departments of Education, Parent-Teacher groups, civic and religious groups, newspaper critics, etc., etc.

The Change

Tom Peters stated that any organization with more than four levels of function was in trouble. Grupe also earlier demonstrated that in addition to the levels in an organization, it is essential that we be aware of the functions and responsibilities at each level. In the hierarchical model shown above with all of the power elements exerting their influence, it is very difficult to determine who has the power and the responsibility for Vision. The Teacher, who should be concerned with all areas; Vision, Process, and Implementation; more often than not is left out of the power cycle.

In the midst of this, and I'll use the term advisedly, confusion, messages which are designed to maintain this hierarchical order are transmitted to the children by the Teacher. Sometimes these messages are not in the best interest of the children. After my experiences over more than 40 years in public school service, I generally get ill when I hear someone say, "After all, the schools are here for the children" because I have seen so many decisions made by the powers that be that are for the benefit of everyone in the system except the children.

Do these messages that are transmitted by teachers actually have a strong impact on the development of our children? Read on ---

A Too True Real Life Story

Several years ago, I was leading one of my favorite workshops for senior citizens. This workshop is entitled *What Do You Want To Be When You Grow Up?* and we look at our station in life and the goals we still have, hidden or out in the open, and what we may choose to do about them. One of my early exercises begins with this statement written on the board, "I would like to _____, **but** _____.
I then invite the participants to fill in the blanks and then to share if the spirit moves them. The "but" in this sentence invites one to give all the reasons, or excuses, for not doing what one would like

How We Got Here

to do. For example, "I would like to read classic books, **but** I don't have the time."

In this instance, Mrs. Anders, a bright, young lady (I later learned that she was 92 years old) volunteered and said, "I would like to paint, but my second grade teacher told me that I had no artistic ability." "Wow," I said to myself, "What a great example to make my point." I then changed the sentence on the board to read, "I would like to _____, **and** _____.

The "and" invited her to list the actions that would enable her to realize her goal. We filled the first blank with "paint' and then, in the second blank listed the possible actions:

   ...I will take an art course.
   ...I will buy an easel, paints, canvases, etc.
   ...I will set up a place to paint in the house.
   ...I will set up a time schedule.
   ...I will join an art group.

I would like to say that Mrs. Anders went right to work and fulfilled her dream, but it didn't happen. Every session thereafter, I asked if she had begun her new journey and she would just sadly shake her head. The message she had integrated over a period of 80+ years was so strong that she was not able to change it even though she wanted to do so. After all, the message had come from her second grade teacher who was, in her eyes, omniscient.

The Messages

Some of these messages come to us from our teachers, others are created by us as a result of those messages. The source is unimportant - the message itself and its acceptance are critical. Remember that any message that someone lays on you becomes the same as your own message when you accept it as fact. If

The Change

someone says you are "lazy", you have the choice of accepting it or rejecting it. If you accept it, it becomes your message and your subconscious mind will register that you are indeed "lazy".

Our task, as adults, is to recognize these messages, reevaluate them, come to realize what they actually mean in our lives at this time, and then accept them or to actively replace them with new and more positive messages. Here are some of the messages from my school experiences:

Making mistakes is bad and must be avoided at any cost.

Jimmy has just gotten his arithmetic paper back from the teacher. The paper is literally dripping with red marks. Jimmy being human crumples up the paper and throws it into the waste paper basket. Miss Taken shouts, "Jimmy, get that paper out of the trash right now. How are you going to improve if you don't correct your mistakes?"

Elsewhere in this book, Dr. Grupe has narrated a true story in which a technician made a mistake costly to the company and how it was perceived by his boss and treated as a learning experience rather than something to be avoided without fail. I believe that making mistakes is an integral, essential part of learning - if you are not making mistakes, you are not pushing the limits and not growing. If Jimmy is not making mistakes in his arithmetic work, he is not being challenged.

Another important aspect of making mistakes is that it tells the teacher, boss, mentor where the learner, subordinate, student can be assisted and helped to grow. "Ah, Betty's quote on the Peregrine printing job hasn't allowed enough funding for the special handling it requires. I've noticed that she has made the same type of error in previous quotes. I'll sit down with her and show her how that has to be figured."

Adult Interpretations of This Message:
- *I must do everything right.*
- *I must do everything right the first time.*
- *If I take a chance and make a mistake, I'm in bad trouble.*
- *Don't take chances - no risking.*
- *Someone 'above' me will always be watching me and catching me whenever I make a mistake. (NIGYYSOB)*

(In *Games People Play,* Eric Berne describes a game in which the boss, spouse, teacher, or whoever, watches like a hawk in order to catch the victim making a mistake and then shouts gleefully, "Now I've Got You, You S.O.B.!" - NIGYYSOB)

My friend, Barbara Davies, gave a speech at our Toastmasters, International Club a few years ago entitled, *Everything Worth Doing is Worth Doing Poorly...At First.* We all blinked, and then moved along with her as she went on to demonstrate the wisdom of that statement with examples from her own life, e.g, learning to drive a car. Did you do everything well the first time you drove a car? No mistakes? Your Dad said WHAT to you when you tried to shift gears without stepping on the clutch?

Don't take risks.

Jimmy couldn't avoid the arithmetic assignment, but he could avoid volunteering in any situation in which he had a choice. The best way to avoid making mistakes is to not take the risks inherent in the more difficult tasks. Young children don't understand that very well and they will get into trouble by blundering along trying out the world until the negative reactions catch up to them. Then many of them back off and stop playing the game. Adventurous souls keep taking risks and they come to understand that you often have

The Change

to suffer the consequences - but not all of us have the courage and stamina of a Thomas Edison; who, by the way, had a very unhappy school experience.

College students by this time have psyched out the system and are experts at dealing with it. After all, they must protect their Grade Point Averages (GPA). Follow me into a college classroom and watch the experienced experts at work. It's the first day of the new term and the professor has just handed out the course syllabus.

Professor: You will note that there will be a mid-term exam and a final exam. There will be a term paper due on May 3.
Student A: What percent of our grade will the exams count?
Professor: The midterm will be 25%, the final 35%, the term paper will be 25%. The remaining 15% is attendance, class participation, and short quizzes.
Student B: Are those 'pop' quizzes or will you warn us each time?
Professor: Quizzes will be announced the week before they're given.
Student C: What will the exams be based on?
Professor: On all of the text and outside reading, but mainly on my lectures.

This will go on until all the rules are established including the desired length of the term paper, type of tests that will be given, if extra credit work is possible, etc., etc., etc. Some students may see the handwriting on the wall and the next day the registrar is kept busy processing 'drop' slips.

Adult Interpretations of This Message:
- *Never volunteer to do anything. (Personally, I really learned that when I was in the Navy)*
- *Everything has to be done by my Boss's rules; I can't be creative or have ideas of my own.*
- *I have to protect myself from people who are 'above' me.*
- *If I don't like the rules, I had better move on to something else.*

How We Got Here

Do what you're told to do, when you're told to do it, the way you were told to do it and you'll be O.K.

This is pretty self-explanatory - the teacher is in charge and the student is to take and follow orders - that's the way it is. For some reason, (usually stated, "After all, they're just kids and they can't make decisions for themselves - we have to do it for them.") we don't work on developing leadership and independence in our children. We are looking for good followers, or as indicated by behavior modifying teachers, "I like the way Mary is working on her assignment" hoping that the other children will want similar recognition by imitating the way Mary is acting.

Common comments heard in the workplace are:
   From the Boss, "Leave your head at the door when you come to work. I'll do the thinking around here." and "Don't ask questions, just follow the plan."
   From co-workers, "It's not your job to question the bosses." and "Who died and made you Boss?"

Adult Interpretations of This Message:
- *The Boss makes the decisions - I carry them out.*
- *It's not my job to question what the bosses tell me to do.*
- *If something goes wrong, don't blame me - it wasn't my idea!*

Sit still and be quiet.

Let's look into some of the rooms in this school. Ah! here's Mr. Bates in our 5th grade. He is a good "disciplinarian" - he runs a tight ship. The Principal likes him because he doesn't send any kids down to his office. Most of the children's parents are happy because their children are learning "discipline." As we walk into his class we see children sitting very still in their seats and there is no talking, whispering, or other forms of movement or noise. That is,

The Change

nothing except the voice and movement of Mr. Bates. Oh, yes, there is something else present - fear.

The child's role in the learning process and in most of the operations in a classroom is a passive or at most reactive one. Angie does only what she is allowed or told to do by the teacher. Even within those guidelines, she often has to ask for permission, "Mr. Bates, may I sharpen my pencil?" "You were supposed to sharpen pencils before class." "But I've written a whole spelling lesson and my pencil is dull." "The rule says that you sharpen pencils before class, but I'll let you do it in this case."

Adult Interpretations of This Message:
- *If I don't make waves, I won't get into trouble.*
- *I don't do anything unless and until the Boss tells me to do it.*
- *If I don't know what to do, I'm safe if I do nothing.*

What you learn in one place has nothing to do with learning about something in any other place.

As a curriculum "expert", I am always amazed at how our schools have managed to separate what is learned in one subject from what is learned in all the other subjects. For example, Mrs. Conerton's third grade class has just completed an excellent lesson in Science on the objects that are attracted to and not attracted to magnets. The children working in pairs tested their magnets on everything in the room, one child using the magnet and the other taking notes in their science notebooks. She completed the session with a categorizing process and the children arrived at the generalization that magnets attract only metal objects, including other magnets, but not all metal objects, e.g. pennies and dimes.

They have experientially and meaningfully learned the concepts and words; magnet, magnetic, attract, repel, north pole, south pole, metal, non-metal, category, groups, research, and experiment. And now Miss Conerton, following the school schedule and curriculum guide, says, "Get your Spelling books out and let's look at the new words for this week. The words are light, might, bright, slight, tight, ..." The lesson for the week is the \ight\ grapheme resulting in the long i sound.

By the way, if the children misspell any words in their Science notebooks, they will remind Mrs. Conerton that, "You shouldn't take any points off because this is Science, not Spelling."

Are these kids smart, or what?

Adult Interpretations of This Message:
- *I'm a tool maker - I don't know anything about the painting department.*
- *That's not my department.*
- *That's not in my job description.*
- *I just do my job and let the other guys do their jobs.*
- *I don't have stock in this company - I just work here.*

You're not O.K. until you learn everything.

Being a pole vaulter or high jumper must be psychologically very difficult because every contest is ended by a failure. Jorge won the high school dual meet with a leap of 6 feet 3 inches, but he failed to make 6 feet 4 inches three times. So it is in school - no matter how well you do in math, you don't know everything and sooner or later you are confronted with failure.

Instead of celebrating our victories, we are constantly confronted with the message, "You may have learned this, but you're still not O. K." (The message should be, "You have learned this and next time you will learn something else that is even better.") This is called **Encouragement**. On the contrary, school vocabulary is full

The Change

of Illness Messages and Terms, e.g., Testing, Diagnosis, Remedial, Prescriptive. These words are used in hospitals and doctor's office to indicate that someone is sick and needs help in order to be cured. In the school environment, do they mean that someone is not O. K. and needs help in order to be cured?

Many times teachers have heard children say, "I keep making mistakes; I guess I'll never learn." The teacher immediately says, "Oh, no, you can do it - I'll help you," because that's what teachers believe and work for. I hope they never change.

Adult Interpretations of This Message:
- *I'll never learn what the Boss knows.*
- *I'm O. K. right where I am; I don't want a promotion.*
- *This is my level of ability; I'm just that good and no better no matter what I do.*

This message is sometimes based on the Fear of Succeeding Syndrome - I can handle this level with some success, but I'm afraid of what will happen if I try to go higher. Observe that successful basketball coach in that small town in Texas. He has found a good level of accomplishment, but he has never gotten to the state finals in his division. His subconscious mind is telling him, "If you get to the top of this division, you will have to go on to the tougher division and I don't think you can be a success there. You had better level out here."

Don't be different from the other kids in the class.

"Why can't you be like Gerald?" - You must always be compared to the others in the class. People who are different are called nerds, retards, and other bad names. I sometimes wonder how Bill Gates, Neil Simon, Neil Diamond, and Robert Oppenheimer did in our schools. I know how Albert Einstein struggled in the

German schools - which reminds me that much of the roots of our schools are found in the German school system, especially the theories and practices of Johann Friederich Herbart which were brought to the United States by Charles and Frank McMurry.

Adult Interpretations of the Message:
- *Dress, act, speak, and behave as others do so you will blend in.*
- *Creative people are strange and I certainly don't want to be called strange so I had better not be creative.*
- *Don't rock the boat. If you do, it'll probably sink right out from under you.*

If you don't have your work done, someone will fix it for you."

This is the Codependency Model - There is a strong sense of codependency in many of our teachers. They simply can't stand to have Sean sit there and do nothing even though he didn't bring his book or finish his assignment. "All right, Sean, look on with Charles. Make sure you get this paper done tonight." A correlative message is, "Since you're 'slow'; do something, anything, and I'll tell you that you're doing fine."

Teachers are in a constant bind - "I must keep working with Jessie and help her to become the best student she can be and she is working hard and improving <u>and</u> one of these days I'm going to have to tell Jessie that she isn't good enough to go on to the next grade level."

How long and how hard do you work with a subordinate before you must decide that he is not going to succeed in that position? When do we give up on the people we are mentoring? When do we tell them they are failures and the organization has to do without them or they are not promotable?

The Change

Adult Interpretations of This Message:
- *I do only what I have to do to keep my job. You're crazy if you do any more than that.*
- *Don't kill the job - it'll still be there tomorrow.*
- *Let's see how far I can push the Foreman before he loses his cool.*
- *If I don't do it, the Boss will have someone else do it.*

(These last two utterances could get you into trouble much quicker in the workplace than they would at school)

You don't have any say about what is going to go on in this classroom.

**"If you don't know where you're going,
you're going to end up somewhere else."**

One of the most requested workshops conducted throughout the business community is the one on Goal Setting. Both Dr. Grupe and I have spent years teaching adults the skills and processes of setting and achieving goals. In addition, I have worked with thousands of elementary teachers on lesson planning with goals, aims, and objectives built into the system.

In reality, most teachers have very little decision-making power in curricular and administrative matters. Sometimes we seem to be focussed on one point, viz.:

A Decree From the Top
"We need to have our children perform well on the achievement tests so we look good to the board and to our parents. Your job is to teach them what they need so that they will get the right answers on the tests."

Moreover, the children in the classroom are entirely out of the loop when planning is done. They do what they are told to do because "After all they are too young to know what's good for them." Once in a while we find an enlightened teacher who helps children set personal, learning goals but they are usually swimming upstream in the education milieu.

We are all aware of how ineffective and low in motivation we are when someone other than us sets the goals. It is difficult to commit our heart, soul, and life to aspirations held by someone other than ourselves. And, of course, there may be some resentment when that someone else who is directing our career lives has less ability or knowledge than we do.

One day I was observing a very fine, older student teacher. She had just completed giving her 5th graders a thorough lesson on the placement of the decimal point in the multiplication of two decimal fractions and I suddenly sat bolt upright when I heard her say, "On the next page, 'They' want you to multiply the two factors and place the decimal point correctly."

When we got together for the post observation evaluation, I asked her, "Who are 'They'?" She blinked and said that she didn't know. We concluded that 'They' are an ethereal entity that helps us explain why we do or don't do something. You know, "We have to get that out on this shift or 'They' will be ticked off." or "I would like to be a more creative teacher, but 'They' won't let me." I suggested that she might say, "I would like you to complete this work" or "You will want to complete this page so you will have a better grasp of the operation."

Adult Interpretations of This Message:
- *I have no responsibility in carrying out the orders that someone else gave me.*
- *Why should I bust my back to make the Boss look good.*

The Change

- *I'd get that job done right but 'They' wouldn't know the difference or even care about it.*
- *I would like to improve this situation, but 'They' won't let me.*
- *I don't have the slightest idea why we do it this way and I couldn't care less. As long as 'They' don't complain it's O.K. with me.*

Do your own work; don't work with others.

Interpersonal relationships and tasks are not encouraged in many areas of our schools. Sometimes in high school we may be given a partner in the Biology Lab but basically we are on our own in our schoolwork. We are told that COMPETITION is where it's at. Besides that parents often get concerned that their child's grade is to be partly determined by the work of another child. "After all, the world out there is competitive and you have to learn how to compete and win."

In business, on the other hand, cooperation is often necessary for the job to be done correctly and expeditiously. Imagine the Managing Editor saying to his two best reporters, "Both of you go out and cover that debate between the incumbent, Clark, and the challenger, Kent, and I'll publish the better report."

In fact, if you observe adults in operation, you see them being most effective when they are working together on projects such as ridding their community of crime, electing a new board member, collecting money for that child who needs a heart transplant. Also if you observe their participation in sports competition, you will hear "How many strokes you giving me?" "How many pins do we spot them each game?" and "I ran the 10K race for the fun of it and set a new PR (Personal Record)." We chose, and have the option to choose the areas of our lives in which we will compete. We make sure that we give ourselves a chance to be successful in our competitive endeavors. We don't extend that option to children in school.

Johnny Wooden of UCLA, arguably the best college basketball coach of all time, never talked to his team about winning. They practiced long and hard to become team players; to play together. His goal for the team, for each player, and for the coaches (himself included) was to be a little bit better today then they were yesterday. If they did that, they could compete with the other team and have a good chance of being the winners. (Anthony Robbins calls this CANI - Constant and Neverending Improvement)

Adult Interpretations of This Message:
- *I take care of my business; you take care of yours.*
- *I won't get credit for my input if I work in a group.*

There's only one right answer and the teacher is the only one who knows what it is.

Somehow we adults raise a mystique about how much we know in the minds of children. My oldest granddaughter, as a child, was convinced that I knew **everything**. Well, she's 12 years old now and she has amended her evaluation of the situation. This conviction among children that adults are omnipotent and omniscient is especially strong in relation to their early teachers. "Miss Carey is so smart - she knows **everything**!" Jennifer says about her Kindergarten teacher.

These early experiences remain quite vivid in our memories. They seem to be relived in other experiences as we encounter new masters, such as our first boss or manager. He knows so much more than we do - we will never get to be that smart. Our next boss is also a master (and we haven't figured out that we are much more than we used to be).

The Change

Adult Interpretations of This Message:
- *I'm afraid to try because the Boss knows all about it and I'll probably foul it up.*
- *My Boss is an expert in that area, I'm not going to make any suggestions and look silly.*
- *I would correct the Boss, but I don't want to embarrass him.*

What you are learning now is not useable now.

"You have to learn your multiplication facts because you will need to know them someday" - (not today, but someday.) We used to call that "Cold Storage" -- learning facts, skills, or concepts that are put into the freezer until you need to use them. Sometimes we don't pull them out of the freezer at any time. Ask your friends how to divide one common fraction by another. 2/3 ÷ 4/5. (The answer is 5/6; there are 5/6 of 2/3 in 4/5) Then ask them the last time, other than in a math class, they divided one fraction by another.

I recall teaching 12 year olds how to take out a mortgage on a house and I regularly see 10 year olds reading numbers into the billions (and they aren't even paying income tax yet!). You can probably top this by listing the number of times you attended those workshops (not any of Dr. Grupe's of course) and the information was not only not useable at the time but you couldn't even imagine that it would be useful at any time. So:

Adult Interpretations of This Message:
- *We have just completed a communications skills workshop and what a waste of time and money!*
- *Management brought that seminar in and they didn't even attend.*
- *Management sat in but they aren't using it so why should we.*
- *It was pretty good stuff, but I don't see how we can use it until we get a new line of computers.*

How We Got Here

If it's not going to be graded, it's not worth doing.

Children learn very quickly what is worth doing and what is not worth doing in school. Much of the time, worth is determined by whether:
> 1) It will be on the next test.
> 2) It will be sent home or displayed at the next open house.
> 3) It will be graded.

Worth also may be determined by whether one is given a 'reward'; a sticker, a piece of candy, a smiley face. I recall watching a student teacher setting up a good lesson on proofreading a paragraph with a class of 5th graders. The students asked her, "What do we get if we get it right." She replied, "Nothing, just do the work." The very quick response was, "Then we won't do it." She said, "Yes, you will" and they decided not to test her courage and got to work.

Again, Aren't these kids smart? When we use an extrinsic reward system with people, they soon find a way to subvert and/or take advantage of that system. After all, despite what some psychologists would have us believe, we humans are much more than smart rats. Our thinking and creative abilities are different *qualitatively* as well as *quantitatively from rats, cats, pigeons, etc.*

We must work with children so that the Joy of Learning is the only 'reward' that is needed. Any teacher who is in touch with the feelings and the spirit of his children recognizes those magic moments when a child's eyes light up and the smile shines as she says, "Oh, I got it!" No candy, sticker, etc., can (or should) follow that.

Adult Interpretations of This Message:
- *They don't evaluate me on this part of my work, so why worry?*
- *I did the job the way they wanted it done and I expect a bonus.*
- *Why should I work on that project? I won't get any credit.*

The Change

Be neat in everything you do.

Since the time we discovered the specialized performance of our bicameral brain - Left Brain/Right Brain (See Chapter 7), I thought that our schools would change many of our **teaching practices** and institute more **learning practices.** They haven't and I don't see very much change in our business world, either.

Left brain oriented people tend to be neat, organized, punctual, sequenced, literal, and neat. They like to make and use outlines. Right brain oriented people tend to be opposite. Instead of outlines, they find a 'mapping' diagram more usefull. Personally, I use the 'Pilot' system in my office - I pile it here and I pile it there, and I know exactly which pile the stuff I want is in.

Unfortunately, our school system is invested in left brain activities capped by those marvelous achievement tests which demand the right answer and only the right answer. They ask convergent questions (with their own "correct" answers), such as, "Why did the American colonists object to the Stamp Act?" Is the correct answer A), B), C), D), or E)? Highly intelligent, highly creative children do not score well on standardized tests for two reasons, 1) They either play around with the answers or bring too much information to the task (It could be A; but wouldn't C be a neat answer; and that biography of Sam Adams said something that points to B...) and 2) Because they play around or cogitate, they don't finish the test.

Creative people, of the right brain persuasion, ask divergent questions, such as, "How could this historical episode be used by our Congress to improve our government's views on taxing?" You won't find that item on any standardized test. Creative children have messy desks - they aren't lazy; they just don't think the same way as the left brainers and they often pay the price to live in our neat, organized world. I have never heard a teacher compliment a child for having a stuffed-in desk or a messy paper.

How We Got Here

Our left-brained school system cherishes right answers, neat papers, acceptable forms, and narrow thinking. Creativity is acceptable only in select areas, such as Art (if the school has an Art program).

Adult Interpretations of This Message:
- *I know I haven't researched this project to the depth that I should have, but if I present it an official enough form, highly organized, my Boss will buy it. (Form over Substance)*
- *I keep my desk organized - it hurts my production but I'm afraid of what the Boss will say if he sees a messy desk.*
- *Sloppy people don't get promoted.*

The Workplace/The Schoolroom

There are so many more messages that our children get as they grow up and many of them start out with "Big boys don't ..." and "Nice girls don't..." I wonder how many grown men have buried their emotions and developed ulcers from "Big boys don't cry." I was happy that the girls on the softball team I coached didn't heed this one, "Nice girls don't get dirty." By the way did you notice that these admonitions are all stated with a negative verb? We don't tell children what to do as much as we tell them what not to do.

I call these messages 'Double Negative Instructions' because they tell children (and adults) what not to do. "Don't run in the halls" is a double negative - running in the halls is a negative so we attach another negative which is supposed to make it positive - it doesn't. "Let's all walk down the halls" is the positive statement.

We come finally to a message that is well meant but is stated and enforced so stringently that we can become immobilized if we live up to the letter of the law: "Don't talk to strangers." In my private business, I have many associates and a big part of their job is making cold calls and meeting new people. They can't afford to have that message in their subconscious computer banks.

The Change

- ■ The School and the Workplace have much to learn from one another; they are not dissimilar, in kind or needs.
- ■ Learners are Learners and Seekers are Seekers; we find them everywhere - in Schools, in Offices, in Warehouses.
- ■ We break some of them down, but we don't mean to do that. We just haven't learned how not to do that.
- ■ We haven't learned how to nurture and cultivate our Risktakers. We must learn how to do it and then do it.

We each have a big job to do - Let's do it together.

**There are two lasting gifts we can give our children;
One is roots, the other is wings.**

Anonymous

REFERENCES

Berne, Eric *Games People Play,* New York: Grove Press, 1964.

Dewey, John *Experience and Education,* New York: MacMillan and Co., 1938.

Fiske, Edward B. *Smart Schools, Smart Kids*, New York: Simon & Schuster, 1991.

Fulghum, Robert *All I Really Need to Know I Learned in Kindergarten,* New York: Ballantine Books, 1986.

Maslow, Abraham *Toward of Psychology of Being,* Princeton, NJ: Van Nostrand, 1968.

Peters, Thomas J. and Waterman, Robert H. *In Search of Excellence*, New York: Warner Books, 1983.

von Oech, Roger *A Whack on the Side of the Head,* New York: Warner Books, 1983.

2 Responding To The Challenge

> *Work is Love made visible.*
> Kahlil Gibran, *The Prophet*

Most companies and organizations begin with a vision - a dream to satisfy a customer need. Such a business usually starts out with dynamic teamwork because the vision is fresh. As it grows, systems are set in place to standardize and maintain production of goods or services. Over the years the original vision can be lost in the midst of process and procedure. When this happens, front line workers are alienated from joy in their work because they cease to be motivated by the grand vision of the company.

As a company grows - front line workers are the key to providing input to management as to what the continuing processes need to be to keep the original vision alive. Management must keep the vision ever in mind and front line workers must be respected for their ongoing ability to help define the needed processes to bring the vision into reality at the consumer level.

The following dialogue, though perhaps an extreme example, reflects what can happen when that respect for the process development potential of front line workers is not understood and nurtured by management.

The Change

FOUNDER: Years ago I had a vision to make this product. Soon there were five people in our company. We worked together like a team. Before long there were 50 employees. Then, it seemed, nobody really wanted to work. We would tell them what to do and it seemed they didn't want to listen.

WORKER: I just put in my eight hours a day here because you don't dare to value my judgment and ideas. When was the last time you were serving customers on the front line of this department?

FOUNDER: I established that department.

WORKER: I know, 15 years ago.

FOUNDER: I developed the procedures and policies for that department.

WORKER: And I'm sure they were great for their time, but they are still being used. Today's customers' needs are not being met. But I'm not going to tell you about it because you just might kill the messenger. I'm emotionally distancing myself from my work - because it's one endless mechanical circle - with me and the customer often left to fend for ourselves. I put in my time and then I'm gone. I've got friends and hobbies that give me emotional satisfaction - because my job sure doesn't.

FOUNDER: I didn't know you felt that way.

WORKER: You never asked me how I felt. You were always too busy telling me what to do and getting on my back if I didn't do it right. So I put my feelings, my creativity and my ideas about how to do the job better - on hold. And I just do what you tell me to do.

Responding to the Challenge

FOUNDER: I've tried working with you in many ways. Remember that productivity consultant I brought in last year?

WORKER: Oh! Do I ever! A high priced guy who had never been in this business before and who then took your place for awhile and started telling us what to do. He was very objective, that is, he treated us all like objects. Want to know a secret?

FOUNDER: Tell me.

WORKER: A group of us got together in the department and figured out ways to keep the department running in spite of the useless and irrelevant directives coming from your consultant.

FOUNDER: But he did a good job. Your department had a 20 percent increase.

WORKER: In spite of him! You know the most fun I've had working here was when our department got together and figured out how to keep the department running.

FOUNDER: You mean the consultant..

WORKER: He didn't know what was going on.

FOUNDER: I can't let you all make the decisions in this company. I'll lose control.

WORKER: You already have. Have you talked to many customers recently?

FOUNDER: Well, no. I hardly ever get out in that area, but my top management tells me...

The Change

> *WORKER: Chances are they tell you what you want to hear. We hear the truth everyday when we're dealing face to face with the ones who ultimately pay all our salaries - the customer. Let me ask you a question - if our entire department came to you as a team, would you listen to us? Would you let us help you develop policies and procedures for our department that will really work and serve the customer? Think about it. We give you a big chunk of our lives by working for you. When you treat us as just a part of the machinery - you get a lot less than you bargained for - you lose the skills, talents, desires and dreams we would be willing to share with your company - if you will respect us, train us, listen to us and, sometimes, get out of the way and let us help you.*

Obviously the consultant being referred to in that exchange did not understand or utilize techniques involving employees in the process of company growth. So often management will hire consultants with approaches that fit the current company mold. And this is done to create change and improvement?

Companies not bringing their employees into decision making processes that relate to customer satisfaction are missing an opportunity to 1. get *results* and 2. provide the environment for greater employee satisfaction in their work.

An astute CEO with whom I spent some time mused about the Employer-Employee relationship. His deeper understanding led him to respect his staff greatly. "I provide an office for my staff," he said "and specially equipped vans and tools they use for servicing client needs. The office is mine. The vans and tools are mine. I can take them all back."

"The one basic thing the employees provide to me." he continued, "they never get back. They give me 8 hours, a part of their life that is gone forever."

Responding to the Challenge

Old and New Views of Employees

It is the work environment that can make the time valuable to both the employee and the one paying the wages. From many years consulting with companies, I have gleaned two sets of employee views toward their company. Companies that limit employees growth and ownership create an attitude as do organizations that make training and sharing of decision making processes an important part of the company environment. One attitude leads to the death of the company - the other to new levels of growth and flexibility.

Old: What I do at work is basically laid out for me.

New: Through continual training in my job skills, decision making processes and problem-solving techniques - I am given more and more responsibility for developing the processes through which I provide the customer the goods or services.

Old: The focus is on the policies and procedures that surround the production of the goods or services. Because of diverse and changing customer needs, there have been times I have wished to please a customer - but it was not within my power to do so.

New: The focus of my company is on customer satisfaction. We are given creative license to do whatever it takes, within broad guidelines, to please the customer.

Old: As a front line employee, I have received most of my training from other front line employees with more experience.

New: As a front line employee, I have been amazed that upper management has worked with me one-on-one and in groups sharing the mission of the company and showing me that

The Change

> they are personally concerned with my training and my success. All the training programs I have been through with the company have been conducted by highly trained company employees zealous about customer satisfaction.

Old: I am never approached and asked how the job I am doing could be done better. I am usually only approached when I have violated a rule or policy of the company - when I have not conducted my activities according to processes set by management. I have a list of three improvements in what I do that would streamline my activities yet get the same amount accomplished. I am afraid to talk to management about the ideas because I may be wrong.

New: I am regularly asked about potential improvements I have developed to better serve the customer. I am not asked to fill out a form about it. I am personally approached and listened to by management. They really know how to listen! If it is necessary to go outside of broad guidelines to serve a unique customer need in a real emergency, I know that I will not be fired for doing it. I will be asked to visit with management as to how my decision helped the customer and why I made the decision. If it was a good decision, it may be allowed in all stores. If not, it was a learning experience for me and makes me a more valuable employee.

Old: Once I mentioned a new idea to my supervisor. Later it was implemented and he took credit for it and was given a raise.

New: I know that I can approach management - my coaches - with any idea I have for improving my work and customer satisfaction. One thing that motivates them to listen to me is that their promotions are not based on their good ideas - but on how many ideas they can stimulate from their employees by creating an atmosphere of freedom to communicate.

Responding to the Challenge

Old: I look forward to Friday quitting time. I have some interesting hobbies and sports that I really get excited about.

New: I really feel that I own my job. Management has proven to me not by words but by their daily actions that they really believe I am the most important person in the company. My mind is important. My ideas are important. It took some adjusting at first to get used to working for a company that treats me this way. Now my friends joke with me because I'll spend some of my own time in the evening or on weekends just thinking about and coming up with new ways to improve the operation of my position with the company. I own that job. It's more than a salary - it's a continual opportunity to show what I can do - what I am capable of. When people really believe in you and listen to you - it really changes your worklife.

Someone Listened

Creating an atmosphere free of fear where the employee can communicate with management begins to tap into a creativity that is just waiting to be utilized. What can happen when management really listens? Let's get down to the dollars and cents value.

From an article in the May, 1992 issue of *Governing Magazine* are excerpts that reflect the magnitude of change possible through ground floor feedback:

"John Sharp thought the idea was 'not much more than a public relations gimmick,' but with Texas state government staring down the barrel of a $ 4.6 billion budget shortfall last year, the state's new comptroller was willing to try anything. At the suggestion of a staff member, Sharp had a toll-free hotline installed to allow Texans to call in with suggestions for saving money.

The Change

"To everyone's surprise, the calls poured in - more than 4,000 in the first 20 days. While callers could remain anonymous, Sharp says the suggestions were so detailed that it was obvious that most calls were coming from inside government. 'They were mainly from mid- and lower-level employees,' says Sharp, 'the people who have struggled day in and day out with the Texas bureaucracy.' These people 'know more than anyone about what would help them do their jobs better, but they had never before been asked. We asked.'

"The process took an army of auditors. More than 100 were borrowed from 16 state agencies and the private sector. They pored over budgets and followed leads gathered at nine public hearings across the state. When the legislature authorized the undertaking, lawmakers hoped the auditors might find savings of as much as $200 million to help defray the budget shortfall. 'We found that much on the first day,' says Sharp. The Texas Performance Review's findings included 195 recommendations projected to save the state $ 4.2 billion. Nearly two-thirds of the recommendations got through the legislature, making up $ 2.4 billion of the projected budget shortfall and eliminating about 1,000 jobs."

This fairy tale response began to change the complexion of how one state government viewed the value of feedback. According to the article the review process is now a permanent part of Texas State government, and the comptroller says hundreds more suggestions are being evaluated. The toll-free number is still averaging 30 to 40 calls a day.

The Thermostat Syndrome

What a power we have in the creative abilities of the people who are right on the front line in our organizations. The people who build the products, those who provide the services. Because changing customer needs will be the constant status quo of the future, processes must change quickly also. When we glean

Responding to the Challenge

constant feedback from those closest to the customer, we move away from a thermostat mentality.

What does a thermostat do? If the room gets too hot or cold, it automatically adjusts temperature back into a comfort zone. If we are into a process or a habit and we venture into trying something different, we will have a natural inclination to move back into our old habit pattern. This is natural but not always useful. Of course feedback can be painful to management if it doesn't paint the picture we want to see. But the price today for staying in a too tightly regulated comfort zone is business failure.

The need to push past the fear of real communication in an organization simply cannot be overemphasized. We will spend the bulk of Chapter 4 dealing with techniques for deepening the level of communication.

The Envelope of Fear

I can remember when I was fourteen years old - one of the first times in my class I had to get up and recite a memorized piece of poetry. You know what happened? I'm probably the only person in the world who has experienced this... I stood up in front of 30 classmates to recite, opened my mouth and guess what came out? Nothing. I forgot every word of the poem. You talk about being humiliated - filled with remorse! I sat down totally ashamed. For a number of months and years it was very difficult for me to participate by sharing my ideas in groups for fear of experiencing that same horrible moment of making a big mistake in front of everyone.

Finally to push past the envelope of fear, I would raise my hand before I gave myself the chance to be afraid. I responded immediately. When you do that, particularly as you're working on your own individual private growth, this creates a great power

The Change

because it allows you to build new habit patterns that begin to give you the freedom to move past fear.

Howard Gitlow and Shelly Gitlow in *The Deming Guide to Quality and Competitive Position* emphasize the importance still placed by many in management upon organizational processes as opposed to people potential development. "What these managers are ignoring" they write, "is that their job is dealing with employees' problems, eliminating their fears and encouraging the development of people...Their fears are a barrier to their emotional well-being and their job performance."

They also report Deming as saying that the fundamental problem in American business is that people are scared to discuss the problems of people."You look awfully happy today," management has historically said, "what's wrong - don't you realize you're at work?"

In our level of communication, we must wisely work within the constraints of the company as it is, hopefully, transforming its communications environment. We know deep inside how wonderful it feels when we have the comfort to share our thoughts and ideas in a non-judgmental environment:

"I respect your ideas. Yes, that idea has merit -let's look into it more. That one I don't believe will fly, let me tell you specifically why. But you'll have other great ideas and I'm looking forward to them."

Such fearless communication must begin with the CEO and then it filters down to permeate the entire company. If the CEO is afraid of truth - who will sacrifice themselves to give it to him/her?

The smell of communicative fear at the top leads to a spider web of double binds throughout the organization. The middle manager says, "If I stretch the rules to please my supervisors' needs in his

Responding to the Challenge

department, I'll be taking the chance of upsetting my General Manager. But...if I don't take the risk of ruffling the GM's feathers - I'll have a supervisor who doesn't respect me - because I haven't provided the resources I know his people need to put out the best product."

The employee is in the same bind, "If I get creative to please the customer, my manager may not understand and I'll be in trouble." Witness the time I ordered a cup of yogurt at one of the many thriving yogurt shops springing up everywhere. "A medium size, please," I said, as the clerk was busy at the machine - obviously making a large one. "A medium size, please," I repeated. She had filled the large one up about half - a medium sized portion. She gave me a rather strained look, dumped the contents of the large cup into the sink and made a medium sized from scratch. "Why didn't you just dump the yogurt from the large cup to the medium size?" I asked. After all, she could have checked with me to see if that would be OK. It would have been a clever thing to do.

"When we make a mistake, we are to start over again." She intoned as though part of a liturgy. Indeed, she may have been thinking "I've done what the manager instructed me to do, even though I could have pleased the customer and saved the store money by doing it the other way. But, it's not my problem."

Work - A "Mushroom" Job?

Is work a cross I must bear? Is it my burden? Haven't we all walked into a business and were treated by the clerk as through we

The Change

were an unnecessary interruption? Believe it or not, most of the time such a slight is not intentional. The clerk didn't walk in to work that morning and say "OK - I'm going to be the most obnoxious clerk in town today." Most of the time it is not intentional - it is habitual. It's encultured. It's the way we perceive ourselves feeling and acting when we find ourselves where we don't want to be.

Peter Block sums the issue up best in *The Empowered Manager:* "The price the organization pays for giving such emphasis to authority is the feeling of helplessness it creates. If it's not my fault, I can't fix it. This is the collusion between the management and the people working for them. Managers take comfort in the fact that there are people under their control who are forced to submit to their wishes and this gives them the illusion of power and influence." Block continues, "Subordinates take comfort in the fact that when things go wrong, it is not their fault; and the fact that they pay for this comfort with their own helplessness is a small price to pay." A "small price" that is, until the customers go away and don't come back.

Now we all know that we can get great mushrooms - very tasty succulent, mushrooms by growing them in a dark environment and feeding them what's left over - manure, if you will. People do not grow well this way. In a Directive-Driven culture, we are paying wages to people to use only a portion of their mental powers. We're getting less return on our investment from people who have much more that they would be willing to give if they were in the right environment.

Effective team empowerment focuses on results, not behavior. Behavior is important, but let's put it in perspective. When we look at the paralysis of process, we find that when a process that is generating a certain type of behavior within an organization continues to develop that singular behavior, which no longer gets us the results we want - we must shift the vision, the expectations and set specific new goals.

When the motivating vision changes, behavior begins to shift. When we communicate to employees the overall vision of the company and provide them ongoing training so they are truly skilled at what they do, then providing them resources to refine the processes, we're encouraging them to develop the behaviors necessary to create the end results that are needed to satisfy the client.

One metropolitan library brought in consultants to improve the "image" of the library services. The consultants informed the library personnel that they should smile more and engage customers in eye contact to a greater degree. To make sure they did that, the consultants explained, they would post a lookout from time to time in each library, noting the smiles and amount of eye contact. If the appropriate amount of customer interaction did not occur, the librarian's job could be in jeopardy. The library employees were transformed into fear-filled robots.

True, effective behaviors should be practiced. But it is imperative that people know why. As one wise marketer once shared with me, when we know the "why", we'll figure out the "how". When the vision of the company is shared and people know why it is essential that they please the customer, then they are ready for an "image" change that they can own. A change that comes from inside.

Empowering Your Staff

A cab driver is an excellent example of an empowered employee. After being picked up, each fare has a special need. To be taken to some place where, perhaps, the cabby has never been. Within the guidelines of a general system - the street system - the cabby creates the best route to please the client. Because he is skilled in

The Change

knowing various route possibilities, he is creative in his behavior as to how to respond to the customer need.

Communication begins with the customer communicating to the front line worker who communicates needs to the supervisor who communicates needs to middle management who communicates needs to upper management who communicates to CEO. If the loop is broken - valuable resources needed to satisfy customer needs will not be brought into place. If anyone fails to be a critical but respectful listener - the system breaks down. And the system, like a river, has to be kept flowing on a daily basis. Communication is not stone. It is water. It flows, melts, changes and must be kept moving, unblocked, daily.

Unless individuals can love what they are doing and have freedom within their work environment to focus on customer needs along with a freedom from fear in communication - quality will not happen in the long run. In order to have quality in a constantly changing environment, we've got to be creative.

Organization -- Equals Work Shadowed by the Fear of Failure

Organism -- Equals Freedom for Growth and Success

If any of you readers are purchasing agents or managers involved in purchasing or allocation of equipment, I think you'll relate to this challenge. Isn't it a real headache to spend thousands of dollars on the latest equipment and six months later find that it has depreciated 50 % because a new piece of equipment has come out that will do more and has a lower initial cost? Technology is changing so fast that equipment value can be swept away.

The only thing that we can bring into a company that grows is

Responding to the Challenge

people. Their capabilities through *Attitude, Interpersonal Communication Skills* and other related training can allow them to appreciate in value. The growing companies of the future will be nurturing that one asset that can keep growing and changing and creating - the human mind.

No work environment or personal set of experiences is perfect, we're always going to have challenges - but being able to transfer those challenges from an expression of fear or reluctance to exuberance and, heaven forbid, fun - that will propel our economy into the next century in fine style.

It is so critical for us to build an attitudinal foundation that will allow Total Quality Management and Self-Managed Teams to grow and prosper without getting gridlocked in the old habit patterns that are not tailored to fit in to the quality focus. Can we have the courage to change - to re-evaluate our systems? It's through courage and willingness to change that we can transform our businesses and organizations.

Here is the horizontal organism that works for the customer:

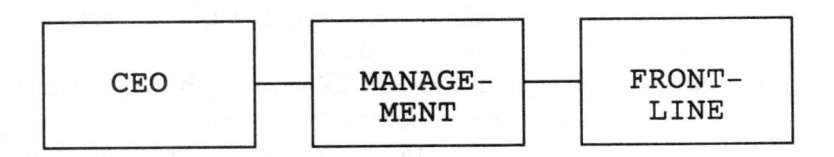

| CEO | — | MANAGE-MENT | — | FRONT-LINE |

We have the same components in the horizontal organism as the vertical organization but with expanded or different functions.

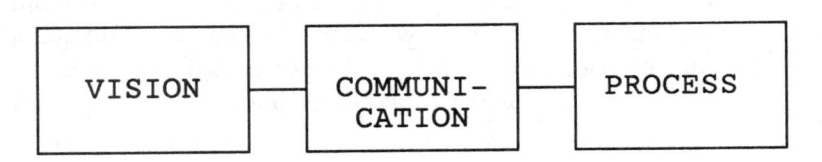

| VISION | — | COMMUNI-CATION | — | PROCESS |

The Change

CEO/Upper Management has a strong focus on the future. Looking at trends, visualizing the position of the company in a year, in five years. The vision and overall goals which are developed are communicated through the organizational facilitator to the front line. Middle management becomes a communicator and a coach, breaking down the broad vision of the company and challenging the front line to continually develop and refine the processes to bring that vision into reality.

The Front Line

Those who touch the customer or the client every day - they are the people closest to receive the feedback as to how well the company is doing in service. Who are the people in a company who are closest to the customer? Who are the people getting immediate feedback on client needs? Those on the front line. Those individuals, when given proper training, can be very instrumental in developing the processes through which a company grows.

One CEO illustrated the front line/customer relationship quite succinctly: At the company headquarters he would frequently direct the attention of a new manager to view the busy street directly below. "A lot of people out there" he would muse, "How many of them are coming up to our office to spend their money?" "None, sir." the fledgling manager answered, "Obviously, they go to our stores scattered around the country." "Obviously" the CEO added,"and our job is to support the clerks all those people come to with their money."

One aspect of the "Moment of Truth" as Tom Peters terms it, is rarely with the management - it is the interaction between front line and customer. The customer goes away with an attitude and a feeling about the company because of the person who wrapped the machine, or put the last pieces together or handed it to us.

Responding to the Challenge

Management begins creating its "Moment of Truth" with its internal customers by moving away from creating processes and then directing the processes to be implemented by the front line. They shift from that directive role to the role of organizational facilitator. A system - an organism if you will -is then created. Beginning with the vision of the company, the communicating of that vision as it relates to each manager's department and then the development of the processes by an empowered front line.

Quality, as perceived by the customer, in the new horizontal framework is very quickly fed back to management - to the organizational facilitator - to the coaches. I will refer to management many times as coaches. I encourage those who are sports minded to think about their favorite teams and consider what would happen if the coaches suddenly became directors and gave everyone exactly what they were supposed to do with no variation. A coach could not do that. Who would have the mental ability to be able to foresee every possible move in any game?

Yet a coach must empower each of those on the team within a framework - the game rules - to be creative in a very systematic way to do the things that need to be done during this very fast moving situation known as a sports game. We can begin to incorporate this concept as we look at business. The fact is that we are having to play a faster more creative and competitive game than ever before.

The Super Computer

We need a Super Computer on our team to cope with constant changes in consumer needs. Darold Treffert, author of *Extraordinary People*, outlines the qualities the perfect computer would possess: "Where is there a computer a mere three pounds in size that can store somewhere between one hundred trillion and 280 quintillion bits of information...? Where is there a computer

The Change

that can not only store massive amounts of information but that can independently correlate, associate, analyze and actually create new insights and ideas from it? Where is there a computer that can truly learn, all by itself and on its own, without being programmed by some outside force to create that 'learning'? Where is there a sophisticated computer that can run as long as 100 years without repair, needs no surge protector, never needs to be booted or formatted, replaces all its parts continually without loss of data and without down time and has its own built-in back-up memory such that it can lose up to 90 percent of its capacity and still not lose stored data?"

Manager: We've just outlined the potential of the last person you hired.
Employee: We're talking about your capabilities.

Earlier in this century, we could sink into long term habits and static skills and get away with it. There was a time when you could go to work for a company, learn one skill, basically provide your services with that skill for, say, forty years and then retire.

Today the average entrant into the job market can expect to have to change or significantly upgrade their skills from five to seven times during their working life. Our wonderful friend technology has put us in this position. The most vital skill to learn now is how to change with the least amount of stress. How to change, to learn and to grow.

Managers will become communicators of a company vision, a coach encouraging change as it becomes necessary (which will be often) and, going one step further, evangelists for the company gospel. Management not modeling the behaviors they are asking of their employees will be ineffective. If the vision doesn't truly inspire you - you can't pass along the inspiration. To have that kind of vision the CEO/Upper Management must look past the quarterly reports to the long term needs within the industry. This is not easy. But keeping the vision keen through longer term strategy provides an important flexibility that can give a company the edge in today's market.

Make Haste Slowly

As I work with companies that have gone onto the "bandwagon" of TQM and Self-Managed Teams, I find CEO's and owners who slow down when they see - really sense that they will have to give up control over the processes. The beads of sweat appear. The excuses come pouring out. The quality initiative is sometimes sabotaged by shortened time frames or attempting to make changes upstream rather than from the top of the organization on down. I have seen management dump their processes on unsuspecting employees, who basically are told "You are now self-managed in these areas. They are your babies now" with no specific training or time to become familiar with the fact that the transition is a long term growth process. When things then start fizzling, the initiative is cast aside with a disparaging, "Well, we gave that program our best shot." It must be done respectfully, slowly and incrementally. When it's done that way, a culture has an opportunity to constructively reshape itself.

It is most important to consider that transition of process accountability is done incrementally as front line employees are given training in interpersonal communications, team dynamics and problem solving techniques. How long does the transition take? It's never fully finished.

There are always new things that can be done by those who touch the customer to make quality a reality. But the job of developing the processes for serving the customer is not "dumped" into the lap of the hapless employee. It is transferred, project by project, piece by piece, as the employee becomes more comfortable using the

The Change

tremendous creativity that he or she possesses. A wonderfully communicated vision can make everyone in the company excited and euphoric but it must then be broken down to smaller elements of implementation.

As a small boy I can remember watching the clouds from the back seat of our 1954 Buick. As long as I looked up that high, I didn't know if we were going fast or just barely moving. With my eyes only on the clouds I could not gauge distance or speed.

Over the years, I have heard so many talk about the wonderful things they have planned for their businesses. Things they hope for and wish to have. And when I hear that I think of those times when I looked up into the clouds. It was only when I came down to earth and looked at the road that I realized where the car was going. It was only then that the benchmarks became visible to determine whether indeed the car was going 10 mph or 50 mph. Unless our visions in life are broken down into yearly, monthly, weekly and daily tasks - they remain like the wispy clouds in the sky. They are beautiful to look at - but remain far away and unattainable.

How can the transition from vision to real implementation begin? In simple ways. One company that had a tight rein on all front line activities also had a company newsletter. However, everything in the newsletter dealt with the management perception of employees and consequently, a lot of the employees didn't even take the time to read it. It was produced outside the company by a contractor.

"We're not getting the support, readership and participation in our newsletter from employees," management moaned to me. "Is this supposed to be a company newsletter?" I asked. "Of course" came their reply. "Then let the employees who make up the bulk of your company write, print and publish it. Give them the resources to do it." I advised. "I don't believe any of our employees have

Responding to the Challenge

experience in that area" came a quick reply. "Then they will have fun learning." I suggested.

At a meeting with employees, management's message was this: A company newsletter should be produced by the company. If you want the newsletter to continue, we will give you ownership of the newsletter or we can just let it die. You put together your own teams and decide who's going to be the editor and who's going to be the proof reader and we'll provide the resources to have it printed. You determine the publication schedule, the contents and select the people who will be the reporters to bring all the material together.

Over the next year there was a slow but powerful transformation of the newsletter. At first quite amateurish but building momentum as each month passed. Interestingly, employees - who became reporters, also interviewed management and the paper began a more objective view of the company. Management/employee communication began to improve. But the greatest power was unleashed in allowing the employees to really feel an ownership and pride in their project.

From that point, management can continue to allow ownership of other job elements on an ascending scale. Let one success prepare the employees for more. Portions of work can be just as rewarding and exciting as hobbies. The company benefits because more of the process development is where it belongs, with those closest to the customer.

Coaches Ask More Questions Than Give Directives

That headline is a slide in my program. When I got the slide back from the computer graphic company, a misprint had occurred. The slide they sent me said "Coaches Ask More Questions Then Give Directives." After studying the error, it occurred to me that the

The Change

person who transferred the slide probably assumed that was the only logical way the sentence could read as opposed to "*Than* Give Directives."

As front line people become more comfortable developing and being creative in the processes that are customer-driven and are given the resources to implement the processes - management continues the empowerment by asking well placed questions. How will that approach work? Where will you place these people in the team? Those on the front line who are becoming increasingly involved in the development of the processes to please the customer are approached by management as experts. They are asked questions about how things will be done both to stimulate their thinking and to show respect for their knowledge and understanding of what needs to happen to produce satisfied customers.

- Directive-Driven cultures tell employees what to do.
- Transition cultures tell, skill train, and begin to get feedback from employees.
- Business Organisms grow by asking questions and getting employee feedback.

Responding to the Challenge

Positive Learning

Dr. Peter S. Pierro has spent a lifetime as an elementary school teacher and college professor. Over those years, he has developed a set of principles of learning. Learning, not teaching, because it is the learner not the teacher who makes the final, crucial decision on whether she will learn. He says (only half jokingly), "College students have learned in their educational careers two important operations, 1. How to sleep with your eyes open and 2. How to yawn with your mouth closed. They, not I, determine whether they will learn the course content or not. I may be able to coerce or reward them using the grading system, but in the end they make the decision whether or not to learn." Here are his principles:

1. Learning is the basic process. Teaching is the enabling of learning to take place.

2. Learning how to learn is most crucial.

3. Learning patterns are unique. Each learner has his/her own personal learning pattern.

4. Learning (education) is the process of drawing out rather than putting in.

5. Learning is an active process and the learner must be actively involved.

6. While both are important, asking questions is more important than giving answers.

7. Learning is goal oriented and purposeful.

8. The best motivation comes from within the learner and from the learning situation. *Learning is its own reward.*

The Change

9. Knowledge of success is better than fear of failure.

10. The learner's interest in the task is the best indicator of his/her readiness to learn.

11. Learning is affected by both the learner's internal condition and by the external environment.

12. Learning must begin where the learner is, not where we would like him/her to be.

13. A reasonable number of repetitions of worthwhile information helps establish its acquisition; excessive repetitions are counterproductive and encourage rejection of the information.

14. Learning occurs best when the skill or information learned can be applied by the learner to his/her own real life.

15. Knowledge of the facts are readily forgotten unless attitudes and principles are included with those facts.

16. Love and joy are better motivators than fear and rewards.

17. Learning activities must be related to the unique learning pattern of each person and not to some logical, standardized pattern.

18. Learning may be improved and accelerated when the learner is in communication with people who are significant to the learner (e.g., a mentor).

THE MASTER PRINCIPLE: Learning how to learn is the most important goal of education.

Responding to the Challenge

Left Brain/Right Brain

We outline in detail in Chapter Four, Module Two, the characteristics of the two hemispheres of the brain as they relate to personality patterns. Here, we will view the left and right hemisphere of the brain in order to see how they come into play to create the empowered employee.

We know that the left hemisphere in the majority of individuals controls verbal skills and ability to create orderly processes. It creates the verbal building blocks so vital in a literate society.

The right hemisphere is visionary. It is non-verbal and it is emotional. It is these three things: vision, non-verbal expression and emotion that have not been emphasized in the work environment in the past. Yet these are the three areas that are most tapped into and that flourish to the greatest degree in our hobbies and many of our after work activities. So the old saying we have heard about "Park your brain at the door when you come to work" is half right. One hemisphere of our brain is literally not required in a Directive-Driven culture. What a waste. Eight hours a day, five days a week being in a position to share only half of our potential with the company that provides us a living.

The entrepreneurs, the ones many times who own or start up companies brought both hemispheres together in their work. The key to the entrepreneur is that they literally see, feel, smell, and taste the vision they are working toward. They have made a deep emotional commitment to the vision and they exercise a childlike enthusiasm in what they do. They have taken the childhood power to dream and deeply fall in love with what they do and brought it up to adult speed. They then use that power to create the future. What I have done is briefly outline steps to empowerment as they are performed by the human mind. *Empowerment must follow this pattern or it will not work.* Let's look at each of these steps closely:

The Change

VISION

A vision is a view into the future. It is a picture of what will be at whatever point we are projecting toward. A vision is an end result. It is not specific as much as majestic at this point. It is a belief in the possible. It is a stretch of the imagination. Part of the power of a great vision is that it is a step into the creative.

An Historical Overview of The Power of Vision

Throughout history vision has been the generating force for the accumulation of knowledge that now provides our current level of technology.

Someone dreamed of a possibility and stepped out to explore. Always such dreamers have been pioneers, slighted by the "established" view of what was conceivable during any age. In the first century A.D., Julius Frontinus, a Roman engineer, brushed off the possibility of new innovations with this sweeping statement " all considerations of works and engines of war, the invention of which has long since reached its limit, and for the improvement of which I see no further hope in the applied arts."

The belief that nothing more is possible continued to manifest its seemingly eternal nature almost 1800 years later. The New York times wrote of the distinguished Samuel Pierpont Langley (1834-1906) "We hope that Professor Langley will not put his substantial greatness as a scientist in further peril by continuing to waste his time, and the money involved, in further airship experiments. Life is short, and he is capable of services to humanity incomparably greater than can be expected to result from trying to fly."

It is applied VISION that has brought us the four Quantum Leaps that are reflected in history.

Responding to the Challenge

QUANTUM LEAP 1 - Navigation: Expansion of the Physical World

Some curious ancestor stood on a beach looking out onto the interminable seas. "What is out there? Where would it take me? What would I find?" Likely the search for the answers to those questions would cost the first of the curious their lives. The price for the development of the art of navigation was dear. The sea swallowed thousands. But learn how to sail by the stars we did. Shipbuilding became an art. A vision creating desire made it all happen.

QUANTUM LEAP 2 - Printing: Expansion of the Knowledge World

From the very beginning of oral and written language, certain ones knew that knowledge meant power. For the high priests of the Middle Ages, knowledge of the language and reading skills set them apart from the masses who held them in great esteem.

"Saint Augustine, writing in the 5th century, refers to his mentor, Saint Ambrose, the Bishop of Milan, who was so learned that he could actually read without moving his lips. For this astonishing feat he was regarded as the brainiest person in the world." recounts Alvin Toffler in his book, *PowerShift*.

Gutenberg, considered the originator of modern day printing, "must have been a man of monumental persuasive powers, for even after his widely publicized bankruptcy another Mainz official was willing to stake him to a full set of printing equipment." according to Daniel J. Boorstin, author of *The Discoverers*. Gutenberg had a burning vision. Such a vision became infectious despite riots in the streets by hundreds of scribes who feared losing their well compensated profession of laboriously hand-copying books.

The Change

THE MOVEMENT OF VISION INTO REALITY CONSTITUTES THE GROWING PAINS OF SOCIETY.

QUANTUM LEAP 3 - Industrial Revolution: Expansion of Human Physical Power

Machinery began multiplying the power of human muscle a thousandfold.

ELECTRICITY created the expansion of time by bringing "more" of it into the workplace and home through artificial lighting. Electricity also led to a multitude of new inventions, often by accident. An electric generator could work as a motor, as was haphazardly discovered in 1873. "A workman setting up Gramme's exhibit at an exhibition in Vienna mistakenly connected one generator to the wires from another already in operation. To everybody's surprise, the second machine began to spin." Recounts DeCamp "As with Bell's first transmitter, the inventor's genius lay in seeing the possibilities opened up by an accident that a less agile mind might have brushed aside."

AUTOMOBILES AND AIR TRAVEL both compressed the time for travel and the boundaries of physical space. Before those innovations "A trip to see friends ten miles away was likely to be an all-day expedition, for the horse had to be given a chance to rest and be fed. No wonder that each region, each town, each farm was far more dependent upon its own resources - its own produce, social contacts, amusements - than in later years." explains Frederick Allen in his book, *The Big Change*.

EACH QUANTUM LEAP IN KNOWLEDGE AND APPLICATION BROUGHT FORTH BY VISION FEEDS THE NEXT: Navigation brought more people with different ideas together. Printing allowed the ideas to be shared for a longer period (past the lifetime of the teller of the tale) and over a

Responding to the Challenge

further distance. Through the accumulation of printed information, science developed generations of knowledge of physical laws that, applied, created new solutions to physical labor challenges.

QUANTUM LEAP 4 - Computer/Communications Revolution

Instantaneous global communication. The beginning of the "global village". The transfer of printed materials to electronic "books" and storage. The replacement of sequential, organizational left hemispheric human brain functions with computers processing and organizing information with the speed of light. The Age of Information Overload. Constant technological changes resulting in the rapid Birth and Death of industries.

QUANTUM LEAP 5 - The Era of Sorting Out Priorities

Humankind has synthesized the motive power of the person with ship, auto and airplane. We have multiplied the physical power of humans a million times over with machines. We have magnified our ears with radio and our eyes with television and, finally, with the computer we have replaced our need to personally organize and calculate. However, the right hemisphere of the human mind can never be replicated because it is the "originator" of the visioning process that has sparked the innovations that we list here.

Our next Quantum leap will occur when we, through introspection, begin to sort out and make the best use of the innovations that Vision has brought forth. These Offspring of Vision can become our demons of the year 2000 or the instruments for a true revolution in the global quality of life.

Company Visioning

When I take the company CEO/Upper Management through the visioning process, I have them make a list of what they feel their

The Change

client needs will be in two years or five years. Then write a screen play in which your company is providing and exceeding those client expectations. Obviously the projecting of client expectations into the future must be a combination of viewing current needs with a creative extension of trends into the future. Note I used the word "screenplay." I want a full scenario to be created. Not a wish list, not a ledger of ideas. I want the new reality to be written in the present tense - as though it were already happening.

These questions must be answered: How is the client pleased with what you are providing? How is your company prospering as a result of these changes? How has intercompany communication improved to bring about the enhancement of consumer quality? And, most vital, why is this vision important to you personally?

The screen play tells through human interaction and, indeed, drama - how it feels to be in this new future. Having a vision puts "failure" in a new perspective. Remember when you were quite young and you learned to ride a bike? Remember what it was like? Did you fall off a few times? We made mistakes, we fell off, didn't we? We pursued our vision to ride that bike. But it was OK to fall off. And at six years of age, we knew quite well that it was OK. We were in a learning process and failure was a part of the education. As a child we naturally recognized that vision creates a new reality.

Riding the bike happened before we were able to ride the bike. Right? Think about it. Is there anyone reading this who learned to ride a bike who didn't see and feel themselves in their mind riding before they rode successfully? Without a vision - failure accomplishes nothing. With a vision - failure is an important part of learning.

When a vision of such magnitude is developed and deeply accepted by CEO/Upper Management - then it is time to communicate the vision truly, honestly and sincerely to middle management and

Responding to the Challenge

supervisory personnel. Their task is to break that vision down to an understandable picture as it relates to each department. Then from that refined vision comes specific goals and objectives. But the vision is not the process - the vision is the Trigger to unlock a very great power.

The Vision "Narration"

It is essential that we integrate our values into the narration of the vision. In my estimation, a values description and mission statement are most powerful when they are part of the one narration. The power of a richly painted vision combined with the emotions felt from positive achievement - open the floodgate of creativity.

While there is an overall vision which must be created by the CEO and Upper Management reflecting a future customer-driven reality which is to be expected, sub-visions within departments and groups should constantly be developed as circumstances require behavioral and perceptual changes. In relation to departmental visioning: As outlined in Chapter Four, Module Five, an issue is brought forth by a team.

THE VISIONING CHALLENGE: A new computer program was introduced to the department without allowing the department staff an opportunity to provide preliminary input on the impact such changes might have on their job functions and how the transition to the new program could best occur. Because the department employees determined they were not adequately included in the change feedback loop, they felt slighted. An "us and them" attitude was given root to grow.

Based upon this information, the team may construct a vision as to what the impact will be when effective feedback systems are in place when new computer programming changes are about to occur.

The Change

The written vision could be something like this:

"Our comfort level is much higher with the new computer software we are now using because we were consulted by management while they were still in the decision making mode in relation to the software. They first filled us in as to the impact they felt the software would have on our job activities. We were then asked, based upon the information they provided, how we would see that software being best integrated into our work activities.

"Our feedback gave them additional perspectives relating to specific activity changes that would occur and how our scheduling and our attitude relating to scheduling would be effected. We were approached respectfully for our input. Management showed that they value us as expects in our work activities. They emphasized that any software change would be transitioned based upon our input as to the best speed for the changeover."

Here we have a description, in present and past tense, of a new approach taken by management communicating to create ownership of change among the workers in the department. How can this vision become reality next time such changes are contemplated by management?

The team developing the vision must then shift to a left-hemisphere sequential mode and design the processes which they feel will enable such a vision to become reality. Is there a time frame? Perhaps. What are the specific steps? Several will be listed. It is vital to remember that the VISION must be developed before the PROCESS. The vision can remain constant while the processes to bring the vision into reality may have to change rather often due to new circumstances.

Responding to the Challenge

Here are some preliminary steps in the process the team may list:

- The vision has already been written, so the team agrees as to the nature of the problem.

- A meeting with management is held with the employees stating their reaction to the last computer program software changeover.

- During the meeting there is a desire to listen to management's reasons for conducting the changeover. Then employees share with management the employees' team vision as to how they would like to experience the next such changeover.

- A series of work sessions with management is held defining the changes in behaviors that will allow better initial communication of change information and appreciation of the time-line needed for the changes to be as focused, effective and nonstressed as possible.

How often will these meetings be? How many meetings will be needed? How will the meetings be spaced to have minimal impact on work scheduling? Who needs to be spoken to? How will the employee's work to communicate the message of their needs? How will employees be prepared to respond to several possible management responses to their requests? All of these variables become a part of the process development toward bringing the vision into reality.

The vision is an expression of the values and attitudes of the employees. It reflects the level of ownership they wish to exhibit in their work. Generally, it should not be subject to modification. Only the processes are flexible - not the vision. If the employees' vision is truly customer-focused, the chances are quite good that

The Change

the values and expectation embodied in the vision are going to be of long term value for the company. It is a dynamic and growing organism that allows and encourages their employees in all areas to unlock the power of team visioning.

EMOTION

This is the Second Step toward Creating the Future. After the mind creates a vision, there must be emotional commitment or the vision dies. After the vision, emotion is the building block for making the future happen. Do we have the courage to dip deeply into the pool of emotional commitment that each of us has? Or do we sit by the pool, sort of dip our feet in and get them wet a little bit. Dare we dive in? The deeper we go into the pool of that emotion the more we touch what we really desire out of life. The closer we come to seeing our real potential.

The power we have through emotions cannot be a well-directed stimulus unless we have enough information within our vision of the future to direct that emotion effectively. Witness the actions during the Era of the Black Plague which haunted Europe centuries ago. Mothers, themselves ill with the plague, would embrace their noninfected children - thereby dooming them to the same fate. Through the deep felt emotion of love, the mother held her children and, because of ignorance, gave them a death sentence. EMOTION NEEDS AN INFORMATION TRACK TO RUN ON - JUST AS A POWERFUL TRAIN MUST BE GUIDED BY TRACKS TO ITS DESTINATION.

Fortunately, today we have a deluge of technical information and innovations about which we can become emotionally committed to achieving the tasks at hand.

When an informed, knowledgeable vision is combined with emotional commitment - we can literally move the world.

Responding to the Challenge

In one story, a small boy is playing on a piece of heavy equipment in a motor yard where his father works. The lad climbs up on a mammoth earth moving machine, sits in the cage and plays with the steering wheel.

"Vroommm....Vrooomm." the lad sounds. While playing, the lad's elbow hits a switch and the motor roars on. Suddenly play turns to fear. The child's foot catches on the emergency brake and releases it. The behemoth is moving and the child is frightened out of his mind. In the few seconds before the child's father jumps up and turns off the machine, the child is thinking of how he only wanted to play. He did not want nor was he ready for the responsibility of the real power. He just wanted to play.

The power that we have as individuals and as groups of individuals functioning in companies when we deeply emotionalize a vision is more than profound - it is beyond words. It is the power that humankind has used, albeit rarely, to transform society to a higher level.

Because such a vision-emotion combination is so powerful - we instinctively avoid it. If we don't use it, we don't have to be responsible for it. We play games when we just dip our feet into this great power. We energize our lives when we dive in. Emotion is the flame that ignites vision.

Vision and Emotion

And what are Vision and Emotion? They are the energies of the right hemisphere of the brain. If you want your employees to fall in love with work, you must seduce the right hemisphere of their brain. Sound clinical? I suppose it does, and the caveat is that you, CEO/Management, must first seduce the right hemisphere of your own brain with a grand vision. If you are not evangelical and modeling the vision of which you speak - the smart right

The Change

hemispheres of the employees won't be fooled. The right hemisphere is that part of the employee's brain that becomes activated about 4:45 p.m. on Friday - when they go deeply and emotionally into that vision of the bowling tournament that will start at 7 p.m. And when they are focused there, they are focused unbelievably. The body may still be lingering at work - but the mind is where the vision and emotion is.

We understand the meaning of enjoyment of focus almost instinctively when we deal with hobbies, pastimes or recreations. When we do those things we love to do - how does the time pass? On a Saturday, we're engrossed in a sport or hobby, we look at the clock and it's ten a.m. and then we get back to what we're doing. A "few" minutes later we look again and it's 1 p.m. Where did the time go?!! The time bandit struck.

When we have an ownership vision combined with a deep emotional commitment toward what we're doing, it alters the structure of how we focus on what we do. We focus more deeply, more richly. Our perception of time is altered. We have all experienced this: either because we are where we don't really want to be and time drags - or because we are having so much enjoyment with what we are doing that we are trying to grasp and hold on to time.

Now, consider what it would be like to arise Monday morning, with a vision and a challenge, an emotional high and a joy to go to work. We're eager to achieve because we've fallen in love within an empowered environment. We have ownership, control and the opportunity to build and be developing the processes that are allowing the company to earn a profit, to grow, to remain competitive in this constantly changing marketplace.

Does it sound unreal that we could really fall in love with what we do?

Responding to the Challenge

Left Hemisphere-driven organizations are losing a richness in enjoyment and creativity that is costing them dearly. If you are a business owner, ask yourself this: Did I begin my business because I was forced to work for myself, or because I was pursuing a dream?

NEW INFORMATION

There is a system that the mind uses to create our future. It is a simple system and it is quite uniform. But it is not well known by many. Two parts of the system we have already touched upon.

1. Ownership of a Vision

2. Emotional Commitment to that Vision

Those are accomplished through the power of the right hemisphere as illustrated:

Vision
↓
Emotion

RIGHT HEMISPHERE

Once the vision and emotion begin to work together, a transformation of the mind occurs. Millions of nerve endings in the nerve bundle known as the Corpus Callosum transmit desires in the form of electrical impulses to the receptive left hemisphere. We live in a world of possibilities. But we see in life only the possibilities that we expect to see. To the rest we remain blind. That's OK as long as the possibilities we expect to see give us a

The Change

vision rich enough to accomplish what is really important and meaningful to us personally and in our business affairs.

Our logical, rational, conscious vision of life is ruled by the visual and emotional focus of the right hemisphere. Once the right hemisphere generates the vision and emotional direction to give us growth in our personal and business opportunities - a powerful process of achievement is more than 50 % underway.

The way the vision-emotion transfer to the left hemisphere occurs is an identical process - whether we are relating to an individual or a group of people in a company. Ideally, the company communicates the vision from CEO/Upper Management to middle management to supervisor to front line in such a way that the importance of each person to that vision is understood and each person is given a stake in the development of the processes through which they will play an important part in bringing that vision into reality.

When this is done new perspectives and opportunities spring up throughout the organism (remember, "Organism" means empowered company). A new excitement and vitality fills the organism. When we are an emotional part of bringing the vision into reality - our right brain begins to present to our conscious mind "new" information that will aid us in our efforts.

Let's illustrate how this dynamic works. Have you ever purchased a new car? Go into a showroom, open the door of a new auto. Put your hand on the leather seating and begin feeling it. Within a few seconds you may hear a soft melodious voice behind you saying "Doesn't that feel good? Go ahead and sit in the car. Notice how soft those seats are. We have one out on the lot just like it. Would you like to take a test drive to really give it a feel? Here are the keys, just take it out for a while."

Responding to the Challenge

All effective salespeople know that when you create a vision in a prospective customer's mind, an expectation of what they want, and when that vision becomes attached to emotion, desire - then the customer is 90 % sold. At that point the desire is transmitted to the logical left hemisphere of the brain to be justified and to find ways to make it possible to fill that need.

" Well, I can't afford the car." You say to yourself at first. "There just isn't any way. I couldn't pay my bills if I got that car." But you are instilled with a vision and an emotional desire - you want that car. You become willing to pay the price. "What kind of creative financing do you offer?" you ask.

It is indeed a wonderful vision to see yourself in a new car. It is also a significant emotional commitment to pay the kind of money necessary to purchase one. Once you make that commitment and drive the car home, something magical happens. That day driving home and the next several days, you see cars just like the one you bought every time you turn the corner. "Where did these cars come from?" you think. "Did everyone go out and buy the same kind of car yesterday?"

What you are experiencing is occurring because when we have a vision with emotional commitment, we begin to see information that is related to the vision. The other cars were already there, they were just not important to us consciously until we made the buying decision.

In a similar manner, when the company shares its vision and gives ownership of the processes so emotional commitment can be shared, front line people become creative, they become creators. They become visionaries instead of robots -they can take advantage of the opportunity they have been given to utilize the right half of the amazing tool we have as human beings, the brain.

The Change

Activation of the right hemisphere of the brain through visioning and emotional commitment can do more than just release "new" bits of information to our conscious awareness. Such activation makes it much easier for us to achieve what I call "Emancipation"- the ability to see with new eyes the habits that may be holding us captive to end results we don't want. Through such emancipation we see clearly what we were doing wrong in our interpersonal communications and emotional expressions with others.

The Emancipation process can be quite painful as we perceive, perhaps for the first time, how we have not communicated well and indeed have hurt others with our behavior. Such emancipation allows us the freedom to learn behaviors that are more responsive and sensitive to the needs of others. Through the growing pains of such an experience we can move into very satisfying personal development and can indeed exceed our expectations.

Another way of expressing this is that when we emotionally commit to a vision of change within ourselves, the depth of our commitment to Serve better, to Communicate better, to be more Sensitive can cause the right brain to give us what can only be called Revelation. It is an experience that is difficult to articulate. It is a shift in our perception of who we can be. We see ourselves clearly and many times we won't like what we see. We are then free to be willing to and capable of change.

IMPLEMENTATION

As new information begins to flow into the organism we perceive consistently how we can improve the processes to provide better customer service. Perception of the new information then leads to its application/implementation.

Responding to the Challenge

In the next illustration, we see the fully functioning right and left hemispheres of the mind synergistically energized to flow together - sharing their different abilities in a way that multiplies capabilities.

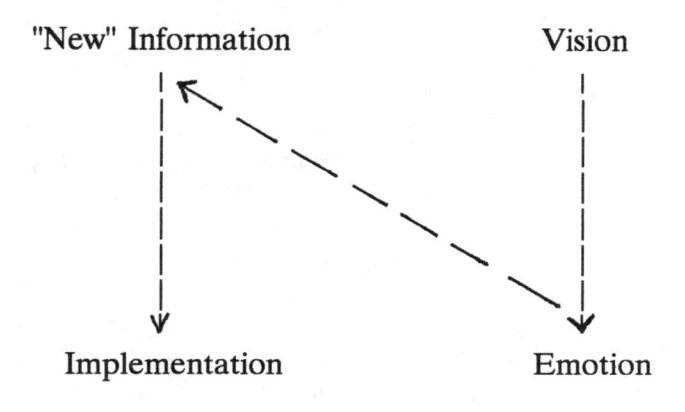

```
"New" Information              Vision
       ↑╲                        │
       │  ╲                      │
       │    ╲                    │
       │      ╲                  │
       │        ╲                │
       │          ╲              │
       ↓            ↘            ↓
  Implementation              Emotion

  LEFT HEMISPHERE         RIGHT HEMISPHERE
```

You are beginning to see that in the Directive-Driven culture, three steps to the proper functioning of the creative mind have been circumvented. When no vision is given, no emotional commitment is possible and no new information needs to be seen to serve the company or the customer. Only implementation of tasks and directives occurs.

"I just work here. I just do my job."

While consulting with one company still functioning in the Directive-Driven mode, I discovered that recently their entire computer system had been out for a day. That computer outage set their customer service back several days. I inquired more and discovered that the night janitor had noticed a large wire out of it's casing and laying where it could easily be tripped over. No one was

The Change

called. Nothing was done. The next day the cable was accidently broken with the resultant computer outage.

The night janitor was asked about the problem. Did she notice it? Why didn't she report it? She was grilled by management. But during the interrogation she gave them a printed company form - her job description. Nowhere on it, she reminded them, did it say that she should report loose cable. And, besides, she felt afraid to bring up something that didn't relate directly to her tasks. She hadn't wanted to bother them with something that was probably a "stupid" thing. The "stupid" thing she didn't report cost the company $15,000. The non-reporting was not her fault. The culture of the company stressed only implementation.

In a company functioning as an organism, the vision would have been shared by management. In summary, the broad vision of the company and then in more detail the operational vision for the department in which she would work, broken into smaller goals and objectives. Then, of course, she would be given "ownership" of the area in which she would clean. She would be asked to put together a plan for proper cleaning of those areas - how does she think it can best be achieved? She is to share that plan with management. Such sharing allows management to appreciate her skill and make suggestions.

Why share the company vision with the janitor? Neurologically speaking, we could be quite technical about the electrical structures of the brain that change when the vision is shared, but the reason

Responding to the Challenge

is really simple. The company shares the vision with the janitor in order to share the joy. To share the joy and challenge of where that vision is taking those in the organism. True, the janitor is not personally involved in most of the goals and objectives of that department. But her ignorance of them gives her no opportunity to be excited about what is being achieved. And her knowledge of them has deep psychological impact. What that janitor is doing is vital. She is an important person. She will be treated as such - with respect. Anything she finds that would interfere with the vision, goals and objectives of the company as they relate to serving the customer should be shared with those who can help. There is no fear in that sharing. Everyone in the company is there for an important purpose. Everyone will be listened to. Communication flows as a river. The lifeblood of the organism flows rich and deep. That company grows and customer expectations are exceeded, time after time.

It becomes more obvious to see the differences in motivating power between the Directive-Driven and the organic environment. Yet for many in the behavioral field the question of "How do we motivate people?" has been an issue as illusive as smoke. Do we reward them? Do we punish them? Are people just inherently lazy?

If any of us go back to the feelings and actions related to our hobbies and pastimes, it becomes quickly obvious that we are not inherently lazy. Workplace environments have been tying one of the employee's legs behind his back. A rather painful thing when you think about it. Then, with one leg tied uselessly, management has been asking them to run as fast as they can. The workplace behaviorists are there at the sidelines offering rewards for the fastest or punishment for the slowest. Within that restraining system, employees will hop as fast as they can. But they are travelling with half their power tied behind their back. No wonder it's fun when working for a Directive-Driven organization to come

The Change

home, untie the other foot and enjoy what humans were made to do - Run. Be free to use their full abilities.

In a Directive-Driven organization, when we have someone come into the workplace and they put in their eight hours a day, five days a week: they are merely asked to implement information - to implement a process that they have no part in designing whatsoever. We are literally tying one side of their brain behind their back.

In order for quality to exist as a system, each person must be functioning freely with both hemispheres turned on. As the front line touches the client, receives feedback as to needs, the front line's ability - not just to react but to be proactive and develop creative ways for satisfying those customer needs must be activated.

The Power of Focus

Once I received a coffee mug from my wife. On the mug were the words "Wherever you are, be there." How cute, I thought. A few years later, while glancing at the mug, the meaning really hit me. Indeed, I was guilty of not focusing on what I needed to be doing at any given time. How easy is it to put in our eight hours a day, yet not focusing. Are we scanning in our mind what we are going to do tomorrow? Or what we will do that evening? When we are where we don't want to be - where is our focus? It's on getting out of there, doing something else, putting in the minimum, putting in the time. The customer is a cross to bear, etc. In the organic environment, enjoyment and focus is possible. Even then, it's not always the easiest thing to do as Mihaly Csikszentmihalyi explains in his book, *The Psychology of Optimal Experience*. "At least as much as intelligence, it requires the commitment of emotions and will. It is not enough to know how to do it; one must do it, consistently, in the same way as athletes or musicians who must keep practicing what they know in theory."

Responding to the Challenge

But when we develop the self-love and the self-discipline to begin to evolve (refer to Chapter Three for more on these personal transformations) our perception of our worklife will start to change. The key to quality is when everyone in an organism is so excited about the vision as it is broken down into goals and objectives that focus becomes fun. We cannot be fully focused unless we've fallen in love with that vision. Unless we feel personal ownership.

I came across a wonderful illustration of this several years ago. One of my business associates worked with his father who has a music ministry. As a young child he began touring throughout the country with his father. He would sing and aid his father in the many needs of the work. As he related this story to me, he stressed that he had, indeed, been going through the motions. "Well, Dad wanted me to do this or that," he said "I was reacting to the needs of my father's organization - a ministry to people who were really in need. But it always felt like work."

Because of one event when he was seventeen, all of this changed, he recounted. They had travelled into a town and were working with some disadvantaged people who were having alcohol and other substance abuse problems. "At that time I saw a person's life really change before my eyes through the ministry and that's when I really realized what my father was doing. It was no longer something I was doing because my dad said I needed to do it. Now I wanted to do it because I saw the end results. At seventeen, I no longer worked for the ministry - I became a part of it." That's the power of having ownership in a vision.

Whatever we do, we owe it to ourselves to fall in love with what we do. That creates a tremendous power of focus. When we have that focus, we can be where we are deeply for that period of time - with far greater productivity and enjoyment.

The Change

The complexity of today's technology is ironically helping us move into a position where work must become enjoyable. Repetitious work will be given to robots. Creative focus will become the skill supreme for the American employee of the future. Only an organic environment will allow such skills to thrive.

As Csikszentmihalyi outlines in *The Psychology of Optimal Experience*, "The brain surgeon operating in a shining hospital and the slave laborer who staggers under a heavy load as he wades through the mud are both working. But the surgeon has a chance to learn new things every day, and every day he learns that he is in control and that he can perform difficult tasks. The laborer is forced to repeat the same exhausting motions, and what he learns is mostly about his own helplessness."

Certainly not all the American workers of the year 2000 will be surgeons. But they must have ownership over the processes they utilize to please the customer if quality is to keep our nation competitive. Ownership allows enjoyment which allows focus. And focus allows us to create. Employees with the "helplessness" mindset react to customers. Employees with the focused mindset create new possibilities for pleasing the customer because they have fun using their creative abilities to do so.

If you really want to compete with someone, try competing with people who have fallen in love with what they do. You virtually can't keep up with them - because they are in another dimension. They are beyond competition.

When Storm Clouds Gather Birds Scatter, But Eagles Soar

Responding to the Challenge

Because they fly above the mundane, eagles have a vision - a perspective that none of the little birds that are just scampering around have any idea concerning. Within the next few decades our business and economic environment will give us many storm clouds with which to deal.

Are we going to choose to be eagles? Will we give ourselves permission to love what we do and develop the power of focus? Or are we going to be little birds down on the ground scampering about in fear of the thunderclouds - reacting? Victims are reactive. If things change and it's somehow negative - then woe is me.

Victors create real companies, Organic Environments. They love themselves enough to give themselves the gift of self-discipline to focus on what the vision of the company really should be-serving the customer in an anticipatory creative fashion. What if your company does not have a vision?

Several recent surveys indicate that there is very little anticipation or planning for the future among many companies. Cost control is used as a reactive tool. In one survey only one percent of businesses were thinking in terms of managing their future. Only one percent with special teams charting the direction a company should go with it's business. The vast majority using rear view mirror approaches.

Restructuring Habits

Habits can change. Habits, attitudes, processes can bind companies into directions that lose most of the human potential to be great. Change the habits and you redirect the power. The mental re-creation process begins when we as individuals create or buy into a vision of what we want the results of our efforts to be. The vision should be written as a screen play - a drama of human achievement. You are not writing about how others will change -

The Change

you are constructing a future in which what you do has been altered. A future in which your habits and priorities are different in order to achieve new and better results.

Quite simply, how do you know what to change? I do not advocate change for change's sake. If you or your company are not getting where you want to be going, odds are 100% that your habits and the direction of your energy must be altered to get the results you want.

First, you stop what you are doing and ask yourself; Why am I doing this and where is it taking me? Second, in addition to introspection, be willing to get counsel from someone who has achieved what you really want to achieve. Few people will slam the door if you humbly ask for their advice. Find someone knowledgeable and bold enough to put a mirror in front of your face to show the flaws in what you currently are doing. Be sure you have the courage to change before you do this!

Let's deal with the "will power" issue. Research is showing that will power to quit doing whatever just doesn't work that well in the long run. It's great at first - when we white knuckle it and stare at the habit we want to break as though we were daring it to come back and bite us - and it usually does.

The problem with will power is that we are focused on fighting what we are thinking about all the time. It becomes a love/hate relationship. To change a habit, focus on the new actions or circumstances you want for yourself. Don't push against the habit with will power trying to demolish it. Just walk away from the habit and embrace something different. Put your time and attention into the new behaviors. What we think about the most is what we ultimately create.

The first step in the habit recreation process is visualizing the

Responding to the Challenge

change that we want to happen as though it has already happened. We sense through our creative ability the positive results that will occur as a result of this new reality. Because we sense the changes and feel them as though they had already happened, we put a deep emotional investment, a depth of commitment, into making the vision real.

It may be a very specific vision, e.g., certain levels of customer service emanating from your department. It may be more generally on an emotional level, e.g., better and deeper communication between staff members. However, in either scenario, create the end results in your mind ahead of time and write them down. If the vision is personal development, show your vision to only those who will support you. If your vision is part of the group visioning process in your department - encourage one another daily to keep the mind focused on the end results. Be ready to prop up a co-worker's sagging attitude. It may be her turn to prop up yours tomorrow. Be mirrors to one another in the department in a positive way.

Personal Commitment

Whether your vision is personal or departmental, there is no greater power than the vision that is backed with an affirmative answer to this question: "Would I pursue this dream even if I received no financial reward?" That seems like an absurd question since we all must work to earn a living. But how much more powerful we are when we love what we do:

1. Because we are well suited for what we do.

2. Because we have discovered elements of what we do that we enjoy.

If our emotional commitment is not brought to life through one of

The Change

those two elements, best that we find other employment. Life is too short to not be alive with a vision.

When criticism is given to another co-worker, you first channel in on what is important to that person about their work and honor that. Support other's successes while giving critique. Virtually all correction within a department should be based on keeping the vision in focus and working toward the specific goals that come from breaking down that vision into time and activity increments.

Creating the Future is a choice. It's a choice each of us makes individually and as companies. The choice is made each day: to create our future or have it created for us by reacting to our environment. Perhaps as you are reading this, you are ready to vision your screenplay of excellence. The decision may be made today. But, each day the decision has to be re-confirmed. Each day we re-commit to simply react to circumstances or create our own circumstances.

Depth of Communication

We understand that for a business organism to flourish there must be depth of communication. It means we have the freedom to speak what we feel in relation to the vision and needs of the company. To the degree that we seek to uphold the vision of growth for the organism, we are respected for our feelings and our ideas - we are honored as a creative individual. Part of the self-discipline that comes into play in depth of communication is focusing that communication into the issues that create customer satisfaction - the end result of all efforts.

Communication should be free, relaxed but also exciting and disciplined. Seems like a paradox? There is nothing wrong with getting excited about pleasing the customer. That trait should be nourished and honored. Such excitement and emotional feeling

Responding to the Challenge

about the company vision is an expanding emotion. The discipline is nourished by the respect for the importance of the vision.

Business meetings are short, intense, deeply felt and very effective. People listening, really listening to one another. Respecting differences. Focusing on the important goals and objectives and creatively doing what must be done to bring the vision into reality. That is where discipline and joy are blended together.

Breadth of Communication

We must be able to communicate fearlessly but in a focused fashion with anyone in the organism up to the CEO. In the business organism of the future, vision will be modeled by CEO/Upper Management as well as being explained in detail as certain goals and objectives are formed with each division and department. Such upper level modeling is critical. "Do what we say, not what we do." will not cut it today. It is suicide. Better to remain a Directive-Driven culture than to "play at" pushing for employee change while thinking CEO/Upper Management can remain in the old mindset. Upper Echelon not modeling true change sticks out as obviously as the truism that gluttony is never long a secret sin.

One company, starting out right, sent Upper Management first through the cultural change training. "Where is the CEO?" I asked. This is always my first question since I will not conduct cultural change programs with a company unless they begin with top down training. I already knew the answer. He was on the front row - right on the firing line, fully participating during the two days of management training. That news filtered down through the grapevine quickly.

This particular CEO, in addition to being a great human being, was clever. He publicly admitted during the seminar several of his own

The Change

failings in his approach to company development. He listed instances and gave illustrations as to what he had learned in order to better serve the company. That news filtered quickly through the company grapevine.

When that CEO later called a meeting of front line personnel to overview what they would be experiencing in the employee cultural change modules - they were ready to listen to him.

Remember, in an effective cultural change process such as the one outlined in Chapter Four, management is beginning to give up "control" over what they never really had: The attitude of the worker. The "control" that is management's real responsibility is to create an environment in which people can creatively grow and nourish the company. This high quality type of "control" is developed through depth of communication.

Time Table for Change

Do I have to tell anyone reading this that we live in an "instant" society? I really believe that if they came out with a headache remedy that promised instant relief even before you took it - people would buy it out of hope that it would work. Can you image the ad "As you reach for our new improved product, you'll feel instant relief." Certainly things don't happen instantly in the real world of human change.

When I spoke recently at a personal growth class in a Middle American city, I encountered a room full of baby-boomers. I asked, "How many of you were raised on a farm?" No one raised a hand. For a vast majority of American workers, we are not an agrarian society. We have forgotten what the farmer knew. When a quality cultural change is birthed by the initial freeing-up of communication within a company, it takes time for people to become comfortable with the new attitudinal systems being put into place.

Responding to the Challenge

Farming Perspective

Farmers don't stand out in their fields and stomp up and down in frustration because the fields are not growing fast enough. They have the wisdom to understand the process that's involved. Believe me - as managers, you are farmers.

If you are a good manager, you are a nourisher of those seeds of creativity, capability, skill and excitement that virtually all employees possess. There are phases to quality cultural change:

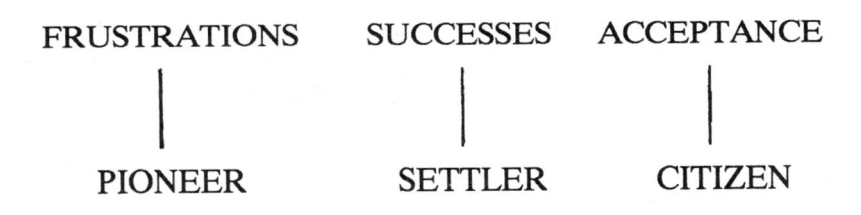

FRUSTRATIONS	SUCCESSES	ACCEPTANCE
|	|	|
PIONEER	SETTLER	CITIZEN

In the beginning Pioneer phase, employees are looking carefully to see if management itself is modeling the changes they are beginning to talk about. If it does, the employees will begin to listen. That's the first key. Then as habits clash with change, frustration sets in. Best to have a sense of humor at this point. Growing pains hurt. Here, the overall vision of the company must be kept clean and crisp and ever before the employee. Encourage more than criticize. Prune the flock when necessary because not every employee will decide they want to be part of a joyful interactive environment. Let those who wish go find another Directive-Driven environment in which to exist. Those who remain gain progressively greater "ownership" over their jobs. They begin to create the processes through which they touch the customer and get constant customer feedback to create an ever ascending level of quality.

The Change

In the Settler phase, those who have taken ownership of the vision and have begun to break that vision down into specific goals and objectives, will begin to see things slowly coming into place. New ideas emerge. Some of those ideas totally transforming what was considered the ceiling for customer service and innovative ways for manufacturing and marketing. Success begins to make the focused effort worthwhile.

Finally comes the Mind Shift that eventually all those who are part of the business organism will feel deeply. The Change has really happened. A realization sets in even more deeply than before - that it really could happen. We're becoming successful through a new way of dealing with one another that is so less stressful than before. It is really OK to have fun while striving diligently toward higher customer service through high quality standards.

Quality is a journey of the human spirit. It's endless. There is no end to what customers are going to need or expect a year from now, or five years hence. Those companies that choose to survive and really come to life will be pleasing the customer and surpassing customer expectations because they have transformed themselves into organisms thriving upon respect, human understanding and focused passion.

Let's define the new technology upon which companies are built...

It used to be that whoever had the best equipment, the best facilities, prevailed. It was a time before global information made everyone capable of possessing the same level of hard goods technology. The "technology" that is now beginning to dominate is best described as the DEPTH OF RELATIONSHIPS. Relationships between management and worker - Relationships between company and supplier - Relationships between sales and engineering.

No longer hiding in little cubicles, organizational departments are learning from one another and learning, most of all, that the whole is much greater than the parts trying to work as "Lone Rangers." They are learning through depth of relationships that an organization functions far better when it is an "organism" sustained by the blood supply of honest, open, and perceptive communication.

Remember, to create our economic future: trust, open communication, DEPTH OF RELATIONSHIPS are tools of the new technology that has the power to transport our economy into the next century in fine style.

REFERENCES

Sylvester, Kathleen, "The 2.4 Billion Dollar Suggestion Box." *Governing Magazine,* May, 1992.

Gitlow, H.S. and Gitlow, S.J., *The Deming Guide to Quality and Competitive Position.* Englewood Cliffs, N.J., 1987.

Block, P. *The Empowered Manager: Positive Skills at Work.* San Francisco, Jossey-Bass, 1987.

Treffert, Darold A. *Extraordinary People,* New York: Harper and Row, 1989.

Frontinus. *Strategematon, III,* Introduction.

DeCamp, L. Sprague. *The Heroic Age of American Invention,* New York: Doubleday and Co., Inc., 1957.

Toffler, Alvin. *Powershift,* New York: Bantam Books, 1990.

Boorstin, Daniel J. *The Discoverors,* New York: Vintage Books, 1985.

Allen, Frederick Lewis. *The Big Change,* New York: Harper and Brothers, 1952.

Csikszentmihalyi, Mihaly. *Flow - The Psychology of Optimal Experience.* Harper and Row, 1990.

3 Personal Dynamics for The Change

> *The unexamined life is not worth living.*
>
> Socrates

The purpose of this chapter is to look closely at the dynamics of personal change from a metaphorical view. Life is a story. We learn through stories. Stories awaken the childlike power of possibilities that lives in each of us. One of the wonders of writing is to be able to creatively take an important concept and through word pictures expand on its meaning and application.

The Challenge

Here you are - you have trained for years to become an accomplished mountain climber. Now, you are several days into what will be one of the greatest challenges in your life. The mountain you are climbing is truly a test of your will, your determination and literally your love of yourself and the worth you place upon your life. You have been told that at the top of this mountain is an ageless piece of wisdom that will transform your mind. You've been told that if you will exercise the determination to pursue it, if you will believe deeply enough that you can achieve it - this piece of wisdom will be worth as much as all the knowledge you have ever received in the past.

The Change

Your muscles tighten as you continue with great tenacity to climb this rugged mountain, braving stiff winds and occasional pouring rain. You have all the right equipment, but your strength is taxed as you reach solid, high walls with few handholds to grasp and even fewer footholds. You continue to climb. Half way up, you become aware that the air is thinning and you realize that this is going to be a task that will truly pit your life against nature.

A few hours later, you pause, exhausted. Suddenly, the realization hits you that there is really no way you can make it to the top - unless there is some change, some transformation, some miracle. But you desire with all your soul. You vision and believe. You will pay whatever price you must.

As your faith reaches the very climax of your ability to feel and desire, you sense a change happening. Your legs become lighter. Your entire body more compact. Your arms begin to expand and surge with tremendous strength.

You are becoming an eagle. Suddenly, elegantly, you lift off the side of the mountain and on graceful wings, you ascend to the heights. In sweeping motions, you move higher and higher toward the summit. Then you soar a few feet above the peak. You open your eyes wide as you look into the horizon above the highest mountain. In that golden sky are the ageless words of wisdom for which you have risked all.

You Owe It To Yourself To Fall In Love With What You Do

This is the universal truth upon which literally all success and happiness in life is based. This is a debt that each of us personally owes not to our company, our spouse, our mother or father. We

Personal Dynamics

owe it deeply and continuously to ourselves. It is the greatest debt we will ever strive to repay. The miracle of being a human, is that we indeed have the capacity to pay that debt and, in so doing, create our own future. By visioning the future that we desire and then by falling deeply in love day by day with the processes that are necessary to get us to that future, we fulfill our reason for existence.

We owe it to ourselves to fall in love with what we do, even when we're in interim positions, when we're doing things that maybe are not immediately involved with our major goals - we can still find an enjoyment and happiness within as we move through the more inconsequential activities toward higher levels of achievement. We realize that the final determinant of our happiness is the person we see in the mirror each morning.

If we cannot fall in love with what we do - we have three other alternatives.

1. Find the profession or activity in our life that we can fall in love with.

2. Find areas in what we do that we enjoy. And look with new eyes at our present activities, finding pleasure where we once found only complaint.

3. Or be a victim for the rest of our life. But a victim is not alive even though physical death has yet to catch up.

The mountain we are all climbing is our life. Miracles seldom occur when real people are on real mountains. But in the mountain climbing world of personal growth and change...miracles are floating around everywhere - just waiting to be desired and brought into reality.

The Change

> *The most important factor in the complex equation of the future is the way the human mind responds to crisis.* In A Study Of History, *Arnold Toynbee points out that the greatest historical forces are set in motion when people decide to pit themselves against serious challenge. Human experience is not a closed circle. It is full of magnificent detours and sudden departures from predicted destinations.*
>
> Norman Cousins

Personal Dynamics

LIFECHANGERS

Program One: LifeValue

Information alone has never brought about profound lifechanges without a corresponding emotional impact. The subconscious mind, directly affected by the non-dominant (right) hemisphere of the brain, is guided and goal-directed by those things which produce the greatest emotional impact upon our conscious awareness.

In the four programs of LifeChangers you will enjoy the opportunity to experience information in a story form. The first LifeChangers Program is entitled LifeValue. The title can be explained only with a story...

A Look in the Mirror

There was an old man lying on his death bed fading in and out of consciousness. During a lucid moment, it suddenly dawned upon him what he had given up in life. The full weight and immensity of what he had missed in life struck him so heavily that he cried. In a way, as we begin to explore and understand the thoughts of this old man perhaps we and the entire universe will mourn.

It began, of course, many years ago. This old man, as is true of all of us, was once a young child. Oh! And the eyes of a two year old - they don't see what we see! They see magic. There is wonder to be explored under every rock. There is a giant or a dinosaur! Behind every tree is a vast area to explore. There is a world revolving in every plant and blade of grass. In all of the little ant cities that the child builds are marvelous, wonderful fantasies about things that can be. Imaginings.

The Change

This old man, when he was a young child of six, would lie in the fields and watch the stars at night and think of the wonder - the wonderful things which could be achieved. One night he would be an explorer - another night a great scientist - and yet another night a great singer - his young mind was filled with all the possibilities of life.

As this young person watched his parents going about their everyday workday world; working at their jobs, coming home each day, following the routine of life - he received a message.

This young man entered school and began to be taught what could and could not be done. Following this line of thinking through during the years in which he was involved in the educational system, he received another message.

The young man's wonderful eyes of magic began to dim and a reality began to form within his mind that there really were limitations, there were boundaries to achievement, to emotions, to what we do and to what we say and to what we can become. "Why?", he would ask. "Because that's what I am being told," he would answer.

Then the young man finished his education and ventured out into the world of work; gaining a job, developing skills, progressing within the business world. And finding himself quickly within the golden handcuffs of routine: going to work, coming back from work, social time, a night of rest, and then repeating everything over and over again.

At times during his young working life, a deep thought would emotionally nag and nip at his soul: "But what about all of the things about which I dreamed when I was a young child? What about all of the possibilities that I explored? Can I step out and try some of these things?" After a pause, he reflected "No, no, that

Personal Dynamics

would not be very safe. Besides, I'm busy now. I have work to do. I really don't have time for day dreaming or play or fantasy. I'm older now."

As his life continued to shape and harden into perceptions of the reality of his own limitations, the nagging of that still small voice inside became weaker and dimmer but it was never totally extinguished.

Now, after many years, upon his death bed, a terrible cosmic realization floods his entire soul. "Why didn't I try? Why didn't I take the opportunity to do some of those fantasies of my dreams of youth. Why didn't I take the time to challenge myself to see if I could succeed? I really always wanted to be a singer. I really always wanted to be an explorer. But I became a business person. That was not bad, but that was all! And it was only all because I let it be all. I was my own worst enemy by setting and allowing such limitations to exist in my life."

"I could have explored!" the old man exclaimed, "I could have saved my money and flown to faraway places. Or, I could have taken singing lessons and satisfied that creative urge I had since childhood. But now the time clock has run out," he moaned, "The game is almost over."

With deep sobs the old man said to himself, "But I was full of fear! What if I had tried to sing and failed? What if I went off to be an explorer and got lost? I feared." And then he smiled a sad smile and said, "Yes, I feared to be the leader of my own life. And that which I feared to do and didn't do, I failed at before I even started."

The Change

> ### *The Past Can Be a Poor Future*
>
> *In a tiny box the old man had hidden away his future. To have pursued it would have required a childlike emotional commitment. He feared to move deeply into his emotions, so he continued to hide his real future by simply reliving the past over and over again; taking the past into more of the future rather than creating the future from the deep dreams and possibilities sensed from his youth. For the sake of a false security, he was willing to be a victim of his past and lose the gift of his real future - his birthright. To cease being a victim means that I must be responsible for my future. Being responsible means I must begin to love myself. Such self love activates discipline to form the future that is the result of my vision.*

As the old man's eyes finally closed in the soft embrace of death, that little six year old boy deep within his mind sat down in front of a beautiful grove of trees near his father's farm and as a cool breeze swept over his face, began to cry over something as silly and childish as broken dreams.

If we open a quarrel between the past and the present, we shall find that we have lost the future.

Winston Churchill

Now, you begin to emotionally understand, in your own personal way, why this first program in the lifechangers series is called LifeValue. But the message calls for another story to increase your feeling of the deepest meaning...

Personal Dynamics

The Value of Time

A Middle Eastern oil baron lay seriously ill. His family gathered around him and counting the wealth in that hospital room, entire countries could be bought and sold. The sheik smiled weakly as he lay in the best bed the famous hospital could furnish - being constantly attended by world famous doctors - available at his beck and call.

One relative offered to fly his favorite meal to him from Brazil. Another offered to bring one of the sheik's friends in from Africa by charter jet for a few moment's visit that afternoon. Money was no object in their offerings to their dying relative.

The sheik paused in reflection and said in a quiet voice, "There is one thing you can obtain for me that I desire greatly, indeed, with all my heart." There was a hush in the room, as they all gathered around his bed and awaited his request with an eagerness to accomplish it.

"Obtain for me another month of life. One more month of life to see my grandchild born." He looked deeply at those around him. "Is that too much to ask? Not ten years, not a year, only a month. Spend all my wealth. Find a way. My wealth is meaningless to me now. I can buy anything in the world by the snap of my fingers." He said weakly " Now, take my wealth and buy me a month."

At first no one dared to respond, then one of his advisors from his youth stepped close to him and whispered "Beloved, when one's time is over, it cannot be bought at any price. It is thrown away in youth, squandered in manhood and not valued until..." he paused, shaking his head and continued, "Until now."

What is time? I don't mean get philosophical! What really is time? It is LIFE.

The Change

A New Perspective

When should we begin to value time? Ideally as soon as we are old enough to understand the two stories you have just read. Because you understand the emotional impact of the stories in your own personal way, today is the day you begin to value your time as you have never, ever valued it before.

If you are a professional person, you will begin to balance your lifestyle and start appreciating the small things you have been missing each day. That sunrise you drive by so quickly. The smile of the small child you pass by. If you are a professional high-achiever, you will begin to take the time to enjoy what you do and just to enjoy being you.

If you are currently not a high achiever in ways that you know would be really meaningful to you, you will begin to consider - what have I been putting off? Is fear keeping me from success? If I knew that whatever I wished to achieve, that I could not fail, what would I go out right now, TODAY, and begin to accomplish, to do, to achieve? The answer to that question will tell you right now, this very moment, what you need to begin to take your precious time and spend part of it doing. Attack life with a passion. You can dream dreams to death - but you cannot work them to death - when you truly work at dreams, they become reality.

Waiting for Happiness

As the story goes...there was a tribe on a small tropical isle in the Pacific Ocean called the Cargo Cult. Throughout the year they waited patiently, hopefully for a big bird to come through the skies and drop happiness on them in the form of magical things.

During World War II, a big bird came over this island dropping everything from mirrors and strange food to mysterious wheeled vehicles. They also dropped bombs. Every year this Cult simulates the conditions that their fathers told them occurred when the great birds dropped gifts. Every year they burn most of their crops to simulate the devastation during which the gifts were bestowed upon their isle. And then they wait. Every year they destroy their only resources in hopes of receiving a miracle. The Cargo Cult are not very happy people. They are waiting for their happiness to come while throwing away the resources from which their lives can be nourished.

Waiting for happiness, like searching the skies for the big birds, is to expect what will never come. Such anticipation is also bound to neglect the possibility for change and growth that exist right now. Today.

People are always blaming their circumstances for what they are. I don't believe in circumstances. The people who get on in this world are people who get up and look for the circumstances they want, and, if they can't find them, make them.
George Bernard Shaw

When we are around those who have fallen in live with themselves by giving themselves the gift of responsibility and discipline, we are uplifted. They don't have to come over to us and discuss the value of paying the necessary price to achieve what is precious to them in life.

Their life is a living testimonial to the fact that they are creating their own happiness by cultivating their garden - their talents and abilities - not waiting for "something" to happen in the future that will give them the happiness they seek. Such people who are tending their garden have a great power - they change us when we are in their presence.

The Change

Steps to Personal Growth

Would you really know who you are physically if you had never seen yourself in a mirror?....

While a physical mirror allows us to see what we look like, the reactions of others to our actions is a reflection of what our behavior looks like. If we want better communication, business and personally, we first should look and listen closely to the reflection found in the reactions of others to the way we now behave. If we are getting consistently negative responses from a certain behavior, we can be reasonably sure that we don't like the reflection of those actions that we see in the reactions of others.

Many times we are so close to our actions that it is very hard to realize all that we are doing. Seek counsel from someone who you believe will give you honest feedback on the behaviors you are beginning to hold in question. Pick someone who will really hold a mirror up to your personality. Expect some pain from truth. But such truth can make us grow. Once we begin to see ourselves...how do we evaluate what should be changed?

If people don't like something about you, it doesn't mean you are flawed...

When we have evaluated our behaviors through the mirror of other people's reactions and had some counseling with someone who will be blunt with us, we then must evaluate the information. Remember, you can't please everyone. There is a basis for a sound evaluation of change which will bring us personal growth. Am I listening to others enough? Am I respecting others? Do I try to win at all costs or do I work for win-win results? Am I moving so fast that I unintentionally use others as speed bumps? Begin to look for and evaluate those behaviors that are keeping you from a closer, deeper relationship with those who can help you grow-

Personal Dynamics

with whom you can share experiences, business and personal, that will allow also a sharing of life experiences.

Why should you go through a problem if someone else already has- and can give you warning signs on how to avoid the pain? Look for deeper communication with those who can guide you. Then choose the behaviors you wish to change. How do you plot the course for change?

If you don't have a road map for personal growth, you may get lost...

I doubt that anyone has set out on a journey where they are driving in which they didn't have a map or vision of where they were heading. When we decide to change a behavior - we should begin first to visualize how we will act with our new set of actions. If we plan on changing our behavior to be more patient, we need to paint a mental scenario as to how we will look and feel being more patient. We can create our own screen play of this , our own movie, if you will - right in our mind. Set the stage for the change. At first we are an actor, we are modeling new behavior - we are, in a way, at first "faking" it until the new behavior becomes more automatic. Our vision of how we perform our new behavior becomes our road map to change. If we are emotionally committed to make the change - the roadway of our vision will get us there. Once we start following the roadmap - how far do we travel each day?

The longest journey begins with one step. Change works the same way...

Nobody changes. NO? Really no. They evolve. When we begin to change behaviors, we still have the ghost of our old way of doing things around with us for awhile. It's like erasing a blackboard. You have to go over the same places several times to get rid of the

The Change

shadow of the former writing. Major behavior changes must be chunked down to daily activities - daily goals of achievement. If I want to become more outgoing and less shy - I don't begin the first day by addressing a forum of 600 people. I may choose as my goal to walk up to one person I don't know at a meeting - extend my hand and say " Hi. Pleased to meet you." That is chunking. It is breaking down behavior into do-able activities. All personal and business growth we wish to be permanent must be chunked down to daily do-able activities.

And by the way, it's our job to celebrate our successes and play them back in our mind. It may be one small step that day, but it's a giant step toward a long term behavioral change. How fast should personal growth happen?

Do we live in an impatient society, or what?

When we want things to happen, we want results now. If you have ever watched a flower grow and bloom, then you know how we change. Having the foresight and patience to nourish our behavior changes day by day brings big results over a reasonable period of time. I've worked with so many harried executives who were not willing to invest a little time in allowing change to really deeply take place. Today is the day of the bandaid approach to life. Quite honestly, you and I are worth more than just using a bandaid.

Personal growth is an evolution of our awareness of how much better we can be to ourselves and to others. We set daily personal goals to bring our changes into reality and then we wait, like the wise farmer, for nature to bring the crop in. And the harvest will come if we have the tenacity to do our part. Personal growth is certainly challenging...how do we stay ready to learn the lessons that will come our way?

Personal Dynamics

Everyone needs some breathing room from constant change now and then, but don't let that time cause you to miss opportunities..

If you stop and think about it, growth is always happening in our life. More now in this day and age, of course, than ever before. A great skill is staying ready to learn - when something worth learning really comes along. Here's the key. Listen..

Listen? Yes really listen. What do I mean? Block out your internal dialogue about what you are hearing and listen carefully. Be a critical listener. Did you know that up to half of what you hear you don't listen to? Try it. Try listening to someone for five minutes without allowing one internal thought to crowd into that listening space. It's hard. It's a skill to be learned. And it's worth learning to really listen. It helps us not miss opportunities that may fly quickly by because we were preoccupied with our own internal conversation. After all, what will help us most in our personal growth, is what we don't already know.

The Price of Personal Growth

There is a price to the development of our potential. Are you willing to pay it? How dear is that price?

Some time back I decided that it would look rather good with my business attire to wear a gold wrist chain. After shopping around and discovering that the real thing - 14K solid gold - was in the thousand dollar range, I proceeded to look at a gold plated chain. I asked the clerk "What is your warranty on this plated chain?" He responded "How much do you sweat?" That gave me a more honest answer than I really wanted.

I purchased the plated chain. About two months later, due to my high skin acidity, the chain looked like something an extra-

The Change

terrestrial had thrown up on. I then went back and bought another plated chain. The price was small - so why not? Thereafter, every two or three months, the clerk would find me back to purchase another plated chain. This went on for about a year.

The next year, while my business was prospering, my wife asked me to hold out my arm. I was immediately afraid I had done something wrong and would probably get slapped. As I held out my arm she, to my amazement, placed a 14K gold chain around my wrist. As she attached it she said "This is what you need." I was deeply moved by that. I was even more deeply moved when I discovered she had put it on my charge card.

Then she sat down with me and detailed with a pencil and paper exactly what I had been doing to myself. "Robert, every three months you've been paying fifty dollars for a gold-plated chain." she explained, "And here, look at what happens after five or ten years. You will have paid a tremendous amount of money - an amount well in excess of a thousand dollars. At the end of that time, what will you have to show for it? Nothing."

She paid a dear price to purchase that solid gold chain, but I can tell you now, years later, it looks just as beautiful. It has to be cleaned, of course, but it's as shiny when it's cleaned as the day it was purchased.

Several days after her "gift", a realization hit me with such impact that I fell to my knees. I perceived what I was doing to myself. Many times in my life I was paying a little bitty price and saying things like "Well, if I just learn how to do that much, I can get by." or "No sense in getting too excited about this. Just do enough to get finished."

I discovered through the symbolism of the gold chain the meaning of paying the greater price now to develop this vision that is within

Personal Dynamics

me, this priceless commodity that is within each of us, our potential. The greater the price that we pay to cultivate, to develop our talents, our skills - the deeper and longer lasting the reward. The greater price we're willing to pay in dedication, effort, concentration and focus not only gets us closer to our goal; it establishes habits and attitudes that make it easier to exercise these growth skills in the future. By paying the greater price now in visioning and emotional commitment we multiply the results over a period of time tenfold, perhaps a hundredfold.

The Value of Discipline

Consider how the price is paid in the development of quality in any profession. We understand the value of that price being paid when we receive services. When you take your car to have it repaired - you want that mechanic to be in love with what they are doing. You don't want them to say " Oh, yeah, we'll get this taken care of". We can tell by their voice tone and mannerisms - the way that they approach the car - if they are quality, knowledgeable professionals.

Mechanics who are in love with their profession will approach your car almost with reverence. They look carefully, they listen, they diagnose. It is as though they are becoming intimate with the machine. It's beautiful. Because they have taken the responsibility to fall in love with what they do - they have developed the discipline of their craft and they exude quality. Witness the professional who drives up to my office in a new Mercedes, he himself impeccably dressed. Eight years of advanced education to become a top craftsman in the legal profession. But he could have been an actor, a writer. We have something to give others - when we cultivate our garden - our potential. Respect and wealth tend to germinate from such cultivation. If I have nothing to give, no developed talents, no skills, no emotional empathy, no wealth - it's ludicrous to assume I have anything to share with you.

The Change

We All Reach "Crossroads"

How important is it to develop quality decisions about what we focus on professionally in life? Some of us learn later in life what we really need to cultivate in the form of talents and abilities.

My "crossroads" came some years back when a client came to my office and literally blew me away - mentally...

As the distinguished black gentleman took his seat, I wondered what kind of project I might be working on with him next. As owner of an audio visual production company, I had worked with him several times. He said over the phone he had simply wanted to visit for a minute. This businessman had led a challenging life. Crippled by a serious auto accident some years back, he walked with a cane. White haired, he look like a black Moses.

"Robert" he said, "You're wasting your life."

I sat up in my chair at his statement. He continued "You have an ability to communicate and teach. Being a business owner in the audio visual field is your current bread and butter, I know. But if you don't use your gift to teach, you will have wasted your life. I'm on a tight schedule. That's all I wanted to say." He then got up and left.

I was in the Twilight Zone the rest of that day, seated at my desk thinking. I knew deep down that he was right; that's what scared me. I had to face the responsibility of what I wanted out of life. I had to face what I had feared for so many years to accomplish. Yet it was what I really wanted to do. I am now a seminar leader, faculty member and, in short, using the gift that was at one time going unused. Sometimes we can fear to step out and be responsible to do the things that we really know would be our first love. Usually we simply put off trying. Benign neglect. If I could

Personal Dynamics

give you two gifts this very day, the first would be to see through the eyes of a child the miracle of life. We hold it in our hands, but we don't see it. It's in front of our eyes, but we don't perceive it - each of those 24 hours that make up the miracle of life.

If I could give you a second gift, it would be to see the miracle of your potential. For each person it is different. The same problem - we're so close to our potential that we don't see it.

Yet the greatest orators in the world cannot give you these two gifts. Only you can give you these gifts. You do that by loving yourself enough to fall in love with whatever you do.

A Journey to Our Potential

Follow me on a journey for awhile. I would like each of you to find that pathway, if you will, that is in your mind. It's a very wonderful pathway that takes you to who you really are. Past all of our mass of excuses, delays and nameless fears. The pathway takes us right to the core of who we are. Take a few moments to travel in your mind to that special place where only you dwell. You and only you know where that is.

As you travel to that place you move toward a wonderful light - dim at first. There are dark spaces, like moving through a dimly lit hallway. You go through the dark spaces and follow the light. At the light, there you are. You, as a child - with all the excitement and marvelous curiosity you possessed when you were six years old. That small child - filled with the power to love, give and to grow.

Move toward that child as you remember yourself to be and hold on to the child. Embrace yourself deep inside. Hold yourself tightly for a moment and just say, "I love you. I really love you. I'm sorry that I haven't been giving you the love that you deserve. I haven't been responsible in developing the discipline to achieve the

The Change

potential of your wonderful gifts. Now that will change."

That small child you are holding is you. You wake up with that child every morning. It's the person with you in the dark, when no one else is around. No human can love that child like you can. Caring people can be supportive of us. They can encourage us. The black gentleman who came and told me a great truth about myself, didn't change me. The change has to come from inside. Love starts out as an inside job. Once we accept ownership of that responsibility and give ourselves also the gift of discipline, our whole life is changed and energized.

What are we losing by not developing our potential? What are we losing by not giving ourselves the gift of discipline? We can certainly go ahead and sleep late when we know that there is something we need to do for our own growth and development. Or we can watch TV and fill that time. Yes, we can just give ourselves a little dab of love. We can let a little bit of fear keep us from stepping out and going to that other position or making that personal or professional decision that we know, in our heart of hearts, is right for us.

You see, that six year old child inside each of us knows what we need. We just haven't been listening. The din of the world has crowded the small voice out. Will we ignore that voice and simply rise to our lowest common denominator? We have the liberty not to grow, that's our choice. I talk frankly with employees every week about their freedom. They can skip skills training, interpersonal communications training. They can stay in a job that just requires some work and no thinking. That's fine. I ask them only to realize the price they will pay later for not paying the smaller price now to learn and grow.

A person who has chosen not to learn and grow emotionally is not a bad person. He or she has simply chosen not to really live.

Personal Dynamics

Whoever you are, whatever your current state in life, you must make your deep emotionally based decision right now to value your time as though your life depended upon it. Finally, it is important to remember that even the clearest best defined vision will not come into reality without a feeling deep within that you love and enjoy what you are doing and that you are doing it for you.

Your vision of the future cannot change others. Yet it can. By changing the way we feel about ourselves and by taking upon ourselves the clothes of new habits and behaviors - we influence the lives of others. What happens in a still pond when a pebble is dropped in the middle? Not a large pebble, just a very small one? A ripple begins and moves wider and wider until it covers the whole pond. You have no idea at this moment just how much you changing you will touch countless others.

To try to make your goals come to life without emotional commitment is something like a person in a cold room lighting matches to create a fire in a large stove that contains no wood. Each match when struck burns for a second and then goes out - leaving the room cold. When we give just casual thought to our objectives - it is like lighting a match. But without the fuel of emotional commitment the flame goes out. Now, if the person in the cold room will take a load of wood and place it in the stove then the match can do its job and soon the room is full of warmth.

In much the same way, emotions are the fuel of our goals. When we give ourselves the gift of emotional commitment toward whatever we set our hand to do - we begin an amazingly wonderful and powerful journey toward developing our full potential.

Think of life as a snowy hill and you begin as a child riding down that hill on a snow sled. Each time you make a decision and turn the course of the snow sled it affects where you go further down the course of life unless you make another change in direction.

The Change

Would the snow sled rider be crazy if he thought "I know I need to make a change in my direction in order to make the sled arrive at the destination I desire, but I'm busy right now. I'll make the choice later. Maybe tomorrow."

CHANGENOTES

In the story, how is the old man being honest with himself?

If you were the old man, what would you have put in place of singing and traveling? Why would they be important to you?

How would you feel with only days left to live?

What would you do during the last week of your life?

List ten activities you would pursue during your last week of life.

Now, make a list of ten items that currently consume an average week of your life in order of priority.

How do the two priority lists compare?

From the list of ten items you would wish to accomplish during your last week of life - number the items in order of priority as to which items you would most fear to seek to accomplish.

Think about the top fear priorities...

What would happen if you no longer feared to achieve these activities?

List an *Activity* of top priority to you that you will begin to achieve *Today*.

Personal Dynamics

Program Two: LifePerceptions

LifePerceptions deals with the fact that our senses will only show us what our brain believes we should be experiencing. Let me share with you an event that really happened to me...

The Van Story

One day I was driving my wife's van as I busily went around town picking up things. I found myself trying to back that van out into a busy highway during the noon rush hour. Let me tell you, there has never been a great love affair between me and that van. As a matter of fact, mechanically, at times I think that van has taken great delight wreaking vengeance upon me by creating problems, but be that as it may - back to the story. I'm trying very judiciously to back this van into the street without getting into a major traffic problem.

The mirrors I have on the van are very small. I have never been able to talk my wife into putting larger mirrors on the vehicle. So I am straining and as I am inching back trying to be able to see if a car is coming from either the right or the left on this busy highway, my stress level is constantly increasing. I am beginning to get a throbbing headache from this whole process.

I had spent five or ten minutes laboriously trying to back out when suddenly I looked in front of me - right in front of me. I burst out laughing because, you see, I was backing away from a department store. Had I been looking not through those tiny limited side mirrors or through the small rear view mirror on the top of the front window - had I not been looking through those but instead had looked directly in front of me - I would have observed a huge plate glass window that was at least sixteen feet wide reflecting all

The Change

of the traffic activity in the highway behind me, giving me a much broader perspective.

Yes, I burst out laughing when I realized what I had been doing to myself. I was laboring backing that van up under the assumption that my little mirrors were my only resource. They were, in a word, my set limitations.

If only I had been more cognizant of potential opportunities - and in this case the opportunity was so obvious. Yet my perception of possibilities was locked into that which was assumed: that you use the rear view mirror and you use the side mirrors to back a vehicle. In this case, however, I had an option. Consciously, however, I did not perceive it - even though my eyes obviously glanced up many times at the large reflective plate glass window directly in front of me.

Suddenly it clicked in my mind that the plate glass window in front of me was all along showing me a complete reflection of all the traffic behind me. I then, with a smile on my face, simply watched the department store window, neatly backed up and quickly drove away.

How many times in life are we missing the *Big Window* in front of us which can give us a much greater perspective of what our capabilities are? Are we limiting ourselves to tools that are only giving us a small picture of what we can really achieve? We said at the start that our senses will only show us what our brain believes we should experience...

The Wrong Key

There was a Texas cattle rancher at the turn of the century who owned the largest herd of cattle in America. His land holdings also

Personal Dynamics

were enormous. This rancher was getting on in years and yet he had no heir to whom to pass on his enterprise. He knew that special skills and tremendous savvy would be required by anyone to take over such a vast responsibility. He devised a test to select the person who would take over the position of overseeing his vast land and cattle holdings.

There were many who applied for this position. As each applicant entered the expansive offices of the cattle baron, they were shown to a room with a large box set against the wall in one corner and in the opposite corner of the room various keys and crowbars laying on the floor.

It was explained to each applicant that within the large box were official appointment papers that, upon being signed by the finder, would appoint him heir of the cattle kingdom. The items laying on the floor on the opposite side of the room could be used to open the box if the applicant so desired. "You have only three minutes to succeed." the baron added.

Each applicant entered the room with these instructions - many ran to the crowbar and with brute strength attempted to force the box with it's huge lock and iron rimmed top open. Others ran to the keys on the floor and quickly tried each key to unlock the ominous box only to find that none of the keys fit the lock. Day after day, each applicant's time expired and they all walked away in utter defeat.

Then one day, a cowboy walked into the room. After receiving his instructions, instead of running to the crowbars and keys, he walked slowly toward the huge metal rimmed box sitting against the wall. He looked at the box carefully from all angles. He touched the box and felt of its seams. He looked carefully through the tiny slit created by the corner of the box almost touching the wall.

The Change

Suddenly he laughed and then he tugged with all his might and managed to slide the giant box a few inches away from the wall. The cowboy then pulled the valuable papers from the box because, you see, the box had no back. The side of the box placed against the wall had been open all the time.

Now, you are beginning to understand that the eyes see only what the brain believes the eyes should see. Perception is a two edged sword. When rightly trained to see many options in life - we will look quickly at many alternatives and then lock onto those that will bring us to our set goals. However, if we set no specific goals then we have set no expectations to which our perceptions can respond.

The successful heir to the cattle baron had a goal of getting into the box not the goal of trying to unlock it or pry it open by brute force with a crowbar as did the other multitude of cowboys. Because his goal was more end result oriented, his subconscious mind was receptive to more available options for achieving his goal. And the cattle baron was wise to devise this test. He knew that the successful contender would be better able to cope with confusing situations and not become immediately locked into useless reactions.

But there is more to understanding the tremendous power of perceptions...

The Assumption Monster

Some time ago, I wrote a technical article for a university in the midwest. I had spent a great deal of time and research and I felt that it was a good article. I sent it in with a satisfied feeling. About three weeks later the article was sent back to me in a large brown envelope with a letter of rejection typed on university stationery. I read the letter carefully - the essence of which was "We appreciate your article but it is really not what we had in mind."

Personal Dynamics

Wishing to take this lemon and make some lemonade, I called the editor at the university and asked simply, "If I rewrote the article, what exactly would you have in mind?" And because of my willingness to communicate and work with him, he gave me the answer to my question.

Then with excitement, I rushed back to my research and produced what I would call a finely developed article on the topic he had suggested - stressing elements he felt were important. I finished the article and mailed it with a smile. I knew that I had followed the tenets that I preach about - being positive in adverse situations and finding the alternative which is always hiding somewhere - that will allow apparent failure to become success.

Three weeks passed and I received another brown envelope from the university. I held this one up to the light before opening it and to my horror, it contained my new article and a letter. I dropped the packet on the desk and wondered why they had rejected my second article after I had gone to such pains to meet all of their requirements. My mind went through a thousand reasons why it should have been accepted. I spent a good thirty minutes in depression. Then I thought "I'll simply call the editor and tell him thanks a lot for rejecting my second article after all the work I've done!"

But first, I thought, I'll open the envelope and read the rejection letter. Then I'll know better what to say to him when I call. I opened the envelope and, indeed, it contained my second article

The Change

and a letter on university stationery. I read it, sat it down, then suddenly picked it up again and re-read it. "What is this?" I thought. The letter read, "Thank you for your second article which we have accepted. We need some minor revisions, if you will be kind enough to make them and send the article back to us."

I read the letter again and again. I laughed and I sat down exhausted. I had been victimized by the same demon of misperception that I teach to avoid. I had assumed that the second envelope, again obviously containing the article and a university letter, was a rejection - I created an imaginary monster to battle.

When the reality of a situation changes, we have a tendency to continue to view the situation looking for and expecting the old reality. Unless we are constantly vigilant, this very moment, to maintain as many options, as many alternatives, in any situation important to us - we will fall victim to the perception monster again and again.

There is a successful solution to 98 per cent of life's challenges if we maintain a wide enough vision to see the alternatives and if we set our goals to achieve the end results we really truly desire.

I read the story of one young lady who, while driving her sports car down a country road, was passed by a man coming from the opposite direction, weaving in and out of his lane as he came around a curve. As he passed the young lady, he yelled "Cow!". This young lady, I understand, was very quick witted and instantly shouted back "Bull!" She was pleased about her quick retort and was still smiling when her sports car hit the cow as she followed the curve in the road.

Never in life assume there is only one meaning to the obvious until you have considered the circumstances carefully.

Personal Dynamics

CHANGENOTES

What incident has happened in your life similar to the van story?

Why did the cattle baron show great wisdom in devising such a test?

When was the last time that you assumed the worst without garnering together all the relevant information?

List an *Activity* you can begin to do *Today* to expand your perception.

The Change

Program Three: LifeFeelings

The Teddy Bear Solution

I provide many seminars for young people about LifeFeelings. Some time ago I developed and conducted "Project Smile" classes through the Job Training Partnership Act to prepare youth for successful job interviews and to teach effective work attitudes and behaviors.

As I begin each seminar, I ask for a volunteer for a very daring demonstration. I don't explain what the demonstration will be but after a few seconds some brave soul will raise his hand. As he reaches the front of the audience, I hand him George. (George is my assistant seminar director - George is a four foot teddy bear.) "Give George a big hug" I say. Perhaps a little embarrassed, the teenager does just that. And is George fluffy! Very cute and huggable!

"How does George make you feel" I ask innocently. "Well, he makes me feel good" most answer. Then I begin to make my point of the entire demonstration. "So George makes you feel good when you hug him. Hmm...that's interesting since George is, of course, not a living thing - and yet you say he makes you feel good." I go on to explain how tricky our language is. That we can even make a statement such as "George makes me feel good" is a linguistic illusion. It isn't logical. Of course it isn't! Because we are the source of all of our feelings - good, bad or indifferent. A wonderful, cuddly thing like George the Teddy Bear can give us a prompting toward nice warm feelings - but we create the feelings.

If I spend an entire day with young people, that is the one central point I want them to remember and understand. You are, and you

Personal Dynamics

always are, the sole source of your feelings. Those youngsters who really got that message left the seminar with their lives changed forever. Responsibility had a different meaning. When we truly become responsible for our feelings - we take responsibility for our life.

The word "responsibility" has taken a beating in its contemporary meaning. The first time I ever remember hearing the word, I was about four years old. My mother came into my room and said "Who's responsible for this mess?" I told her it wasn't me. I was not an only child. I had a little brother. You can't get away with that excuse if you're an only child. They put you away somewhere for treatment if you keep blaming someone else for what you actually did. On an adult level, when we fail to take responsibility for what we do, we give away our freedom to grow and achieve to our full potential.

By the way, I use George with adults too. Imagine the professional accountant or truck driver being handed George and being instructed to give him a big hug. Sometimes I get reactions like "This is stupid." I smile and say, "Come on, hug him anyway." The message I always receive from the victim of this demonstration, whether youth or adult, is that things create feelings. But they don't. We speak a lie and when we think though the circumstances of George or of any experience we perceive - we know the real truth. We create our own feelings.

Isn't our language tricky?

We also find ourselves saying things like "Bill made me so mad at work today." or "I had an argument with Jan last night and she made me feel so guilty." or "That mistake I made yesterday made me so sick." You rarely, if ever, hear someone say "After my argument with Roger, I made a conscious decision that I would feel bad about the evening."

The Change

The Weird Sales Call

Once I arrived to make a major sales presentation to a very influential client. I was well prepared - I had researched all of my facts, the circumstances of his company, making certain my services would fit his needs. Almost the very moment upon entering his office, I noticed his expression was strained. As we began our conversation, he gave an aura of hesitancy and concern. I asked him many questions about his possible need for my services. He answered them all positively but his demeanor kept concerning me for some strange reason.

As the interview concluded, he stated that he would get back in touch. He made no commitments to my proposal. I walked away confused and somewhat disappointed. I played the interview back through my mind a dozen times that day. Each time I saw him again in my mind, I noted his hesitancy and his concern about something that showed through his voice tone and body language - even though he was agreeing with my sales points. I felt as though I had won the battle but lost the war.

For all practical purposes - my day was ruined. I couldn't get the client's positive words yet conflicting body language out of my mind. I thought of a thousand things I may had said wrong or perhaps it was the way I had approached him. What did I do wrong? All of these thoughts continued to fuel my feelings.

It suddenly dawned upon me that I had to be approaching the entire situation incorrectly. Having all of these conflicting negative feelings about this one sales meeting was doing me no good at all. The fact of the matter was that I simply did not know why his positive words did not match his negative body language. The only way I would ever know would be to ask him.

It was not easy, but I picked up the phone, dialed his office and

Personal Dynamics

asked him why his expression seemed negative during the morning's interview. "My wife was in a serious automobile accident last weekend, and my thoughts were really on that," he explained. I wished him and his wife well and hung up the phone. He was not upset with my presentation. He had other things on his mind. But, until I knew the truth, I was allowing his expressions to control my attitudes and feelings as well as allowing my imagination to run wild inventing reasons for his displeasure with my presentation.

To make my life easier, I soon learned to be very straightforward and politely ask a client up front - why the sour expression during my presentation - if that's the reaction I was receiving. At first, it seemed almost rude to ask - but it was the right thing to do.

Lessons Learned

Two other lessons were driven home very deeply to me though this experience: First, regardless of the reaction I receive from another person, I am the gatekeeper of my emotions. I do not have to go away dejected unless I give myself permission to do so. And why should I give myself permission to feel dejected?

Second, we have to be patient with ourselves. We didn't learn overnight to immediately react with negative feelings toward a certain expression or sour voice tone when we experience it. For us to unlearn such negative reactions will also take time and patience.

You can sum it up to yourself with one statement: I own my own feelings. Whatever feelings I create within myself - I own them because I created them. If I allow my feelings to own me - then I lose control of the quality of my own life.

There seems to be almost a Negative Mental Gravity that pulls us toward a negative evaluation of our experiences and abilities. By

The Change

searching for and finding the positive lessons to be discovered in any experience and by emphasizing to ourselves the effective things we have accomplished with our abilities - we begin to flex our mental muscles to overcome this Negative Mental Gravity.

The "If Onlys"

Part of that Negative Mental Gravity I call the "If only" complex. It is a disease that is easy to catch and hard to get rid of. How often do we hear " If only I had a better territory, my sales would be up this year." or " If only I had the education I need, I would get a better job. " or " If only my spouse would support my decisions - I would be more successful." If only...If only...

"If onlys" keep us from the reality of the situation. "If onlys" keep us forever chasing rainbows. The past no longer exists. It's a painful fact - but it's true. The future is determined by one thing and one thing only - what we do right now..today. If our sales are down - we have to do something about it. If we don't have the education we need - it's available. We can go get it - at night if necessary.

The "If onlys" have caused the premature death of millions of good ideas and potential careers. An amazing young lady who was tragically blinded in both eyes during youth, has perhaps more of a reason to use the "If onlys" than most. Yet she has stated many times "I may not have 20-20 vision but I do have a wonderful brain." That resolute lady, by the way, earns her living as a legal consultant.

Happy Time Recipe

Do you want to see many more positive applications of your abilities? Do you want to find many more ways to widen your successes and diminish the negative impact of failure?

Personal Dynamics

Then take into your life the five minute *Happy Time* recipe.

At the end of each workday - while still in your car or as you arrive home, take five minutes and pat yourself on the back for what you did right that day. Was it a lousy day? You still did many things right. You still had successes. Even if you find only one - celebrate and allow yourself to feel a deep and abiding sense of happiness and gratitude with your abilities. there is no one else like you in the entire universe. You are unique and you are wonderful.

Learn positive lessons from your mistakes and failures and then forget about them. But remember your successes and remember - you can and will succeed again. Feel good deep inside about yourself - no one else in the world can do that for you.

And remember this also. Nothing in life is perfect. If you wait until the perfect time, the perfect place, the perfect success to be happy - forget it - happiness will never come.

Practice itself does not make perfect - it makes permanent -that is, it builds habits. If we reach out to try to achieve we will always fail somewhat along the way. Failure is a part of success. Learn from the failure and keep your emphasis on the habit of success.

To be emotionally hurt due to failure is normal but not helpful. Learn from the failure and quickly get back to being happy. After all, if you're not happy and filled with a good , warm rich feeling about yourself, right now - this very moment - when do you plan on being happy?

Remember, you own your own feelings.

The Change

CHANGENOTES

How can you easily make external things "responsible" for your feelings? Give several examples.

When was the last time that you allowed someone else's attitude to determine yours?

How can you "own" your own feelings?

Exercise: Think now, with your eyes closed, of a time that was very stressful and worrisome to you. Take a moment, visualize it, hear it, feel it...

Exercise: Think now, with your eyes closed, of a time that was a great joy to you, a time of achievement, of accomplishment. Take a moment and visualize it, hear it, feel it...

You understand, now, how you "create" your own feelings. You brought back definite feelings through the power of your imagination.

How can you, personally, implement the five minute *Happy Time* recipe?

Why not just wait for the perfect time to be happy?

What *Activity* can you begin *Today* to take control of your feelings?

Personal Dynamics

Program Four: LifeStress

Modern Day Stress

Even though in truth, as we will learn, stress is the result of perception: I want to deal with it separately from our second program called LifePerceptions because LifeStress is the physiological effect of modern day misperceptions or, in other words, perceptions allowed to run wild and harm the body.

I have two business acquaintances who both readily admit to having been victims of stress. The first is a vibrant, energetic young man who rose in the television profession to chief production director at a major market television station. The stress he perceived from his pressure-cooker, deadline oriented environment caused his hair to fall out - he lost weight and after several years became seriously ill.

I visited with him recently. He's now in another profession, he's put on weight, looks great and is no longer sick.

A lady I know in her early fifty's lost her husband several years ago - she also lost an inch in height due to stress and depression ... One noted physician dares to estimate that up to 90% of all illness is related in some degree to stress.

We hear so often from the media all about this age being a stress filled time. Our compressed, computerized day to day living is supposed to heap upon us a level of anxiety heretofore unknown. But is this correct? Is it a valid hypothesis that our age is the worst when it comes to stress?

The Change

The Days of Og

To truly answer this, I believe we must travel back in time and look at the lives of our ancestors. If we go back far enough, we might find a distant relative named Og leaving the sanctuary of his cave. Soon upon his travels he meets a ferocious saber-tooth tiger and will quickly be devoured if he does not immediately respond to the nature of the crisis.

Fortunately for Og, he has a miraculous built-in physical response mechanism that modern day scientists call the "Fight or Flight Response." Faced with such danger, his blood supply leaves his stomach, his brain, and other organs - flowing immediately instead to his skeletal muscles for instant action. At this point, with adrenalin surging through his body Og will fight or, if the beast is large, he will run the mile in a time to fill any Olympian with envy.

If our ancestor Og were suddenly whisked by time machine into our modern age, given a few weeks to view and interact with our culture, and then asked to speak to us about stress: his response would probably be "You dummies, you have no stress. Your stress is an illusion. Unless something is about to eat you - why get upset about it."

And you know what, as culturally backward as Og might be, his words would be absolutely true. Let me repeat one part of Og's likely comment. "Your stress is an illusion."

The vast majority of "stressful" situations in which we find ourselves today are essentially self-imposed from an emotional standpoint. This is not to say that circumstances are illusions. Not at all. However, the manner in which we respond to circumstances is what creates stress - not the circumstances themselves. If we believe that we are going to be fired from our job our "Fight or flight" response will be activated, adrenalin will pump into our body

Personal Dynamics

- and because we do not have to fight or flee, it breaks down to more toxic chemicals in our system and literally poisons us.

Now, remember, I said if we *think* that we are going to be fired from our job. Whether it is true or not, we will experience the same stress as if we were actually in the boss' office being fired. In many ways our biological "Fight or flight" response is outdated for our emotional needs today. However, we cannot change our biology - we can only change the way we think.

The Jogger Experience

Let me share a real experience with you. I was walking downtown in a major city close to rush hour one day and heard the screeching of tires and I was certain I would hear the crash of twisting metal. As I turned, I saw a car swerving to miss a young jogger going across the street reading a paperback book and at the same time listening to a headphone radio.

Just hearing the auto braking and seeing the narrow miss caused my heart to start pounding. The young jogger continued jogging as if nothing had happened. You see, the jogger never knew that she had been only a few seconds from being a fatality. Had those events been seen and heard, she would have no doubt been terrified.

The Paradigm

Now, at this point, let's look for just a second at paradigms. Circumstances around us must be perceived to have any kind of impact - stressful or otherwise. Those circumstances that we do perceive we then decode within our personal paradigms. A paradigm, in this instance, being a set of rules framing our boundaries of emotional significance and comfort. The way that we see our reality.

The Change

Why are paradigms significant? It is through the emotional boundaries which are set in our mind that we interpret all aspects of reality. Reality is not the same for every individual. Think back to the lady jogger who doesn't perceive her close scrape with death. Reality in a broader sense is somewhat different for each of us due to the paradigms we have formed as a result of our childhood training, our experiences, and the inward conclusions we have drawn from both training and life experiences. There are literally as many "realities" - or zones of comfort - as there are human beings in the world.

Because of culture and many shared experiences - a tapestry of that reality in each area of the world is similar. Geography can help create a shared reality - a shared security - as can language. Indeed, we have an innate desire to fellowship with those whose perceptions of reality are closest to our own, because in those circumstances we feel safe and secure - nonstressed.

We desire those relationships - because we feel secure and accepted - many times without weighing the cost. The jogger may have felt very much in the groove with the youth set by jogging with headphones and reading at the same time - but the jogger's attempt to fit in with a group fad - could have been fatal.

Paradigms can be very valuable to us in allowing the direction of our energies to not be lost in the conscious attempt to understand and deal with a myriad of perceptions which are not of value to the end result we wish to achieve. If paradigms seem a bit confusing, it's just that our set way of looking at things, our paradigms, if you will, are either our helpers or our worst enemies. They either bring into our view information that will help us achieve our goals or they will make us defensive and stressed in situations that do not support our beliefs and values.

Our paradigms are like boxes that our mind fits into. We move

Personal Dynamics

around, we get comfortable and we feel safe and secure in this box. Once in this box we become effectively blind to other things outside. If a circumstance comes along which is different from what we are used to in our box we are intruded upon - we are moved out of our comfort zone and we are then *STRESSED*.

NEGATIVE STRESS

Our modern day stress is usually the physiological response to the perception of fears or dangers that intrude upon our paradigms but often do not really come into existence.

The Grocery Store From Hell

One day my wife called me at work while I was quite busy on an important project. She asked if I would go to the store right then and get some bread and milk. I explained I would be delighted to do this later that evening as soon as I was finished with my project. Her voice changed, and she said "Please bring me the bread and milk" in a tone that was very easy to understand. At which time I said, "Dear, the motor's running. I'm on my way."

So I left where I wanted to be, got into my car, and went to the grocery store - where I didn't want to be. I was a man with a mission. Quickly getting a cart, I must have left friction burns on the store tile floor I was moving so fast. I got the bread and milk and headed for the checkout counter. There was a line - and it

The Change

stretched all the way back to the meat counter at the opposite end of the store. I got in line thinking, "Why is this happening to me? I was so happy doing what I wanted to do at the office. Now I'm here, in line, where I don't want to be. Woe is me! Why is this happening to ME!"

During this time, the two children belonging to the lady in line in front of me were salivating and nipping holes in my pant legs. I'm standing there looking into the misty distance at the young checker (couldn't have been more than 18 years old) slowly checking every item. He would hold up every second or third item and say, "Mrs. Jones, have you bought this item here before? This is interesting. Could you tell me a little bit about it? I thought about buying it myself. Could we visit for a few minutes about it?"

After that checker-customer conversation happened several times - or at least it was my judgment from the distance that it was happening - my stress level was building higher and higher. At this point I was ready to walk up to the front of the line, put my lips to the checker's young ears and say softly through clenched teeth, "Could you do me a great personal favor? Could you check me out during my lifetime?"

Finally, I got to be next in line. This precious lady in front of me, bless her heart, pulled out food stamps to pay for her purchases. At this point, I had lost my judgment. I was quite insane with stress. "Here I am now" I said to myself, "Still waiting in line while someone spends my tax money." I was the supreme victim.

Then I took this wonderful attitude home. You can imagine my six year old son, greeting me at the door with "Hi, Daddy!" I bark "Get out of my way kid, if you want to live to be seven." The little child walks away, morose, depressed, because daddy has brought this wonderful attitude home. Daddy chose to be a victim. When we are where we don't want to be, we tend to victimize ourselves and

Personal Dynamics

blame our surroundings and our circumstances for the fact that we are unhappy. When we are victims, we react to circumstances rather than to the realities of the experience. We literally give up our ability to positively create our future.

We only become proactive, we only create our positive future when we decide that wherever we are - emotionally, mentally, physically - we're going to be in a positively focused frame of mind. The more powerfully we positively focus, the happier we can be. Whenever we are in a situation where we are thinking only of where we would rather be or where we were yesterday, we give up our opportunity for happiness at that moment. We give up our ability to live fully in the present.

If I had gone back into that store with a different perception, things could have gone quite differently. As I walked in, got the bread and milk, and saw the long line; I could very easily have said to myself "Thank goodness for the abundance we have in this country; that we can be in line to purchase an unlimited supply of food. What a tremendous blessing that is."

I could have, if I had chosen, been filled with gratitude rather than frustration. It was probably the young checker's first day on the job. He was going slow to make sure he did it right. As I was viewing him from a distance, he really was not holding the items up and asking Mrs. Jones what she thought of them. He was looking at the bar code and making sure the price was correct.

But you see, I was ready to condemn. I was eager to judge. That was my job as the victim. These "trigger" reactions I responded to at the store will not go away immediately if I find myself in that situation again. It will require conscious thought on my part to begin questioning why I feel the way I do and to begin to visualize and expect from myself new behaviors in those circumstances.

The Change

The lady and her two children? Little did I know that the dear lady had been laid off from her job and was out eight hours a day diligently searching for employment. On top of that, one of her children had cancer and was on chemotherapy. If I had known her story of bravery and determined effort, I would have given her my groceries. But, you see, I didn't want to become aware of that kind of story. The world that day was out to make me miserable. As a victim, it's never my fault. It's the fault of everything and everyone around me.

When we see ourselves as a victim, we put ourselves in a very tiny box with no options other than to feel miserable. We are worth more than that. We have no business treating ourselves that way. Victimization creates a negative focus that almost always leaves us with much less than we should gain from any experience.

The Seminar That Wasn't

Once I was getting ready to leave for a seminar that I had paid quite a bit of money to attend. I was looking forward to the information - very excited to be at the evening seminar. About 4:30 PM I arrived home from the office. I changed into another suit and headed for the door. I had a good hour start to get to the seminar location which was only 30 minutes away. My keys, I thought, where are my keys? I looked here, I looked there. No keys. I looked in all the drawers. Finally, I looked under the dog, under the cat. Where are my keys? Finally, 45 minutes after beginning the great key hunt, I found them.

Now I had 15 minutes to get to a seminar and there was a 30 minute drive from my house to the meeting place. As I rushed to my car I thought, "There always are a few others who will be a little late. Being a few minutes late will hardly get them past the housekeeping material." I roared out of the driveway and soon onto the interstate highway - five miles up the road all the traffic

Personal Dynamics

was slowed to a crawl due to an overturned truck.

There I was, seated in my car, travelling at a snail's pace. The vision of arriving an hour late was becoming a reality. When I walked into the seminar room, everyone was already seated as the program had started long before. As I moved to the middle of the crowd and took a seat, it seemed all eyes were slowly following this tardy student.

All during my time at the seminar, I'm thinking about the long line of traffic, the search for my keys, my frustration at being late. Why did all of this have to happen to me? To this day, I cannot tell you what was covered during my time at that seminar because I allowed myself to take on a victim mentality, I lost focus on what was happening in the present. My focus was on the "troubles" which, by the way, were in the past. The time I searched for the lost keys or spent in traffic could never be brought back and given to me. Yet I was replaying those experiences rather than focusing on the seminar and learning.

We imagine the problems into existence or make them bigger than they actually are - and that is sufficient to create chemical changes in our bodies which, because we cannot dissipate the "Fight or Flight" response chemical changes by indeed fighting or running away, lead to the suppression of our immune systems as surely as does the dreaded AIDS virus. The vast majority of times our stress that leads to illness is unwarranted and useless.

POSITIVE STRESS

So far we have always referred to stress as a negative experience and indeed stress resulting from fear of possible negative results is physically destructive because the mind creates illusions that activate the fight or flight response in our bodies for no constructive reason. There is a positive stress. Such stress is found

The Change

in the act of creating and achieving that which is based upon positive goal setting and planning. Positive stress is what we experience as the excitement of being in control of any creative process - from carpentry - to sales - to management.

Positive stress is a stress that the body can chemically dissipate without physiological damage - such stress is helpful in moving us toward achievement. To further explain the difference between negative and positive stress - let me give you two examples in the sales arena - the first being an example of negative stress:

"I know that Mr. Jones is going to be a tough cookie when I present this proposal today," our salesperson says to himself as he nears the client's office. He hasn't done his homework or planned for today's meeting. Unfortunately, our salesperson has spent several days visualizing ahead of time the problems he feels he will most likely encounter with his client. He has built up a great deal of fear and is actually dreading the meeting.

As he enters the client's office, he is stressed, his palms are sweaty and adrenalin is being pumped into his system. The salesperson's nervousness is quickly transmitted through his body language to the client - who becomes uneasy. The presentation is unsuccessful and the salesperson leaves commenting to himself "Ah...this just isn't my day. That client's attitude toward my product really makes me sick."

The salesperson functioning under negative stress has failed to set positive goals toward his product presentation. He has allowed negative fear goals to develop an unhealthy stress situation around his anticipation of the sales meeting. As the salesperson left the unsuccessful presentation, he continued to feel out of control and he blamed the failure of the sales meeting, "It's just one of those days" and he projected his ill feelings as being the fault of the client's attitude.

Personal Dynamics

Now, for the salesperson who is functioning under positive stress.

The salesperson says to herself as she nears the client's office, "Several of my associates have told me that Mr. Jones is not an easy person to visit with concerning our products. Well, I believe that they may not have focused in on his real needs in the areas that our products serve. I've done some research into Mr. Jones business and talked with several of his staff before this meeting. I believe that my presentation will meet his needs."

She has also been visualizing the actual meeting in a very positive way. In her mind, she sees and hears herself giving the presentation to Mr. Jones. She sees Mr. Jones' interest and acceptance of her proposal. She visualizes all of this before the actual meeting. Upon arriving at the client's office, she enters very confidently, relaxed but excited and...the proposal is very impressive to Mr. Jones who senses the salesperson's active interest and effort to clearly define his company's product needs. But Mr. Jones says he wants a few days to make up his mind.

As the salesperson leaves the office she smiles and says to herself, "I certainly hope Mr. Jones decides to go with our company - otherwise he will really be the loser."

The salesperson functioning under positive stress set the goal of being prepared for the presentation, did her homework, and looked forward to the sales presentation with anticipation and excitement.

The Change

When the sale did not occur as the salesperson had hoped - she left in a positive frame of mind - she was still in control of what she had control over in the first place - she had given the best presentation she could and the ball was now in the client's court.

Life is not perfect, yet many live in a constant low level negative stress situation which is harmful because they expect constant perfection from themselves and from others. As we move along on the journey toward our professional goals there will be bumps in the road, that's just a part of life. To be upset or impatient during the process of achieving a long range goal is many times as useless and counterproductive as allowing ourselves to be stressed while travelling at a rapid rate of speed in our vehicle between two destinations - making good time - but upset because we're not already there.

We have the same physical makeup as our ancestors who literally had to fight for their existence. The chemicals our body sends into our system at times of stress saved the lives of those who lived centuries before us because it gave them extra strength and energy to fight or flee from danger. We live in a different society. Most of our stress is self-created in the form of worry and regret. We can control how we react with our environment. We can control our emotions. Through self-directed goal setting, we can unleash the energy of positive stress -that's the excitement of reaching out to accomplish challenging activities that are important to us.

Positive stress does not harm us - it invigorates us.

Move away from negative stress - don't be a victim. It's your choice. Use positive stress to motivate and energize you toward the professional achievement that you deserve.

Personal Dynamics

CHANGENOTES

After hearing the story of Og, how does our age really compare when it comes to true stress?

How can our belief's cause illness?

What does the lady jogger perceive?

What circumstances create an impact upon us?

How is "reality" different for each of us?

What are paradigms?

The Change

What is a good definition of modern day stress?

What is positive stress?

How does positive stress differ from negative stress?

List two *Positive Actions* you can take *Today* to reduce your negative stress level.

4 Creating The Change in Your Company

> *Ask not for whom the bell tolls,*
> *It tolls for thee.*
> John Donne

If I tell you that 2 plus 2 is 4, you can perceive that piece of information intellectually and make an immediate change in your thinking about those numbers. That is traditional learning. If, on the other hand, your heart is beating fast because you are in front of an audience and I tell you to calm down - you understand intellectually what I am telling you is correct but you cannot make the holistic mind-body change immediately. It requires a period of emotional change and thought practice to implement the experiential. The changing of habits and attitudes literally requires the actions of a different portion of the brain to process this unique and more challenging form of learning.

Consulting recently with an area business that has introduced the team concept into their workplace, I noticed all the elements had been laid out in proper order. Information was provided allowing employees access to necessary data about how the team approach will change their working habits. Additional opportunities for cross training and continuing education were provided. The company had

The Change

set upon the course of teaching through the traditional 2 plus 2 is 4 method. The company, however, was sad because chaos had set in...

This company was learning an important lesson about paradigms. An example of a paradigm could be the redecorating of a living room - perhaps adding new wallpaper or new curtains or changing the furniture around or bringing in a bookcase. We can make lots of internal changes within the living room paradigm but only when the room ceases to be a living room does the paradigm itself change. If the living room is suddenly considered a storage room or a garage - the paradigm shifts and living room furniture is out of place. The room now has a new overall application. it is perceived in an entirely different way.

This particular company, attempting to institute team management, changed around the furniture in their business living room (figuratively speaking) without really changing the way that they communicated to and perceived their employees. Here is how the employees heard the message from on high: "We know what is best for you. Our new way of dealing with you can be called team management. Do what we ask you to and you will be following a new pattern of teamwork. We'll select opportunities for you to receive additional training and education. We have decided that this new company policy will empower you to become more committed to the company and therefore more productive."

Initially, several employees simply quit. Others, after the team management consultant left the group for his next assignment, went into a state of expectation saying "What do they want us to do now?" Their expectations and the initial delivery system used by the company to offer the team management concept were based upon the vertical plan, i.e., thinking filters down to the employee. Nothing had really changed except that the employees were now organized into groups looking for a leader.

Creating the Change

If the good fairy could change the way in which the company first presented the team management concept it might have come out something like this: "Just because we are management or own the company doesn't mean that we have all the best ideas about how to sell, produce or deliver our products. How would you feel about increasing your importance by becoming instrumental in decisions regarding your workplace? We feel that you, working as a team, can see areas in which job productivity and quality can be improved in ways that are practical and useful. There are lots of educational opportunities we would like to offer you. Here's a list of some of them. We would like your opinion."

Empowerment and Your Staff

What does it take for a company to move from just rearranging the furniture to a complete paradigm housecleaning? This can occur when company management shifts from intercession to true empowerment. In top down management there is often delegation of responsibility but constant intercession when it comes to thinking. Management says, "I'll take care of the thinking. Thank you." That fosters among those to whom tasks have been delegated a culture of fear and buck-passing. Not a great place for innovation to occur.

Empowerment means believing, really believing that the worker on the floor has a mind and accepting that repetitive manual labor is actually not the best use of a human being.

Within twenty years, those managers weaned in the school of fear and intimidation who do not make a major paradigm housecleaning may find themselves with their backs to the wall, screaming with veins bulging into the faces of robots on the assembly floor. A rather humorous scenario when you think about it.

The Change

A New Dimension

Creating Quality means, most of all, creating a new environment of communication. It's not just that there becomes more communication - it becomes different. Rather than quantitative, it is a qualitative change that moves to a different dimension of human relationships.

The intensive Quality Cultural Change Program outlined in this chapter is only a beginning. Quality - besides being the overall system of the organization - is like a river. You dip into the human flow of communication daily to reinforce, respond to new circumstances and, obviously, to train new people. Mix positive attitude with effective knowledge systems and you can experience quantum leaps in human achievement, your own as well as those with whom you work.

The program outlined herein is a foundation for establishing the level of communication needed for the attitudes toward change and personal growth to be positive.

Each of the five modules in the Quality Cultural Change series is a one day session. Each is recommended to be followed by a half-day follow-up session. This insures feedback is provided after a time of applying the information provided by that particular module. The five module series can be held over a three or five month period depending on the spacing of follow-up sessions between modules.

The first two modules are for CEO/Owner/management only. This program does not flow upstream. That does not work. Upstream attitudinal modification has been tried too many times by organizations in which the management, sensing a "soft" problem, has commissioned a consultant to "fix" the troops. Attitude is not a static little box to be adjusted in the head of each person. Maybe the French philosopher Descartes could believe that several centuries ago, but we know that attitude is a river flowing through an organization.

The third and fourth modules are for staff and the final module integrates both management and staff together to begin moving the "grapevine" of communications into effective management/ staff dialogue.

The Change

MODULE ONE - MANAGEMENT

List two (2) of your expectations for today's program.

Exercise: It is important to take a brief period of time to discuss management's continuing expectations. What do they expect this program to achieve? Many expectations at this point may be somewhat general. Some may border on the negative. It is important for a facilitator to glean varied expectations in order to get a feel for the audience.

What is communication? Define it.

Such a simple question! Yet as I have asked that question to a multitude of groups over the years - many of them professional trainers - I have so often received answers such as " It's making sure that I present all the details" or "It's getting my information across" or "It's making sure the other person understands me." After a number of answers have been proffered, I hasten to suggest that presenting all the details, getting information across and even knowing that the other person understands you will not get the job done. The most effective definition of communication that I can provide is "getting the results we want". When management sets a vision for the company - a customer driven vision - all communication must be to get the results needed.

All languages are dirty. They are filled with generalization, deletions and distortions. Unless we not only hurl information at people but get specific feedback - the chances are quite good that we will not get the results we want. Effective methods of communication are the foundation for the entire series of programs. Without effective communication quality cannot exist.

Creating the Change

> **OVERVIEW**
>
> - Historical Perspective of Directive-Driven Culture
>
> - Why Management by Directive is Insufficient for Today's Technological Environment
>
> - How Intellectual Acceptance of the Possibility of a Quality Environment is Only the First Step to Addressing Cultural Barriers
>
> - An Introduction to the Customer-Driven Empowered Culture
>
> - Time Expectations for Cultural Change

In this section of the Module the information in Chapter One and Two of this book is presented to build a foundation as to what is possible when effective communication and teamwork exist.

Communication as the Lifeblood of the Business Organization

Communication - most specifically the transmission of the vision of end results - is the lifeblood of a successful business. You may wish to spend some time creating a metaphor - and this could even become an interesting diagram - that a business is not a machine - it's an organism that works in a holistic way, just like the human body. That fact makes moot the question of which is most important - management or staff. Making a choice would be as silly as choosing which is most vital in the human body - the heart or the lungs. In an interactive holistic system nothing functions well unless everything functions well.

The Change

Employee and management each have a vital role to play and they are dependent upon each other. Communication within an organization is the lifeblood just as circulation in the human body must continue for life to be sustained. When communication is not flowing - moving the vision of the company goals deeply and richly within an organization (organism!), the entity is going to get sick.

Throughout the five Modules, you will note that many metaphors are used. Stories activate the creative right hemisphere of the brain and can allow us to see new perspectives on old issues. They can allow us to grow not only in knowledge but in understanding of new applications.

Management View:

1. If you could change any current attitude among the employees in your department - what would you change?

2. Very frankly, what do you feel is your greatest challenge as a manager?

3. How should management deal with employee dissatisfaction?

4. Please describe your concept of the "ideal" employee.

At this point, managers will fill out the four question management view. The questions are phrased to reveal attitudinal perspectives. They reveal the viewpoint from which that manager views another set of people. To allow freedom in responding to the assessment, the attendees are instructed not to turn in the assessment form. Their comments are for their own personal use.

However, once the forms are individually filled out - the focus on

Creating the Change

the individual assessment form takes an interesting turn. The entire group is asked to break into teams of 6 or 7 per team. Once in teams, each team is asked to choose a secretary for their team. Each team is then instructed to develop a team consensus on each of the four questions they have filled out individually. The chosen secretary will record the team's consensus on each question and at a selected time will report the information to the entire group.

We have discovered that this system seems to free up the attendees' candor in responding to the assessment form. First of all, they are more at ease discussing what they have written down among their peers. Secondly, their perception of differing views begins to expand as they hear what others within their team are saying. Even if it is a homogeneous group, there will be some differences of opinion.

Another synergy occurs when the secretary of each team gives his/her consensus presentation to the entire group. There is then a larger incorporation of different perspectives. During each secretary's presentation the facilitator will transfer to a flip chart that team's consensus to each question. Many times through this process, management will see other responses to issues they thought were black and white. They will find that others in the teams, whom they admire and respect, will be coming up with different viewpoints on the same question.

This entire assessment process works so well because attendees are given ownership throughout the process. First, they know that their specific answers are confidential to their team. The team chooses its own secretary. This personal involvement increases participation in the process. Through this assessment consensus, management begins to see more clearly their current vision of staff performance and changes they feel are needed. Management expectations of staff are brought to the forefront to be discussed.

The Change

After the consensus of each team to each of the four questions is transferred to a flip chart, the group as a whole looks for a pattern of the main issues associated with the team responses to each question. The group will then choose one or two major issues that represent the group response to each of these questions. The main issues and the consensus issues of each team for questions one and two will be further addressed in Staff/Management Module Five.

Overview of Habits

At this time, we begin to discuss how we all very easily become creatures of our own habits, attitudes and beliefs. Running on "automatic", so to speak, is not a problem as long as our habits are getting us where we want to go. I use a couple of stories that allow the group to laugh at me.

One story relates to a time when the power went off in our home. My wife told me to go get the flashlight. So the first thing I did was go into the kitchen and flipped up the light switch so I could find the flashlight. How deeply we can be programmed to believe that certain things will happen!

In another example, I changed jobs. That next Monday - I got in my car, had my material in my briefcase to head for my new job, and before I knew it - I was in the parking lot of my old place of employment. How easy it is to run on the same tracks.

Brain researchers have identified the cerebellum as the portion of the brain responsible for reacting to imprinted processes. According to Professor Roger Penrose, University of Oxford, "The cerebellum seems to be much more of an 'automaton' than the cerebrum. Actions under cerebellar control seem almost to take place 'by themselves' without one having to 'think about' them."

This "subconscious" portion of our mind runs about 95 percent of

Creating the Change

our life. We program a vast array of things into our life and they become automatic. Everything from the tying of shoes to the way we react to buzz words that are religiously or politically charged.

It is so easy to continue to be freeflowing in our habits and repeat old actions or thoughts even after we have consciously learned something new. "Intellectual" learning has to filter down to automatic response through either repetition or emotional significance.

What Are the "Triggers" That Activate Our Expectations?

Exercise: Here's an example of how repetition can create responses so powerful that we cannot at first control them. You know how difficult it may have been when you were in school and you were asked to study and learn? Surely the day of judgement would come and the teacher would ask for the material to be recited. Let's turn things around now. I'm going to recite part of something and I want you to keep from thinking about the rest of it. Is that fair enough? Can you possibly believe that habits could be so strong that you won't be able to keep yourself from completing the phrase? Here goes..

Hickory, Dickory, Dock - the mouse...

What? You couldn't keep from thinking of the ending?

Let's try again.

Jack be Nimble, Jack be Quick, Jack jumped...

As you can tell from your automatic responses to these ditties which perhaps you have not heard for 20 years, repetition can be a powerful form of programming. The ditties are like triggers they

The Change

set off a programmed response to fill in and complete the "story".

Things which deeply impact us emotionally also can program us to respond a certain way. Repetition and emotional involvement are two powerful systems through which the brain learns. We create what becomes automatic assumptions about people many times through this same process. We assume a person will act the way she has acted in the past or, for some reason, we will have a certain emotional reaction when in the presence of that person. Those feelings and assumptions about others come upon us with the speed of light. They can easily control our voice tone and body language as we respond and many times create in the other person the response we assumed would occur. Our habits can control how we react to people unless we step back and ask ourselves:

"Why am I thinking that way about that person?"

"Why do I have the feeling that I'm going to have that kind of experience with that person?"

Essentially, what I expect of others is what they are most likely to give me. My tone of voice and my body language tell others exactly how I expect to be treated. Those we work with on a daily basis become, in a way, family. If we are not careful, we develop programmed ways of reacting to each other which may not be serving the best communication purposes. We may not be moving where we really want to go with our interpersonal business relationships.

EXAMPLE: When I see an employee doing something that seems really out of line relating to customer service, I may respond immediately and emotionally. This usually does not create a communicative environment. Many times it shuts down future dialogue because the employee fears another negative response.

Creating the Change

Trigger Response: "*Why did you do that! Don't do that! You ignored the customer.*"

By stepping back and acting to explore the reasons for certain actions, we create a more effective environment for positive change.

Creative Response: "*What you did is interesting. Explain it to me.*"

If the explanation reveals a problem with motive or knowledge - give an alternative manner for handling the situation. Begin the suggested changes with this..

Corrective question: "*What would happen if you did it this way?*"

Your manner of teaching indicates that feedback is required from the employee.

A "trigger" that sets off our repetitive or emotional response can be the way a person walks in or their tone of voice. We may assume that they are going to say a certain thing and we're set to react a certain way. Or we assume that we know the motives behind certain actions. It's amazing sometimes the amount of ESP we assume we possess.

We begin to destroy our triggers when we stop and ask ourselves and the other person objective questions about what is happening. It's so easy and yet so incorrect to assume because a person did a certain thing that they have a certain motive. Yet many times we label employees with comments like "You really don't care much about your work do you?" or "You don't think the customer is very important do you?"

The Change

When we stop and ask objective questions such as "What you did is interesting, will you explain it to me?" we are in the business of exercising emotional discipline. We may consider that as part of our job as managers, although it certainly has deeper personal implications. If we say it sarcastically or defiantly, we continue to signal that we are immediately assigning a motive to the actions. The tone of the question must be sincere. We cannot, should not, ought not, must not assign a label to the motive until we have the facts.

Many times the motive of the employee will be sincere, even though it is perhaps sincere ignorance. Again, instruct using the question "What would happen if you did it this way?" and proceed to suggest a better track for the employee to follow. Give plenty of room for feedback and creativity within general guidelines.

Giving employees positive attention and asking objective questions can help minimize employee activities that are created simply to get attention. One person may perform an action out of the desire for power, revenge or just to be left alone. Indeed, a person may assume some type of disability in order to be left alone. If we find ourselves having to ask the question "Why do you always send your stuff in a certain way when I keep saying it ought to be done another way?" we have already experienced a communication breakdown which hopefully can be remedied. People must be noticed on a daily basis for what they do right. Management must continually project the value of the employee. In a dynamic, growing organization mistakes and errors will occur in the pursuit of the realization of the company vision. Without some error there is no growth.

One of the important dynamics to creating positive expectations involves getting a handle on the fear "trigger' which can so habitually restrain us from trying new things for fear of making a mistake. The last thing any business person wants to hear about is failure. Intuitively we have geared ourselves to the point where we feel if there is anything in the world we don't want to hear, it's the word "Failure" - certainly as in "business failure". Yet we all know, when we stop and think about it, that all processes that improve and create positive change require a zone, a buffer if you will, where creative things can be tried and when limited failure can be accepted - a place in which the little mistakes that can lead to great ideas come about.

It's only though failure sometimes that we learn the best systems with which to please the customer and maintain ourselves on the cutting edge of the rapidly changing business society in which we find ourselves today. While failure should be "managed" as it relates to amount of capital, time or human resources that are held in potential jeopardy, even "big" mistakes, when handled properly, can become the seeds for growth.

The Fear of Failure

A good friend of mine who is a consummate marketer gave me a bit of advice once that I have never forgotten. He said that the road to success is always under construction - it's never finished. If you are going to be fearful because the road isn't finished, you'll never start the journey. You build the road as you go.

Many decades ago, as I recall the story, the CEO of a major company dealing with vacuum tubes - the awakenings of what we now experience as the computer and electronics generation - convened a very important meeting. A new generation of test tube was to be demonstrated. The company's prime clients from all over the country were flown in for this demonstration. At that time, flying was still exotic and quite an expense.

As the group assembles, a young lab assistant enters the room wheeling the test tubes on a cart to the location to hook up for the

The Change

demonstration. In front of this distinguished audience, the lab assistant finds himself helplessly grappling to keep the cart upright when a wheel snags upon a power line running across the tile floor. Perhaps you can visualize in slow motion the test tubes made of delicate glass tumbling from the cart and crashing on the tile. Utter devastation. Of course, the demonstration is called off.

The next morning the lab assistant is called to the president's office. As he walks into the room and seats himself, he looks at the president with great contrition and says, " Sir, I know that you are going to fire me..." and at that point the president of the company stands, walks to the assistant, bends down, looks him in the eye and says, "I want to tell you something. That was a ridiculous statement you just made. How on earth can I fire you? You're too valuable for me to fire. I just gave you a $10,000 education yesterday."

Here was one CEO who looked carefully at motive and attitude. Had the assistant's attitude been frivolous, he most likely would have fired him. Obviously knowing the young lab assistant was sincerely contrite - the president used the experience to deepen the lad's loyalty, mutual trust, and respect toward the president and the company. This being a much told story - one version has the lad becoming in a few years supervisor of the research department - as trusted and dependable a fellow as ever worked in the business.

Another version of the story has another CEO many years later finishing the tale and then with a gleam in his eye confiding that he was the lad and that he had worked tirelessly the rest of his life to repay the trust the earlier president had placed in him.

Group Exercise: Ask the group, who in your business or personal life has inspired you? What were their skills or attitudes that make them inspirational to you?

Use of Questionnaires

Within many companies and organizations, this seems to be the age of the questionnaire. Certainly feedback is essential as we will see as we go through this five module series. However, many employees for years have developed a trigger that when a questionnaire is sent out to the rank and file to be filled out, nothing will come of it. As a matter of fact, no action to filled out questionnaires can be a greater morale destroyer than a company might imagine.

It is far better to not send out a questionnaire if you don't really want to know the feedback. As a matter of fact, it is probably better to not ask an employee for feedback in any form unless you are ready to positively respond to her needs. If management is not willing to provide a constructive response to employee feedback it is best just to let the employees park their brains at the door, put in their 8 hours each working day and let your company and the employee travel the road to mediocrity on into competitive oblivion.

If a questionnaire is sent out, within two weeks the company should send back to each participant a summary of the responses, as simple as a typed summary of their feedback to the company. You are not making any changes at this point -you are showing the employee how much you value his opinion. You are in effect saying "Here is a summary of what we understand that you have said. Does this sound correct to you?" Then shortly thereafter, send out a summary consensus of what the employees as a whole feel about certain issues that were addressed in the questionnaire. What if those feelings don't concur with company policy? Sweep them under the rug? Don't talk about it anymore?

If you ignore strong employee feelings about a certain company related issue you are sitting on an emotional time bomb. Here is

The Change

where our paradigm as business and industry must change. We have looked at employees in the past as building blocks. You move a block here or there and you've built something. But people are not blocks. Blocks and machines don't have feelings or the ability to be creative.

The company that sends out a questionnaire and then doesn't follow up is acting in a counterproductive manner. They are saying in so many words "I'm involving you, so now that you're involved, don't bother me." That approach elicits anger, frustration or the nonchalant "Well, it really doesn't make any difference" from the employee. The employee says "I could have written anything I wanted on the questionnaire. It really did not make any difference."

Within four weeks after the questionnaire is filled out, the company should begin to conduct brief interviews with every person who filled out a questionnaire to gauge even more precisely their attitudes on issues relative to the company. Personal face to face concern is a strong psychological boost to an employee who perhaps has worked where she was little more than a number. After the interviews are done, the company's responsibility is to quickly deal with the issues and begin to make further changes that allow employees greater involvement in the growth of the company.

The process is:

> *Questionnaire -> Written Feedback -> Personal Discussion -> Ongoing Employee Involvement in Making Constructive Changes.*

Programmed triggers or expectations employees may have when they are not allowed to be the eyes and ears for their company's growth create boundaries in Employee/Customer experiences.

Creating the Change

"That's Not My Department"

One Saturday I drove to a nearby service station/convenience market that had newly opened. I normally purchase an early edition of the Sunday paper on Saturday afternoon. So I walked into the mart looking for the paper in a bin as I would find it in several other service station marts in the area. After looking in vain, I asked the attendant about the location of the papers. "Oh," she responded " the newspapers are in the pay coin boxes out there."

"Out there" was 20 feet from the front door of the mart. As I walked toward the large steel boxes housing the papers, it occurred to me that most of us carry four quarters at all times, right? While walking back into the mart to get change, I decided to share with that company through their employee a way to keep and increase their business.

Getting the young attendant's attention, I explained, "If you will put the newspapers in the store, I and many others will come in to buy them and also get things like milk, soda pop, candy bars and, if our kids are with us, we'll be forced to buy a lot more than we want. Just the simple incentive created by moving the newspapers into your store can increase your business." I felt I was performing an important customer feedback service to the company until I continued to look into the eyes of the attendant only to discover that the lights were on but nobody was home.

The young lady had no earthly idea what to do with what I had just told her. Her expectation of her job was to take customers' money and process credit cards. The idea that a customer would provide feedback to help her company grow had apparently never been introduced into the pattern of what she might expect to happen during her shift.

The Change

Steps to Visioning New Responses

As we begin to vision ourselves providing new responses to trigger circumstances, we begin a process which will allow us to change our programming.

List A "Trigger" Response You Have Had in the Past

Exercise: The attendees should at this point list a trigger response that they have experienced in the recent past. First, I share my *Assumption Monster* trigger response (the story is in Life-Perceptions, Chapter 3). I then let those brave souls who will volunteer briefly talk about their trigger responses and how they helped/hindered them.

Visualize Yourself Stepping Back, Thinking, Then Responding From the Perspective of Empowerment

Exercise: They should now take a challenging trigger response they have experienced in the past - one that has not been productive for them - and vision themselves changing that response.

Let them write a story illustrating the circumstances in which they were tempted to immediately respond a certain way. But they step back - they consider - and they decide on a different behavior.

"What you just said makes me want to shout in your face. But, wait. Let me ask a question, cool down, and deal with the facts of the situation. The way you are 'poorly' dressed, the way you walked 'arrogantly' into the room - causes an emotional response. But, wait I'm assigning motives! Let me step back, visualize myself asking questions to move my expectations into perspective."

When I write this story, I kick in the power of the pre-frontal lobe of the brain (that part which only humans have) and I visualize the

Creating the Change

end result I desire from my relationship with that person or circumstance.

I see it...

I feel it...

I hear it...

I then feel myself actually living that vision. I begin to change my expectations as to how I view that individual so that I'm sending out different nonverbal signals to that person. Because the right hemisphere of the brain controls our nonverbal actions (body language, voice tone) the only way I can reshape that nonverbal action is to vision a new way of reacting.

In short, we begin to create the way in which we wish to respond to others rather than simply reacting helplessly to triggers that we have allowed ourselves to become programmed into. Obviously this process takes visioning, practice and time. We must blend an intellectual desire and emotional commitment to change our triggers. Unless we are committed emotionally to change - we're just playing games.

Setting Priorities

Exercise: It is amazing how often our business priorities are based upon the organizational structure of the business as opposed to the human resources structure of the company.

List Five Daily Priorities in the Order You Actually Strive to Achieve Them

Which of These Relate to Communication?

The Change

How Do They Relate to Communication?

Here we ask five daily priorities to be listed in the order they are usually dealt with. Are the top ones procedural? Are they repetitious? How many relate to communication? How do they relate? Is it only sending messages down to the front line or a freeflow both ways?

From a Stress Standpoint, How Do You Handle Project Closure?

How Many Balls Can You Juggle at the Same Time?

How many balls can you juggle at the same time? Some of us who have more than two or three balls in the air want you to know that you had better not come over and demand my time because I'm going to cut you off short or bite your head off. When your time is taxed with projects and an employee comes to you and says "I've got this problem, I really need to talk to you", how do you respond?

Trigger response: You scream at them and say " I'm busy right now, can't you see?"

What you must do is be disciplined enough to take 15 seconds, look them right in the eye and say:

Creative response: "You're important to me and what you have to say is important. I want to get with you tomorrow. We'll spend time going over that. When would be the best time when we can get together?

Actually, I have timed it as taking about 10 seconds to say those

Creating the Change

words. You positively reinforce the employee's importance. Give him your full attention for 15 seconds and you can create enough good will - he will be happy to come back tomorrow. However, you must keep your promise. When you and the employee set a time - it must be good as gold.

What if they say "This can't wait!" Then you must say to yourself "This must be high priority." Either stop what you are doing or lead them to someone who can immediately help them. Sometimes in the heat of battle you must make what I call dirty decisions, "If I stop what I am doing I will cause damage. But If I don't stop what I am doing and see about those employee problems I will cause damage. Which will cause the greater damage?"

Weigh it and make an immediate decision. As business structure and customer driven needs continue to change the nature of organizations; a rule of thumb for the future is that those crises involving attitude and good will had best be taken care of ahead of procedural matters because attitude and good will with both external customers and internal customers (employees) are the ingredients that you can't buy and that will set you apart from the competition.

When an employee comes to us with a crisis we must keep our expectations open. "Oh no! If I stop and work with him. It will set me back an hour" may not be true. You may get to the core of the issue in five minutes and assure him that you'll have the information needed by noon tomorrow. The less we tense up in fast paced scheduling, the more we can stay creative in dealing with interruptions. They will happen, you know.

The Company Meeting

The issue of company meetings should be addressed. As I work with organizations across the country I hear time and time again "I'm sure that communication is important but we've got a tight

The Change

production schedule. We just don't have room for social time." For many companies meetings become just that - social time. I can sympathize with their complaint. But when we talk about successful employee communication, empowerment or self-managed teams, we are dealing with very focused activities.

In all meetings and communication there must be a focus on the company vision for customer service and how to achieve it. That focus must come about in conjunction with the emotional and intellectual needs of everyone involved. If I feel a certain way about what is happening in the company, I need to feel free to communicate my feeling without fear. However, I do not need to feel free to talk at length about my uncle and his health. True, that is part of me but it's not relevant to the vision of the company, and in the long term, to my paycheck.

We must have freedom, however, to get personal in our communications about our feelings and our judgments as they relate to our work. In those areas we need to feel that we can unload. We've always done so in the past, but we've communicated with our peers through the grapevine. That took care of our emotional needs but did not help the company. The company needs the grapevine in the main line of communication. The company, however, will only earn the right to have the grapevine when each person feels without fear to communicate their feelings and needs as they relate to company issues.

Creating the Change

How Committed Are You to the Company Vision?

The company vision means in a nutshell: How we serve the customers' needs. A company exists to fulfill customer needs. Do we always strive to be true and faithful to those needs. Mouthing commitment while speaking otherwise in a different setting eventually can come back to haunt us. Years ago there was a clown who had a kiddie radio program. Both kids and parents thought from his program that he was the kindest, most child-caring person in the world. One day the clown thought the microphone was off at the end of his program and he said - for all the world to hear - "That'll do the little *@*#* for another week." Needless to say, his program didn't last very long after that. He lost customer loyalty.

I cannot emphasize too strongly to management: If you want to play act - go to Hollywood. We do ourselves and the company a disservice when we do not become deeply committed to the vision of the organization. Emotional commitment and excitement are the keys that unlock our creative potential. If we cannot reevaluate and find areas within our work that create excitement for us - we may well need to find a company with a vision that we can become excited about.

Our Focus of Interest?

We all see things through the filter of our personalities. (There will be more on this in Module Two) Suffice it to say that minor personality differences and variations in the way people do things need not be divisive elements. Many times they become so, however. The key to successful communication is keeping all eyes on the goal of the vision. Before I spend my time trying to change the way you do something, I must pause and ask myself "Is the job getting done?

The Change

Is the attitude right?" My interest as a manager must be in cultivating each employee's ability to work toward the company vision. I am first of all most interested in their attitude and secondly, I am vitally interesting in each utilizing their unique talents and abilities in a synergistic way toward the goals of the company. I am an orchestra leader and an orchestra leader doesn't worry about how each person holds the instrument. They are interested in what?... The ultimate sound of the orchestra.

The Issue of Separateness

The management at a major automotive facility discovered that having an executive diner was creating an attitudinal problem which was far more damaging than any of the prestige that was gained by having a separate diner. The message received by the rank and file was one of separateness. We are different from you - so we are separate from you.

Organizing

One large company with many small rooms housing various departments literally knocked down the walls - not metaphorically - but with large sledge hammers. That was done quickly. What took longer was the breaking down of the psychological walls that such surroundings had help create. Little communication had been generated between departments - little sharing of information because of intense rivalry . The tearing down of the walls was a way for the company to say "We need to be competing against our German and Asian Competitors- not within our own company."

Creating the Change

ASSIGNMENT:

During the period of time between this module and the follow-up session become aware of at least two triggers in your daily business experiences. Become aware of two circumstances where you found yourself immediately reacting to someone or something in a programmed manner.

Develop and begin to visualize a new way to cope with those circumstances if the results you have been getting from your programmed reactions are not satisfactory.

FOLLOW-UP SESSION:

Management teams will discuss triggers they have noticed over the time since the last module. What kind of action plan can begin to change those triggers? Elicit examples from those who feel comfortable speaking to their particular challenges. Request each team's secretary to make copies of the one or two issues of consensus to the first two questions of Management View and give a copy to each member of the team to be used during Module Five.

The Change

MODULE TWO - MANAGEMENT

> *People are not stupid and they're not children.*
> *They can handle tough communication;*
> *They deserve the truth.*
> Carolyn Zachary
> Director, Public Relations
> AT&T Capital Corporation*

Communicating the Company Vision - Why is it Important?

Common sense would tell us that there is a big difference between our destination and how we actually get there. ("The map is not the territory") But in the business world sometimes the two get confused. Virtually all companies begin with a vision - perhaps a certain product or service to fill a need in society. When the company was small the vision was constantly in mind and processes were developed to move toward and sustain that business goal. As companies grow larger and older many times the processes that were once used to move toward the original goal become bureaucracy and tradition. The processes themselves begin to become the goal and the original vision is lost.

There are warning signs that this is happening: Management says, "Fill out these forms", Marketing says, "Sell what makes the most money." What all these actions are losing is the sight of real customer needs. The vision must be on customer needs. Processes to get there must be constantly changing with the customer in mind.

---

*Quoted from an article by Gary Stern in *IABC Communication World*.

Creating the Change

Departmental Competition

Are you a sports fan? What would be the characteristics of the worst teams? How well would those teams function if the players didn't communicate key information to each other? What if the players plotted to see how well they could one up other players on their team?

Relating to this concept, Dr. Peter Pierro shares a story:

"As a basketball coach, I learned very quickly that in order to win (that is, to compete successfully), I had to teach my players to cooperate fully - it is often called Teamwork. After they learn to play together, we are ready to take on the competition.

"I was once involved in a sports situation in which competition among players backfired to the detriment of the team. I had just taken the position of assistant basketball coach at a small high school (100 students) that was rightfully famous for its great teams. I had watched them play several games the year before and they had been well coached and seemed to be highly motivated. Unfortunately, in one of the games I saw, they had lost a tough game in the finals of the sectional tournament. If they had won, they would have been one of the sixteen teams contesting for the state title - there was only one level at that time.

"They were doing quite well the first half mainly by getting the ball in to their excellent center and he was scoring almost at will. In the second half, the ball wasn't getting to him and the guards were taking most of the shots. They were not hitting too well and the opponents took the lead. Toward the end of the game, the ball begin getting back to the center, but he had turned "cold" and the time ran out before they could recover the lead. I remember wondering, 'Why wasn't that terrific center getting the ball? They should have won.'

The Change

"At halftime in the first game the following year, I was taking the shot charts and scorebook to the dressing room when one of the guards (who had been in that final game) asked me how many points he had scored. I blinked and said, 'I won't tell you' and moved on. The other guard, who had also been in that game, stopped me and asked how many points he had scored. He got the same answer.

"Then the light came on - the former coach had set up a competitive system. The top scorer each game and ongoing throughout the season was rewarded. So, when the center started putting up big numbers, each of the guards said, 'Wait a minute - it's my turn to catch up' and the game went down the drain.

"In this case when individual competition came into the picture, it was misplaced - it destroyed cooperation (team-work) and in turn it negatively affected the competition with their opponents. You may rest assured that the player competitive model was discontinued - we saved our competition for our opponents."

There are other pitfalls - what if, instead of looking at the other team as the opposition, the players spend their time in confrontation with their own coach? What if, instead of trying to build up enthusiasm and ownership among the team members by assigning responsibilities to build players' skills, the coach simply tells them what to do with no variance allowed for the display of creativity and exceptional skill. How would a team like that play?

We still have too many teams like that playing in the United States economic league. But instead of calling them teams - we call them businesses. Let's play like a winning team. Competition is a killer when cooperation is needed. If we want to have competition, we want to be competing with Germany or Russia. We don't need to be competing with other departments within our organization.

Creating the Change

Vertical Chimneys

It shouldn't take Santa Claus sliding down vertical chimneys to get information from one department to another. Whether departmental non-communication is from a lack of understanding or competition - it is non-professional. The damage caused by information needing to go through different departments that lack communication between each other is illustrated in the story of the potential customer who called an auto dealership and wanted a radio installed in his car.

He was routed to the sales department and made arrangements for the installation of the specific type radio he desired. "No problem," the salesperson said, "just bring your car in this Saturday and we'll get that puppy slipped in for you and get you a good deal on it."

The customer arrives at the dealership on the Saturday. He goes to the service department. "You want what?" the service manager asks incredulously, "No, we didn't get an order for a radio installation. Sure we can get the radio but it will take about a week and we can install it for you, no problem."

Next Saturday the customer calls the parts department to make sure the radio is in. "Let me check with the order clerk," the parts manager says "Well, apparently that order didn't get from service to parts. We can get it in two days for you. Come on in Wednesday and we can take care of you."

The customer is back on Wednesday. The radio is in the parts department. After an hour waiting, a service person walks up to the customer in the waiting area, "I'm in service. Is that radio supposed to be installed today?"

About this time we can visualize the customer turning into the character played by Michael Douglas in the movie *Falling Down*

The Change

and going completely berserk. But he keeps his cool, gets in his car and never, never, never comes back. And over the next year he tells six other people never to go there.

Communicating the company vision of how the customer is to be treated and served helps define for each department the importance of their activities as those activities interact with other departments to bring forth the final moment of truth - customer satisfaction. If a company is not effectively communicating it's vision of service - departments tend to develop their own agendas and run in many directions. Most of the time reacting to crisis: Run, run - put the fire out! Run in circles. Run and Shout.

Personal Motivation for Communicating the Company Vision

In their book, *The Winning Performance,* Don Clifford and Richard Cavanaugh term winning CEO's as "Chief Evangelical Officers" and Bill Marriott, Jr. owner of Marriott Hotels has exhorted managers and owners alike that "There needs to be an element of executive evangelism in operation; not only the chief executive but the other senior management must preach, teach and reinforce the gospel of service quality." People want a deeply felt mission in life. They want an emotional reason to personally strive toward quality.

Winning management develops an internal set of motivations for doing what they do and they believe, really believe that even if they were not compensated - if somehow they could still live and put food on the table - they would continue doing what they do because they love it. Is that asking too much? Only if you wish to avoid world class quality.

Fear-Based vs Joy of Creating

Pushing the "envelope" of fear-moving into uncharted areas - trying new things can be as intimidating as was the breaking of the sound

Creating the Change

barrier. Those from physicists to physicians wondered what would really happen to the human body once it accelerated beyond the speed of sound. No one knew for sure. One Brave pilot decided to find out. Because one person, indeed a team, pushed the "envelope" of fear - flight was transformed and new technologies in aircraft design resulted. Companies that motivate through fear will not survive in today's constantly changing global marketplace.

Fear based motivation - and who hasn't worked under that? -is like a black hole. Once you have done well, there is still that emptiness. Because you are still scared that you are going to foul up in the future. You say, "Well, I better do something else, or failure is going to catch up with me." Our personal vision quickly becomes that of "Don't foul up!"

Whereas, the joy of creating, as opposed to being a constrictive emotion, is an expanding emotion which allows us to take pride in ourselves and our lives. It creates a continuing feeling that we are moving in a direction for our sake. Not because we are afraid of some external thing. We are doing what we are doing for our own personal growth. We cease running away from problems and begin to embrace solutions. We focus on our unique growth potential and create new opportunities as opposed to spending all our time reacting to and running away from potential disaster.

Constrictive emotions: Fear, envy, hate, (be creative and fill in the rest) tend to create a low level of stress that can be a killer. Low level stress can be as fatal as AIDS because it gently but firmly suppresses the immune system over a long period of time. Stress does not kill you, it is what stress lets into the body that kills you. Under the influence of constrictive emotions, organizations can develop dysfunctional systems, where the vision literally becomes what they don't want to happen. And sure enough, many times it happens.

The Change

Three Phase Emotional Control

Negative emotional responses which are not rationally considered can create communications problems and ill feelings. If we are in a highly charged emotional situation in which our immediate or long term response is needed the following system may be used:

Phase One: Pause the conversation and say "In order to be of better help to you, I need a couple of minutes to gather my thoughts." Leave the room if necessary, take some deep breaths and put the current situation into perspective. Look for win-win possibilities. Relax and be creative in looking for solutions.

Phase Two: If a next day response is necessary, write a letter to the person who has caused the emotional feelings you are experiencing. You will not give this letter to him. Simply write candidly, sparing no words, how you feel - deeply feel about what you are writing. Put the letter away for an hour, take it back out and read it again putting all the emotion you feel into the reading. Do this three or four times over the evening. The next day, when you must face the situation, you will notice that you have a much greater emotional control over your feelings and the way you express them.

Phase Three: If there is a length of time you have to work out the emotional difficulties - write a letter to the person who has caused the emotional feelings you are experiencing. You will not give this letter to him. Simply write candidly, sparing no words - how you feel. After you have read it the first time putting great emotional feeling into it - put the letter in a drawer. The next day, take the letter back out and read it again. Then put the letter away again. Do this for three or four days and then dispose of the letter.

Through the use of this system you are moving highly emotional right brain hemisphere feelings into the left hemisphere of language which is less feeling and more objective. Through this process you will become more in charge of your emotions when you communicate with the person involved in the emotional circumstances.

Expanding emotions of excitement, enthusiasm, hope and joy create a vibrant energy that is positive and nourishing to the body. A person with a vision - a mission - can put in long hours and remain in good health. Researchers are discovering that positive, empowered motivation related to strong personal goals creates a different chemical discharge in the body.

Expanding emotions and loyalty to a vision and a team can create tremendous success. The lack of which was recently bemoaned in a leading sports article reflecting on the golden stars of baseball and that we don't have such heroes anymore because of the lack of loyalty to a team. Baseball is really regressing, the article relates. It's going down hill because the fan is no longer able to say, "this is my team and I have a connection here with this team. I don't have a connection here anymore...it's all greed and money now." A good illustration of attitudinal decay from the world of sports.

There must be loyalty to our skills and a loyalty successful managers are looking to build with a company that has a real mission, a deep vision. It's awfully hard to be loyal to a company that is going in sixteen different directions. Staff may look at a company and management style and have a definite fear factor in really communicating. That fear creates a division. Through the grapevine true feelings flow from peer to peer while official company communication reflects management's view only. And the twain shall never meet? Such a division between free flowing and traditional communication is many times reflected within each employee. I'm only going to talk to myself about what I know is probably going to happen. I will focus on the reality - not what I would hope for or dream about or vision. I will think about what I am most likely going to have to settle for. I cease to dream, to hope and to be

The Change

willing to strive for something more creative or better. I am no longer alive. I just work here.

One friend who works in the communications field as an engineer related to me how he attempted several times to develop a comprehensive equipment maintenance and preventative replacement program to protect the company against downtime due to equipment malfunction. The company would not consider his recommendations nor give him appreciation for his time spent tackling the problem. "I emotionally died to the company at that point," he explained. "Now I just put in my time."

The Power of Ownership

How many of us, when we go out on a weekend to enjoy a hobby or sport, are filled with fear? Now, that's a silly question. We're filled with just the opposite - with excitement because we have real ownership in what we are doing.

Now, how many of us have failed at fishing? How many of us have failed at bowling? Or basketball? We do it all the time. But you see, we've shifted to a different paradigm or belief system when we're in those type of activities. We see things, if I may use the term, more holistically. We see the whole situation and we realize that part of the fun is just the sheer physical practice or the patience to do things until we get the results we want...until we catch the fish, until we sink the basket. We realize in those situations part of the fun is going through the process to get to that end result.

When companies build a grand vision for service to the customer - they begin to create an environmental framework that people can latch on to. We desire to be a part of something greater than we are. I truly believe there is an innate human desire to be part of a mission that is going to really accomplish something for our nation

Creating the Change

and the world. Generations to come silently await our deep commitment to the future. Without a vision our emotions become diffused - they lack focus.

Old Man Story *(Refer to the LifeValue Section of Chapter 3)*

Are we in our careers because we fear poverty and failure and therefore we just took the first job that came along when we got out of high school or college? Has our career track been somewhat accidental? How many of us sat down at the beginning crossroads of our career and said."You know I'm an incomparably wonderful and capable human being. What do I really want to do with my life? What would give me tremendous joy ? First I'll chart it out - set my goals and then I'll find a way to develop my skills and talents in that area."

The challenge is for organizations to develop a very specific customer oriented vision for their future. Creating that future by paying the price now means moving past the fear to create deep rich communication within the organism (organization). Each of us must - as a microcosm - create an internally developed vision of what we want to make of our life professionally. And our internal customer is the person in the mirror.

Handling Conflict

Disagreement contains seeds of opportunity. As a matter of fact, some other cultures view conflict differently than us. Some cultures view conflict as a normally occurring event that is positive. In our Western culture, we have a tendency to want to avoid conflict even if it means bigger problems later as a result of stuffing the situation in a hole and hoping the issue will not come back out. While we may view conflict as something that interrupts the normal flow of events - others may see conflict as a part of the process to come to final decisions and consensus. The key to dealing with conflict,

The Change

as we will see, is bound up in the arts of sharing power and active listening.

When the grapevine has been integrated into the main line of company communication, employees can respectfully and assertively communicate how they feel about issues. Issues can be evaluated and discussed. The key is keeping all communication aligned with the main goal and vision of the company.

Sharing Power

Who has the power in the company? The owner/CEO? Surely they have the power to hire, terminate and make policy. But who ultimately controls the fate of the CEO and company? The customers. If the products or services are not purchased - the company must make quick changes or die.

Management: Have you ever had power over your employees?

Yes, to give them directions. No, as it relates to creating a long term level of commitment and productivity. The fact is that looking over someone's shoulder or constantly dictating to them means that each employee is no more than the management's best intentions or their best ability at Extra Sensory Perception (ESP).

To really share power means to create an environment where people - like seeds - are nurtured to grow to their full potential. Let's look at an analogy: No farmer ever had the power to make seeds grow. It was the farmer's responsibility, if he or she wanted a good crop, to create a nurturing environment. The growth was always accomplished by the natural force within nature and within the seed. Just as it is with people. As detailed in Chapter 2, front line employees are closest to the power of the company - the paying customers. They must be immersed in the vision of the

Creating the Change

company, given the resources needed to serve the customer. Management must be a coaching resource to the front line employee. Management gains much "power" by doing this. How So? When you merely direct others as to what you think they should be doing - you create an extension of your own limitations.

When you develop an environment for group ownership of the company vision and make yourself available as a facilitator to encourage and train employees in providing customer satisfaction - you multiply yourself synergistically through the creative efforts of all those working with you.

The processes that go into making the "moment of truth" for the customer are best designed by the front line employee. Those closest to the customer must be given the power to please the customer. I have never talked to anyone who went up to the sixth floor of a national headquarters, knocked on the CEO's door and said "I would like to visit with you for about five minutes just to get a feel for your company." From whom do we gain our impression of any company? From the cashier, salesperson or attendant. If they don't have the flexibility, motivation and power to please us - the company is doomed.

The Thermostat...Comfort Zone Listening

If we do not train ourselves as expert listeners - we tend to hear what we want to hear. Just as a thermostat works to keep temperature within a few degrees variation - so our belief systems - our thoughts - tend to work to confirm what we expect to hear and want to believe. We become cynical when we literally block out what the other person is saying because we are so busy loading our guns to fire back. This is counterproductive. Cynicism is the greatest power our ego has to keep us from becoming aware of new possibilities that might make us initially uncomfortable but which would ultimately benefit us. Because we have always

The Change

operated in a certain way - does not mean that is the best way to operate in the future.

At a recent training session frustration was abounding. The organization repeatedly put the employees through "quality" programs on a regular basis to "fix" them. The programs "fixed" them, all right. They were practiced cynics. They said to each other "Well, here's another training program to try to squeeze more work out of us," and then with arms folded, the group dared me to teach them.

I saw what I was up against. These people had been hurt. They had been treated as though a quick fix of "quality" with little or no management involvement would bring up "productivity". These people were no dummies. They knew when an attempt at manipulation by management was going on. If management in the first of the quality attempts had fully jumped on board and began creating a different culture or climate in the organization, that would have been "real". That would have been accepted. But they had been burned several times.

I started off by saying "If you believe that there is nothing you can really learn from what I will present today - you are right." That threw them off a little and perked up their ears. "Even if your management will not allow you to do the things we talk about today, you can still take advantage of the personal growth opportunities that these communication skills we will cover today will provide you. Don't just accept what I say, question it - take what is valuable to you and use it. Don't be a cynic, be a critical listener." And with that the light bulbs came on for some in the group.

As management, we can also become practiced cynics, if we are not alert. It may be a janitor who will suggest to you a better way. Will you be willing to listen? Decades ago in England research was

Creating the Change

being carried out to develop a vaccine. A book was being written on various research techniques. Several scientists collaborating prepared viral cultures to photograph for inclusion in the book. They were left overnight in the lab for a morning photo session. That next morning the cultures were discolored and dead.

Mold spores from a sandwich left by the cleaning lady had been the culprit. The cleaning lady was soundly scolded for her actions. As she left, in her quaint cockney accent she made one comment almost under her breath. In a questioning tone she said. "I'm sorry about messing up your photo session, but when I'm thinkin' 'bout it - seems that mold - it don't like that virus." The scientists were quite perturbed and very busy creating new viruses. They were too busy to really hear what the cleaning lady said. It would be years later before her thoughts about the mold-virus connection became the basis for effective research toward a successful vaccine.

Exercise: At this point attendees in their teams will break down further into groups of three. Each will talk for two minutes about something they did recently. Another in the team will have the responsibility to actively listen to their story and then accurately summarize what they have just said. Each assigned listener must keep their mind clear of their own thoughts to allow them to be a receptive listener. Each team will go through this process until each member has had a chance to tell a story and be listened to. Each group of three will choose whom they believe did the best job of relating back the story based upon the criteria of: most accurate retelling of information, relayed best the emotional and attitudinal feeling of the person telling the story.

Breaking Down Generalizations

Another area of significant concern as a listening skill is the ability to break down generalizations. We are constantly bombarded by information which is so general that we cannot use it to make

The Change

informed decisions. In the most simplistic form you can sense the frustration if I ask you, "Are you Good?" You might well answer "Yes, I am." I might continue by asking, "Are you always good?" You may answer "Not always." I might then ask, "Why not?" Has our discourse really communicated anything? No. The word "good" was never defined. If I ask you, "Are you a good typist?" and you answer "Yes", I might ask, "Can you type 70 words per minute with no mistakes?" You might answer "No." Then I ask, "Why not?" "I need more practice," you answer. Here we have at least communicated the parameters of a need because we have defined a good typist as someone who types 70 wpm with no mistakes.

In Group Exercise Scene One, we see how a failure to break down generalizations creates a barrier to problem resolution.

Scene Two features an effective questioning method for breaking down generalizations and allowing the real issues to rise to the top for analysis and resolution. You will note that this technique requires employee feedback and ownership of part of the resolution process.

Exercise: Pick two volunteers to read Scene One in front of the group and ask the group if anything was really communicated or resolved through the dialogue. If not, why not?

Exercise: Pick two other volunteers to read Scene Two in front of the group and ask the same question. Delineate what was accomplished through the questioning processes in Scene Two. Both scenes relate to the same issues yet bring forth different responses.

Creating the Change

SCENE ONE

Supervisor: There is a problem I would like to discuss.

Director: Certainly, Bill. Sit down and let's hear about it.

Supervisor: Productivity in Division 5 team has dropped for the second reporting period.

Director: Well, two quarterly drops in productivity do indicate a problem.

Supervisor: The Division 5 team has been operational for five years and facilitated by me for a year now. The first six months of this year, as you know, were outstanding.

Director: I know that. And productivity is the key indicator and is your overall responsibility. What's the problem?

Supervisor: The team and I have come to the conclusion that we are not getting the support from upper management needed to implement our production strategies.

Director: I can't believe you would come in here and accuse us of not supporting you. I can show you lists of meetings we have attended in support of your team's work. I can assure you that we have been preferential toward no special team.

Supervisor: Look, I'm not accusing you of trying to stall my team's efforts.

The Change

Director: If you realize that we care about your team, it seems you would spend less time trying to fix blame to upper management and more time getting the team going.

Supervisor: I understand what you're saying. Let me visit with my team leader again and see if maybe we've been looking at things the wrong way.

Director: There you go. Get down to the brass tacks with the team leader. Focus in on productivity. That's what self-managed teams were created for - greater productivity. Get that vision of improvement burning in their minds. They can pick up the pace.

Supervisor: I'll get together with the team the middle of the week.

Director: As soon as possible. Productivity is the team's job and you're the facilitator. I'll be keeping track and remember, Bill, we're always here when you have a problem. We'll work together to meet the challenges.

Supervisor: I understand. Thanks for your time.

Creating the Change

SCENE TWO

Supervisor: There is a problem I would like to discuss.

Director: Certainly. Exactly what do you have a problem with? (NounFocus)

Supervisor: Productivity in Division 5 team has dropped for the second reporting period.

Director: Exactly how has it dropped? (ActionFocus)

Supervisor: A ten percent production drop. We've had a twenty percent drop in the number of team members attending the monthly strategy meetings. Cooperation has gone out the window.

Director: Why do you feel "cooperation has gone out the window?"

Supervisor: Well, quite frankly, the team and I have come to the conclusion that we are not getting the support from upper management needed to implement our production strategies.

Director: What support are you speaking of, specifically?

Supervisor: We feel that you have been attending the strategy meetings but not supporting the team resolutions.

Director: Not supporting the team resolutions? How am I doing that, specifically?

Supervisor: You will agree during the meeting with certain production changes but that's all.

The Change

Director: What do you mean by "that's all?" (Generalization - Focusing)

Supervisor: Later, as a team, we do not receive the resources to implement the production changes.

Director: What specific production changes and resources are you referring to?

Supervisor: Mainly the change to 24 hour shifts with the resources to hire additional members of the team and allow them shift variations.

Director: Let me make sure at this point that I understand what you have outlined: Your team's production is down because the team feels it has not been given the support it needs both in resources and policy from the upper management? (Feedback)

Supervisor: Yes, that is what I am saying.

Director: OK, Bill, before we begin to make any changes - let's make sure we know where we are wanting to go. From your vantage point what will need to happen for this problem to be solved? What will be the hard evidence that it has happened?

Supervisor: Upper Management support!

Director: Outline exactly what you need.

Supervisor: During the first six months of this year, management quickly responded with resources to 80 percent of the strategy plans of our team. We were energized by the

Creating the Change

cooperation and production was outstanding. We want production back to that level.

Director: What is the primary difference between the first six months of this year and the last two quarters?

Supervisor: The willingness on management's part to provide specific resources - that made the difference in productivity because of both morale level and capability to implement strategy.

Director: At this point, Bill, outline the relationship we need to be building to bring District 5 team productivity back to an acceptable level.

Supervisor: We want you to look again at our proposal to change to 24 hour shifts, hiring additional members of the team and allowing them shift variations. (Feedback)

Director: Bill, can we agree that we will look again at that proposal and can we also agree that you and your team will be open to other options that help support the increased productivity of the team? (Summation for Agreement)

Supervisor: That sounds good to me.

The Change

The Role of Representational Systems

In addition to attacking generalizations in our business communication, understanding the representational systems used by those with whom we communicate is essential. Researchers have learned that we are auditory, visual or kinesthetic (feeling) in our way of processing information.

Witness the young supervisor who builds a persuasive argument for changes in his department. He visits with the CEO and verbally offers an extensive argument in favor of the changes - after a few minutes the young executive feels he has lost the CEO's interest. The CEO begins to make comments like "I don't see how that would make a difference." and "Rather than just visiting, I would like to look over your proposals in depth".

Because the CEO was very visual - desiring to see more than hear the arguments - he considered the verbal presentation being given by the supervisor as just "visiting". If you want to get serious with me, give me something to see. The junior executive, who was quite auditory in his method of communicating, left the CEO's office confused. He had done his homework but nobody was listening. In reality, the CEO, highly visual and the junior executive, highly auditory - were like two ships passing in the night - never on the same wavelength.

Read the three stories on the following page and then decide which seemed most interesting to you.

Creating the Change

WHAT IS YOUR **PRIMARY** REPRESENTATIONAL SYSTEM?

VISUAL
The red brick colonial home seemed to loom large as the blue car entered the white paved circle drive. The brown wood shingles on the roof looked ancient and cracked. As the shiny bronze door knob was turned the massive wooden door opened to reveal a vast spaciousness in the master living area not readily apparent from the outside. With deep brown carpeting, the living area was large and dark as a cavern until the lights revealed the deep oak paneled walls and timbered ceiling.

AUDITORY
Rows of birds seemed to be singing the same melodic song as our auto rumbled toward the house. I could hear myself thinking back to all the things my friends had told me about this place. Their words seemed to come back as though I could hear the tones of pleasure. I sensed the growing silence as the car seemed to whistle into the large circle drive. Opening the front door with a resounding click, the hinges gave a mournful moan as I entered the silence of a large living area. The only sound to be heard was the remote ticking of a small clock located undoubtedly in an adjacent room. I heard myself heave a contented sigh as I sat with an audible plop on the nearby sofa.

KINESTHETIC
My hands gripped the steering wheel a little tighter and my excitement continued to grow as I could feel the nearness of the house that had inspired within my mind such a tumble of ideas. My foot pressed lightly on the brake as we eased into the circle driveway. As I gingerly placed my hand on the door knob I could still feel the coolness of the morning on the brass. As I lifted my step higher to enter, the living room seemed to pull me into its unique atmosphere. It brought back to me a bundle of feelings about a home in which I had played - rough and tumbled - years earlier. And now those earlier years seem to have been powerfully thrown back into my thoughts with such ferocity that I could not fight them off.

The Change

As you could probably determine, each story was about the same house but told from a visual, auditory and kinesthetic viewpoint. The story you enjoy most probably was written in the representational system that you habitually use. Here is a list of Visual, Auditory and Kinesthetic words that come up quite often:

Visual	Auditory	Kinesthetic
Appear	Audible	Bounce
Clarity	Babble	Caress
Clear	Boisterous	Catch
Cockeyed	Buzz	Clutch
Colors	Clear as a	Cold
Conspicuous	bell	Feel
Disappear	Discord	Firm
Enlightened	Dissonant	Fumble
Farsighted	Double talk	Grasp
Features	Droning	Grope
Focus	Drumming	Handle
Glance	Earshot	Sensitive
Hindsight	Echo	Hard
Horizon	Give a hoot	Hold
Illusion	Grumble	Hustle
Illustrate	Harmony	Stroke
Image	Hear	Impressed
Inspect	In tune with	Kiss
Keen	Lend an ear	Get in touch
Look	Listen	Lukewarm
Neat	Loud	Toss around
Picture	Muffled	Stumble on
Point Out	Mumble	Poke
See	Murmuring	Press
In the dark	Noisy	Tension
Whole	Pronounced	Touch on
picture	Vibes	Back away

Creating the Change

Exercise: Attendees engage each other in conversation and write down the predicates most spoken to determine the representational system of the person they are conversing with. After they make the determination, each member of the team will take a turn presenting a brief business proposal to another member using the representational system most comfortable to that person. Each member of the team will have an opportunity both to present a proposal and have a proposal presented to them.

The Creative "What if" Technique

Some time ago, I went to a printer to prepare to have one of my books published. The front of the book was going to be a multicolored design bleeding off the edges. I had visualized in great detail how I wanted the front to look. The printer looked at my sketches - wrinkled his brow and said in a low voice, "There's really no way we can do that."I thought for a second and then responded "OK, let me just ask you this, just for the fun of it. What if you could do it? How would you do it?" Now, there was an even longer pause. Wheels were turning.

Finally the printer said "If I could do it, we would have to use a certain width paper, we would have to strip the art work"..on and on he went for about five minutes and then ended by saying "and this would be more expensive. Probably more than you would want to pay. "From all of this I surmised he had told me initially that it "couldn't be done" because he felt the price would be prohibitive. It was higher, yes. But I wanted the front the way I wanted it. And I got what I wanted because I followed up with a "What if?"

Managers, you will be amazed how often you can get the impossible done when you sincerely ask "What if..?" The employee says "I just can't make this deadline" and you say "What if you could, what would you have to do?" The employee's mental wheels start turning and they tell you what it will take - perhaps in overtime.

The Change

Then you must decide if the price for the "What if..?" is a price you are willing to pay. If it relates to customer satisfaction, you had better find a way to pay the price.

The "What if..?" technique can be a miracle worker when it comes to barriers in interpersonal relations at work. The employee says "There is just no way that I can get along with Joe," and you respond "What if you could get along with Joe. How would things have to be different for that to happen?" Note the response. Then go to Joe who says about the first employee "There is just no way that I can get along with Bill," and you respond "What if you could get along with Bill - how would things have to be different for that to happen?" Note the response. In situations of serious conflict this technique can bring forth substantial areas for compromise and agreement. Sometimes you discover the two combatants want the same things - but have failed to communicate with each other.

**Viewing Staff As Customers To Create
An Atmosphere Of Empowerment**

When we make requests of the employees - what do those requests have to do with serving the customer? We honor and respect the position of front line workers when we make sure our requests are geared to uphold and enhance their serving the external customer. How can I make this plain? Everyone in a company: CEO, upper management, middle management, staff, front line are servants to one another in order to provide a unified flow of resources and creativity in serving the final external customer.

The one who is the greatest servant should be the CEO. He/she has the greatest responsibility to service in a leadership/visionary capacity. Upper and middle management set the pace for the vision and goal of the company to be understood and broken down into smaller sub-goals for departments. They spread the gospel of the

Creating the Change

vision to the front line and nurture them with the resources needed to exceed the external customer's expectations. Bureaucracy has no place here. Only requests that relate to the enhanced delivery of goods and services to the customer are communicated through the company. Is that form needed? What would happen if it were never filled out? Would the customer still be served and served well? If so, burn the form. Next form please..what would happen if it were never filled out? Would the customer still be served and served well?...etc.

The successful manager learns to be proactive - to anticipate. What are the customers' and employees' needs that they may not be expressing? We all know that when problems get buried, they seldom grow smaller. How can we keep the lines of communication open in an ever more widening circle?

Are we learning to catch those little non-verbal nuances when visiting with employees and taking the time to ask additional questions to make sure we are communicating? Catching non-verbal nuances happens many times in close relationships, especially in marriage. One partner has a problem and the spouse learns to read enough about it through the tone of voice and eye contact to then ask the right questions. We become sensitive to the thoughts and feelings of that significant other person.

The businesses of the year 2000 and beyond that experience dynamic growth will be, in many ways, like a family. They will learn to read body language and be sensitive to one another. One-on-one lunches with an employee and visiting during company social times are great opportunities to demonstrate that you are all in the pursuit of the vision of customer satisfaction together. It can't be achieved by management alone or by employees alone. The CEO can't do it alone. The company is a body, in every sense of the word.

The Change

Personality Profiles

It cannot be overstated that today in business and industry so often personality and behavioral differences create friction, division and suspicion. Because we are just beginning the upward curve toward ethnic integration (which is addressed in Chapter Five, "Integrating Ethnic Cultures into the Team Environment" by LaJoyce Lawton) we certainly must adjust quickly to understand and accommodate different personality profiles among those who are of our own culture.

Left/Right hemispheric understanding of the functioning of the human brain is become more commonplace. The basic premise being that just as we may be left or right handed, we also have a proclivity to function more in one hemisphere of the brain than in the other. However, such brain dominance is not a mark of genius or dumbness. It is simply a way of viewing reality. As we will see, an organization that captures the advantages of several of the qualities of both brain hemispheres in the choosing and positioning of those hired has a great synergistic advantage over the company that has merely hired clones of the several managers.

Creativity and organizational development must occur hand in hand. Not one after the other. Which is more important in an organization: creativity or organization? Before you answer that question, answer this one: which is more important, the brain or the heart? Here we see why the word "organization" would be better replaced with "organism". There must be synergy in a growing business in today's rapid electronic climate in order to be successfully customer-driven.

The following brief word association exercise has been developed following the neocortical and limbic behaviors of both brain hemispheres suggested by researchers Maclean, Treffert, Ornstein, Penrose and Herrmann.

Creating the Change

Paul Maclean has shown the vertical connection between the limbic system and neocortex to be somewhat indirect - a quasi-buffer separating intellect from emotion. Darold Treffert views the role of the limbic system as that of using emotion to view reality. Robert Ornstein suggests that the integration of both hemispheres creates a synergy of effectiveness. Roger Penrose lists many characteristics that seem to underlie neocortical and limbic functions - those along with additional indicators advanced by Ned Herrmann make up the personality profiles presented in this chapter.

Look through a sample test (pp. 218-219) and see how the scoring works. Then, move through the test quickly (pp. 216-217). Your most accurate scores will come from taking your first guess as you compare the words across the page. For example, you see the top of the test the word "Reasoning" and across to the right the word "Experience". Which one are you? You have ten points to divide between the words. Is it a tossup? Then give one 5 and the other 5. Or, if you feel only slightly toward one and most toward the other - give the least favored 2 and the other 8. If it's a sure thing, give one the 10 points and 0 to the other. Then total your scores and record your four total scores on the separate scoring page. After you have personally taken the test: Look through the sample test that is filled out and scored on the separate scoring page.

NOTE: Such a simple Word Association Test is certainly not exact. Your scores should be viewed as an approximation of hemispheric tendencies.

The Change

BRAIN SCAN

Left Brain-Knowledge (Input)

1

Reasoning	_____
Logical	_____
Communication	_____
Actual	_____
Knowledge	_____
Real	_____
Technical	_____
Present	_____
Analytical	_____
Rational	_____

TOTAL _____

Right Brain-Experience (Experiential)

3

Experience	_____
Intuition	_____
Non-definite	_____
Metaphors	_____
Fun	_____
End result oriented	_____
Ambiguous	_____
Flexibility	_____
Imagination	_____
Dreamer	_____

TOTAL _____

Left Brain-Procedure (Nesting)

2

Detail	_____
Conservative	_____
Sequential	_____
Controlled	_____
Organized	_____
Planned	_____
Non-Ambitious	_____
Dogmatic	_____
Form	_____
Structure	_____

TOTAL _____

Right Brain-Emotional (Expanding)

4

Feelings	_____
Relationships	_____
People	_____
Senses	_____
Music	_____
Eternity	_____
Sensations	_____
Harmonious	_____
Free Form	_____
Charitable	_____

TOTAL _____

QUALITIES OF PERCEPTUAL AREAS

1 "Theorizer" Knowledge Evaluation Score_____	3 "Visualizer" Visual Possibilities Score_____
2 "Organizer" Organizational Score_____	4 "Emotionalizer" Emotional Score_____

The Change

BRAIN SCAN

Left Brain-Knowledge (Input)

1

Reasoning	8
Logical	2
Communication	10
Actual	10
Knowledge	7
Real	0
Technical	5
Present	2
Analytical	2
Rational	2

TOTAL 48

Right Brain-Experience (Experiential)

3

Experience	2
Intuition	8
Non-definite	0
Metaphors	0
Fun	3
End result oriented	10
Ambiguous	5
Flexibility	8
Imagination	8
Dreamer	8

TOTAL 52

Left Brain-Procedure (Nesting)

2

Detail	10
Conservative	8
Sequential	8
Controlled	10
Organized	8
Planned	7
Non-Ambitious	8
Dogmatic	8
Form	8
Structure	8

TOTAL 83

Right Brain-Emotional (Expanding)

4

Feelings	0
Relationships	2
People	2
Senses	0
Music	2
Eternity	3
Sensations	2
Harmonious	2
Free Form	2
Charitable	2

TOTAL 17

QUALITIES OF PERCEPTUAL AREAS

1 "Theorizer" Knowledge Evaluation Score _48_	3 "Visualizer" Visual Possibilities Score _52_
2 "Organizer" Organizational Score _83_	4 "Emotionalizer" Emotional Score _17_

The Change

In the sample test you see the test taker scoring almost equally in theorizing and visualizing. Those two areas will be compatible and easy to cross over one to another. No one scores only in one area. We are all combinations with tendencies toward one or more as being our dominant areas. The highest score you will note is Organizer and the lowest Emotional. This person might fit the description of a manager once brought to my attention.

The Unintentional Insult

Shortly after coming into a company to provide consulting - a secretary confided an event to me. Recently she had finished a lengthy project and submitted it to her manager. After approaching his desk and laying the folder on it, the manager looked at the folder and said in a monotone voice "I'll check the numbers". The secretary walked away and halfway down the hall burst into tears. "He never took the time to even look at me and say 'Thank you'" she later explained.

By a chain of circumstances, shortly thereafter I had the opportunity to visit with that manager about the incident. When I described her reaction to his comment, he sat back, thought for a moment and then said. "Well, what did she expect - angels coming down from heaven with trumpets congratulating her on handing in the work? She finished the work, gave it to me and I told her I would check it out. What does she want?"

His tone was not arrogant but simply confused. He had not meant to insult the secretary. It was just that his personality was not naturally empathetic. "She just wanted you to look at her, smile and say 'Thank you.' That's all" I replied. Her test score, by the way, gave her a high number as Emotional. To her the feelings of empathy and appreciation were as important as her salary. I told the manager, "Smile for me and say 'Thank you'. Ready, now try it." His face cracked as he tried to smile.

"No. Don't grimace. Smile," I coached. His "Thank you" came out in a monotone. "Put feeling into the 'Thank you'" I said. "This feels strange" he confided. "I can appreciate that," I noted, "but with practice you'll get the hang of it and you'll be communicating better to a person with a different personality pattern and getting better results."

Honoring Different Solutions

In a particular educational institution, there was a young lady in administration doing some research work. She had her notebooks and file folders laid out all over the floor in her office. It was her way of doing research. She was very efficient and became very focused in her research processes. The director came in one morning, viewed all the file folders scattered about and became somewhat agitated. "Look, we have an international tour coming through this afternoon," he said "we've got to clean up your office."

With that they began scooping up file folders and by the time the director left her office, she was set back by at least a day in her research because her system was destroyed. She had known where everything was in her chaos of file folders. By the way, the research she was doing was quite vital to both the director and the institution.

What happened in a nutshell is that an Organizer viewed someone who is more visionary tackling a problem in a "disorganized" way and became very concerned, and upset, because they were not using the same type of system to solve the problem. But if they are getting a successful solution there must be mutual respect for the differences between these two personalities and the way they relate to each other.

Now, let's change the scenario for a moment. Let's consider how things would have been different if the director had come into the

The Change

administrator's office and said, "We've got an international tour coming through this afternoon. Let me close your blinds and close your door so that we won't disturb you as we go down the hall. However, please come out and welcome the group, won't you?"

Here the director is expressing by his approach respect and appreciation for the seeming disarray of papers found in her office. He understands that it is her research style. He understood that everything was laid out efficiently for her based on her personality (visionary) and the way she processes information. The director, a more orderly individual (organizer), looks past his immediate desire to scoop up the "disorganization" and yields to the other person's need to use a different process.

Interestingly both the administrator and director were Ph.D.s. Our educational system does not give us much of a grounding in how to work with and appreciate different perceptions and work processes. Personality differences between individuals underlie a great number of challenges and difficulties that we have in our personal and business life. These "small" things have such a tremendous impact on people's attitudes because personalities define our attitudinal relationship with others. It can be advanced that a great percentage of disagreements and misunderstanding are due to differences in perceptual viewpoints. It is many times not a conscious attempt to be uncommunicative or abrasive. But the rub comes when we don't get the reaction we expect and desire.

The Bicameral Brain

In recent times, more has become known about the human brain. We have known for some time that it is bicameral, that there are two hemispheres. Recently, it's come into our field of knowledge that the left hemisphere is where language is controlled - where we receive information and from which we send information. It's also the area involved with our ability to put things into sequence.

Creating the Change

The right hemisphere deals with nonverbal activity - visioning, emotion. The personality patterns we will look at are related to the differing strengths of the two brain hemispheres. These differing ways of perceiving reality do not constitute intelligence levels. These differences involve our perception - the way we view our world. All of us are combinations of left/right brain qualities - although most of us will have one or two areas that are dominant. The use of understanding the dominant differences is to be sensitive to how we relate and communicate to those who see the world in a varied light.

We must resist the temptation to categorize people. We don't want to view a person in such a way that we immediately put him or her into a personality "box." We want to view general tendencies and then look at how those can be addressed when we communicate with those who perceive things differently that we do.

Our "Left-Brain Society"

Before we begin talking about the major hemispheric differences, we must note that we live in a "left-brain society"; a society based on left hemisphere thinking. From the time that we are little children until about the age of eight, we tend to dwell in our right hemisphere. This tends to be very irritating to parents. Gosh, why doesn't little Johnny ever clean up his room? Why does little Linda make such a mess? How is it possible that little Tony can enter into this particular area and within five minutes do away with all the cleaning that mommy has done in the last two hours?

In our society, as adults, as a rule we become very sequential, very orderly. But young children until after the age of eight, really don't have a clue as to where we are coming from. They tend to dwell in a world more feeling and visionary than do we adults. There is physiology involved. Up until the age of about eight a young person can have a very severe head trauma, perhaps a great deal

The Change

of damage to the left hemisphere and the language system will regenerate in the right hemisphere. The brain is quite elastic until about the age of eight. After that time, if such trauma occurs and there is significant damage to the left hemisphere, in many cases, the language system will only partially or not at all regenerate in the right hemisphere.

But you see, we continue as adults with the capabilities of the right brain always available to us - even if submerged by the organizational demands of everyday life. The two hemispheres are connected by the Corpus Callosum, a bundle of nerve fibers, which allows the two hemisphere to communicate. When that bundle of nerve fibers is severed, as has been done in humans to treat severe forms of epilepsy, it is as though the individual possesses two separate brains. Both hemispheres are unable to communicate with each other.

We will discuss the major personality traits in those who are left hemisphere dominant and right hemisphere dominant. On the next four pages, I want to introduce you to four generalized characters who demonstrate these characteristics:

A special thanks to professional illustrator Guy Chism for the four Personality Profile illustrations.

Creating the Change

CHRIS/CHRISTA THE COMPUTER

The analytical person I call Chris or Christa the Computer. Can you envision people who look like computers? Maybe they have a little computer screen with a head on top and they have a cup of coffee as they are looking over streams of information. They love to create systems with given information. Facts are like tinker toys to them. If they do not feel that they have adequate information, it is very difficult to get them to act. This is the type of person who, if you ask them about how something works, will take you back to the history of when they invented the thing and will inform you of every fact about it for hours. Chris or Christa the Computer is vital to our business and organizational systems today.

The Change

ANNE/ANDY THE ORGANIZER

Another strength of the left hemisphere deals with organizational capabilities. You might look at these persons and term them as Anne or Andy the Organizer. You might even look at them as though they were walking filing cabinets. You can see all of these little drawers all alphabetically arranged quite neatly. If you pull one of the little drawers open, everything is arranged in an exact and precise measurement of content and information. This is the type person who keeps our business and industry organized. Put them in a room with an empty file cabinet and a huge disarray of folders and documents; come back six hours later and you will find everything neatly organized. There is a real emotional desire for neatness and order. If these persons are placed in a disorderly situation, they become disoriented until they can develop some order in the environment in order to make them feel secure.

Creating the Change

VICKIE/VINCE THE VISIONARY

A power that Vickie or Vince the Visionary has owing to right hemisphere dominance is the ability to see in whole pictures. Sometimes they can't even express in words what they see in their mind. This is the type person who can operate well on intuition - an entrepreneur who can see new ideas, new possibilities. Very inventive - capable of coming up with things almost out of thin air. Very adept at looking at circumstances from a different perspective. When business changes occurred at a slow predictable rate - this trait was really almost totally relegated to the arts and to those daring heroes who risk all to start a company with ideas ahead of their time. Today and in the future those individuals with visionary traits will occupy an important place in growing organizations. The company will learn to feed off of that visionary ability to come up with creative processes to fulfill and indeed stay ahead of customer expectations.

The Change

EMILIE/EDDIE THE EMOTIONALIZER

The feeling power of the right hemisphere as represented by Emilie or Eddie the Emotionalizer shows that this person, with a bowl of cookies in one hand and maybe even a little bottle of aspirin, is always there to supply moral support - to empathize. This is the type of person who can read body language very well. This person will come over to you on a morning after a rough night - you didn't get any sleep, you have a pounding headache but you don't want to tell anybody about it. Emilie or Eddie will come up to you and say, "You've got a headache today don't you? Things can be rough sometimes can't they? Here, have an aspirin." or "Here, have a cookie" and give you a pat on the back. These are the cheerleaders of an organization. They are equally valuable to a growing vibrant company.

QUALITIES OF PERCEPTUAL AREAS

THEORIZER
"Facts become tinkertoys"

VISUALIZER
"Dreams of what could be"

1	3
• Feels secure with knowledge • Needs to know • Reacts to lack of information	• Feels secure with change • Needs to brainstorm • Reacts to lack of innovation
2	4
• Feels secure with order • Needs to organize things, tasks • Reacts to disorder	• Feels secure with understanding feelings • Needs to "feel" things • Reacts to emotions

ORGANIZER
"A place for everything, everything in its place"

EMOTIONALIZER
"Sensitive to the current state of feelings inside and around them"

The Change

Using the Separate Hemisperes

Just as most of us are either left-handed or right-handed, we will have a tendency toward being either right-hemispere or left-hemisphere dominated. Some of us are ambidextrous and in like manner we are capable of switching quite easily from the perspective of one hemisphere to that of the other.

An example of how this switching can occur and how valuable a skill it can be is the writing of this book. As I put together a rough draft of any section, I cannot afford to view that effort from a left hemisphere sequential, orderly perspective. If I do, nothing gets written because my brain refuses to let the product come out messy and unorganized. In my left hemisphere perspective, to "throw" things on the page is too disorganized and I become frustrated dealing with it.

I must relax, switch to right hemisphere, and just let my thoughts flow out on paper. I can always come back, switch to the janitorial left hemisphere and clean the mess up (an outline is a good way to get that done). But the mess first has to be there to be organized. From my own experience I feel that a lot of what is called "writer's block" comes from one's inability to switch to the free flowing, unconscious power of the right brain thereby allowing whatever is up there between the ears to flow on out through the fingertips into the pen or word processor.

Whether writing a book or tackling tough business decisions, I feel that many times it is better to throw some ideas out and then do housekeeping on them rather than straining to come up with the impossibly perfect concept the first time through. Another option is a relatively simple process called "mapping" or "webbing" which is done by taking a sheet of plain paper, writing the main concept in the center and then send out webs or tentacles to sub-concepts, facts, and ideas. We then have a nice, right-hemisphere picture.

Creating the Change

Whole Brain Synergy

Let's look at how the various hemispheric traits can develop a very dynamic synergy in an organization (organism). I had a good friend who was very visionary - tremendously capable in coming up with new ideas. He teamed with a fellow who was an organizer. Together they made an unbeatable team. Their company grew by leaps and bounds. One, being a visionary, led the way with all kinds of wonderful ideas. His associate, the organizer, followed behind him cleaning up the pieces and putting things in proper order - bringing his grand dreams down to realistic chunks of business activity. Several years later, when they parted ways, the visionary didn't last very long in the business by himself. Without the organizational skills, he was unable to keep the business together.

In the world of sports, the National Football League did a study which proved interesting. The offensive players' lockers were found to be quite neat. The defensive players lockers, by and large, were in disarray. This begins to fall into place when we consider that the offense must always know what to do, when to do it and how to do it, sequentially (left hemisphere). Whereas the defensive player always has to be reading the movement and saying "Ah, they just did this" and reacting with creative moves (right hemisphere). The importance of the synergistic interplay is obvious.

In most companies, particularly those in which self-managed teams are being formed, you want to have the varied hemispheric traits represented among your employees. You want to be in a position to benefit from the varied perspectives provided by each way of seeing a business reality. Remember the story about the elephant and the blind men. One who felt the trunk said "This is a large snake." The blind man feeling the leg said "This is a tree." They came up with several sincere explanations as to what this creature was. But none could grasp the picture. They each attacked the issue singly.

The Change

Many times as we look at clients and their needs we may be "seeing" only the trunk or the foot and not the whole picture. That is why it is imperative to have various perceptions represented in our teams to integrate their views into a whole picture - this is where each person on the team can bring his or her particular talents and perceptions into play for the benefit of the whole organization.

Creating a Unity

Let's look at an example of those with varied hemispheric perceptions working together to create a greater whole. We begin with a start up team within a company. We are certainly looking for new ways to satisfy the customer. We want an input of information that is not static - status quo - but creative and innovative in it's potential applications.

Can you imagine the input that the visionary person (Vince/Vicki the Visionary) can provide the company through creative brainstorming? The dearth of possibilities may then be passed on to Chris/Christa the Computer, who can analyze the possibilities, look at theoretical scenarios and build systems using the best of the brainstorming. These systems can be passed to Andy/Anne the Organizer to organize the systems and perhaps create a series of real life training programs or a set of projects that will become an effective way to address needs of customers.

What have we done? We have taken people with more of a visioning capability to come up with general strategic planning ideas. Then we move to developing theoretical systems using the best planning ideas. The theoretical systems must then be organized into workable procedures and tasks.

Does it have to flow this way? No. Chris/Christa the Computer may develop a theoretical system with current information and hand it to Vicki/Vince the Visionary to be projected out to the potential result of its applications.

Wait. We still have Emilie/Eddie the Emotionalizer. Where would she/he fit into the organization? Every team needs a cheerleader - that person who displays a high level of emotional empathy. When you're down, they pick you up. They are a special confidant to the team members. They empathize with your feeling and emotions.

When we look at these characteristics of the left/right hemisphere as they exhibit themselves in human relations - we are literally viewing a balanced mind. A whole perspective on reality. Each of these parts - Visioning, analyzing, organizing, emotionalizing come into play when and where needed to allow us, whether it's an individual or a company, to create our future - not just react to our environment.

The balanced holistic view gives us the power to be proactive - to develop a vision of where we want to go, develop systems to get there, make those systems workable and be emotionally encouraged along the way.

Most Of Us Are "Hemispheric" Addicts

When we do not perceive how our mind pulls us toward our specific hemispheric tendencies- we are easily addicted to them. That is, we react to these perceptions as an addict would react to the short term favorable feelings created by a drug of choice. We get a comfortable feeling being organized so we choose organizing activities- even if they may not be appropriate to the circumstances. Or our comfortable feeling may come from always trying new things (visionary), accumulating and studying information (analytical) or becoming emotionally involved (emotionalizer) in almost any situation that touches us.

The Change

When we understand how we so easily and automatically tend to react to our dominant hemispheric tendencies- we can begin to become free to choose our responses. We can become aware that we no longer need to be chained to the reaction of our dominant hemispheric tendencies. We can begin to choose based upon the context of the circumstances the importance of organization, analysis, visioning or emotional feelings. Each of these approaches continue to be available to us. But they must be available as choice not as compulsion. Choice is freedom. Freedom is power.

When we function only through the left hemisphere, we put ourselves in a reactive mode. Because the left hemisphere only responds to given information or the status quo. It can develop systems based upon current information and it can organize those systems very efficiently. But without the activation of the right hemisphere, we're not looking at new possibilities - we're not projecting into the future. We're not seeing the variables that will allow us to be creative in our planning as to where we will be five or ten years from now.

Strategic planning from the left hemisphere is like driving by looking through the rear view mirror. You get a great view of where you've already been. But we're rather powerless to direct where we are going. Due to our current fast paced and constantly changing business environment, it is not going to be adequate to just see clearly where we have been. It can be terminally deadly to project into the future just based on where we have been. The future is waiting for those who have eyes.

Can you imagine the strength and power of teams that incorporate all of these personality profiles into groups and organizations that work toward creating the future? Right now too often we are paying employees for maybe twenty five percent of their brain power. We are telling them what to do and they are just implementing our directions. That perpetuates the past.

Creating the Change

The Power of Utilizing Both Hemispheres

As discussed in Chapter Two, a company's responsibility is first to share the vision of where they are going with their employees. This must be done with zeal, with emotion, with great excitement. The employee must be in partnership in designing the processes through which the mission is achieved. That is the key to unlocking the employees' emotive connection to the mission. Being told what to do can be emotionally limiting. Being able to develop the processes to get a mission accomplished is exhilarating. Such employee ownership allows the employee to grow more quickly in skill. When, through ownership, you open up the visioning and emotive aspects of anyone, you have activated that very powerful right hemisphere - allowing them the freedom to be creative.

An employee will leave work and spend hours with a hobby. Doing something they love - a sport. They will be intensely creative. Why do they need to shut that all down when they come into the workplace? As brought out in Chapter Two, that is our prevailing belief system about work. It has to be a drudgery, a drag. Anybody who loves their work has got to be a little crazy. We get off at 5 o'clock feeling totally drained and about the only thing that's going to get us back on our feet is really what we should have had eight hours of in the first place - the opportunity to be creative - to feel part of a larger mission. For the time being, until work changes its complexion, we find that re-creation in sports and hobbies in which we have freedom of ownership.

CEO, management: Respect the perceptual differences of people, pull them into play synergistically so that the varied parts, literally equal themselves many times over geometrically. The power for the company becomes many times more than the individual abilities of each employee. Another pot of gold: divisiveness due to personality differences will begin to change into respect for valuable viewpoints and perspectives that enhance the company's ability to be

The Change

competitive. And make money. And make payroll. Once employees really see the sequence: varied personalities share varied perceptive skills with company, value the results of the sharing of varied perceptive skills, company growth, company profits, profit sharing, money in employees' pockets. Pragmatism in the form of income and job security can change attitudes when all else fails.

The company begins the process of activating the right hemispheric thinking throughout the organization by sharing the company vision with employees and staff. We get excited about the vision and unlock that wonderful childhood power we all have to dream - to expand our beliefs, to be moldable, to change - to try new things. We take the childhood ability and bring it up to adult speed and begin to activate a portion of our mind which has perhaps been dormant. There is a price which must be paid, however, for unlocking that childhood power to dream and fall in love with what we do: We will find ourselves consistently more happy, more refreshed, filled with greater energy and more enthusiastic than we've been for years. When we start enjoying what we do - we become more creative. Can you handle feeling that way? It's a "rough" job that build's world class quality, but somebody's got to do it.

We can easily see what happens when the full power of that right hemisphere is not brought into use. Remember that last year's resolution you made on New Year's Eve? Then two weeks later it was blown. We intellectually (left hemisphere) wanted to change, but without emotion - a real emotional commitment to what we do - those visions fizzle - they die. We've all experienced that. But, hopefully, all of us have also experienced the deep satisfaction that happens when we do put emotional commitment into what we're doing. When we create both that vision and that emotion - we become tremendously creative in coming up with new facts and ideas that can help us organize and finally achieve what we desire to accomplish.

Creating the Change

Now, I'll let you in on a secret. Want to know why the appliance repair people are always so happy, cheerful and enthusiastic when they come around? Think about it - they move appliances, such as refrigerators, away from the wall for repair and they pick up all of those resolutions and positive affirmations that we had pasted on the front of the refrigerator, which then traveled up to the top of the appliance and fell into the bottomless pit behind. They pick up and read those things many times daily. Can you blame them for being so dynamic and successful?

Consider the basic hemispheric traits we have discussed in this chapter. You may be very strong in visioning. You may be very adept at analyzing or maybe you're more of an emotive type person - you can easily read other peoples' body language and you work well with people to uplift and encourage them. Whatever trait may be most dominant for you makes you very important and valuable to an organization.

Companies that go through the process of learning to see from other hemisphere's perspectives and appreciate the creativity that can come from that panoramic view can develop a synergy among their staff and management. It's a oneness that can give them such a unique and competitive edge that other companies may be forced to scratch their heads and say, "How are they coming up with these creative ideas and responding to change so quickly?" The department head in a company asking that question has sixty five people who are all clones. They all dress the same, think the same and even raise their hands in seminars the same (I've seen that happen!) And they expect to come up with new ideas?

How can we be creative in developing the quality that we need into and past the year 2000? Only by seeing with new eyes. You know, we don't need new horizons. We need new eyes. We need to see what's already there in the tapestry of reality that will lead us to where we want to go.

The Change

The next time someone irritates you, whether it's in a business situation or in your personal life - evaluate a little bit about their personality pattern - think about yours - and look at coming to terms and understanding and appreciating the differences in the way people approach solving problems and coming to solutions. In such understanding is unlimited power.

Test Your Skills With This Review

During office conversation, have you heard the following comments from co-workers about co-workers? "I don't understand how they ever get anything accomplished. They never seem to be preparing?" Or, at the other end of the spectrum, "They get into such needless detail about everything."

From whose point of view do we attempt to gain rapport with fellow workers? If we color all our judgments through the filter of our personality - our way of perceiving things - what are we missing?

Without becoming highly technical, we know that the two hemispheres of the brain perform some rather distinct functions. Generally speaking, the left brain is logical, analytical and sequential. Whereas the right hemisphere sees in complete pictures and feels deeply. Just as some persons who are right or left handed , so we each have a proclivity to be right or left hemisphere dominant in our perception of reality.

Christa/Chris the Computer will be the first to say about Emilie/Eddie the Emotionalizer: "If they would be more concerned with the information needed to get the job done -they would be much more effective. I catch them so often chatting with another co-worker about their problems, Or they will just be in a mood because of something they have experienced. They simply let their feelings get in the way of efficiency."

Creating the Change

Emilie/Eddie the Emotionalizer will be the first to say about Christa/Chris the Computer: "They always give me the feeling that my work is just tolerated but never appreciated."

After reviewing the profiles of personalities covered earlier in this chapter take the test on the next page and write in which personality you feel would be saying each statement and to whom they would be referring. The answers are at the end of the test. Have Fun!

The Change

PERCEPTIVE OFFICE CONVERSATION

1. "I don't see how they can come to such good decisions without first more comprehensively researching the pros and cons. Although jumping to conclusions - many times they are right."

Says_____ about_____

2. "If they would be more concerned with the information to get the job done - they would be much more effective. I catch them so often chatting with another co-worker about their problems. Or they will just be in a mood because of something they have experienced. They simply let their feelings get in the way of efficiency."

Says_____ about_____

3. "I don't understand how they ever get anything accomplished. They never seem to be preparing."

Says_____ about_____

4. "They seem always to be messing up their daily schedule by spending unscheduled time in interpersonal conversation rather than sticking to their work routine. They really are violating company policy rather often."

Says_____ about_____

Creating the Change

5. "Gets into such needless detail about everything."

Says_____ about_____

6. "Always running around in circles - organizing - never doing things differently."

Says_____ about_____

7. "Always gives me the feeling that my work is just tolerated but never appreciated."

Says_____ about_____

8. "Never stops to enjoy. Just keeps organizing. How boring. It never looks like they are having any fun."

Says_____ about_____

The Change

ANSWERS

1. Christa/Chris the Computer about Vicki/Vince the Visionary

2. Christa/Chris the Computer about Emilie/Eddie the Emotionalizer

3. Anne/Andy the Organizer about Vicki/Vince the Visionary

4. Anne/Andy the Organizer about Emilie/Eddie the Emotionalizer

5. Vickie/Vince the Visionary about Christa/Chris the Computer

6. Vickie/Vince the Visionary about Anne/Andy the Organizer

7. Emilie/Eddie the Emotionalizer about Christa/Chris the Computer

8. Emilie/Eddie the Emotionalizer about Anne/Andy the Organizer

Now, let's run through a brief evaluation on pages 244-247. It has many similarities to the essay questions relating to attitudes you went through at the beginning of Module One. Here they are structured in a manner which can be scored.

Remember, our personalities and our attitudes are not always the same. We may assume an attitude toward something because we feel we must - while it would be most comfortable for us to approach it otherwise. Our attitudes are developed through belief systems taught us since youth and through personal adaptations to our specific environment. On the other hand, personality patterns tend to be more genetic as well as learned. Our dominant personality patterns constitute areas in which we can move in a free flowing fashion. We can move into other personality areas - but to do so causes some stress - because we are not as comfortable. We can adapt but only with determined conscious thought. Attitudes can be changed much easier than basic personality patterns.

Creating the Change

In this test you will choose a statement or statements that best interpret your perceptual approach to an aspect of workplace environment. These are six questions each having five possible answers. Ten points are allotted per question to be distributed among the five possible answers.

To the question "My department functions best when:" you may assign 3 points to D "Team goals are emphasized" and 7 points to C "When the employees get excited about the 'big picture' - the end results I need." if you determine that to be the scale of preference, with the highest number denoting the highest preference. Of course, if one answer fits you completely give it the entire ten points.

Once finished with the test, total up all your points for each letter. The letters correspond as shown to the attitudes most likely demonstrated by personality profiles.

A - Christa/Chris the Computer

B - Anne/Andy the Organizer

C and E - Vicki/Vince the Visionary

D - Emilie/Eddie the Emotionalizer

The Change

SUPERVISORY QUESTIONNAIRE

1. My Department Functions Best When:

D _____ Team goals are emphasized.

B _____ When each employee knows the specific information they need in order to accomplish his/her tasks.

E _____ I am visualizing in specific detail the end results that I wish to achieve with the co-operation of all the employees. When I bring that vision to whatever level necessary to make them all excited about it.

C _____ When the employees get excited about the "big picture" -- the end results I need.

A _____ When I am on top of what everyone is doing so that I can catch anyone who is dragging his or her feet.

2. If You Could Change Any Current Attitude Existing Among The Employees -- What Would You Change?

A _____ I would make certain that each employee thoroughly understands that I am the supervisor and that their future with the company hinges on their doing what I tell them to do.

D _____ I would want a stronger emphasis on team effort and fair play so that all employees benefit in their service to the company.

B _____ The specific directions laid down for efficient functioning in the department should be followed more closely.

C _____ Each employee should take a greater responsibility to work toward the overall goals I have set for the department.

E _____ I would first look at the way I am approaching each employee to make certain that he or she perceives what I want from him or her and understands in their own terms how they can achieve it.

Creating the Change

3. Very Frankly, What Do You Feel Is Your Greatest Weakness As A Supervisor?

E _____ Sometimes failing to communicate the overall goals I have for the department in a way that is really understood by each and every employee.

A _____ I let my employees get away with dragging their feet and trying to "pull a fast one" to get out of doing the work they should be doing.

B _____ If I do not know or do not communicate properly the job requirements and specific duties that each employee ought to be performing.

C _____ When I get all excited about the goals for the department and that excitement somehow just doesn't catch on with everyone else even when I try to tell everyone how great the end results will be.

D _____ Sometimes I will favor one employee over others or spend more time with paperwork when I should be out with the team getting a feel as to whether everything is running OK.

4. What Do You Believe Should Be Done To Reduce Employee Turn-Over In Your Department?

A _____ If the employees will buckle down and do their work and quit trying to slough off -- I won't have to fire them.

D _____ Each individual should gather around the team efforts of the department and feel that they can come to me for personal help with any problems they may face.

C _____ If each worker will put forth greater responsibility for their own success, they can work their way up the organization.

The Change

B _____ Perhaps a better understanding by each employee of the specific duties of their job so that they can perform it better will help make them more satisfied. They really need also to have as much information as possible about the benefits that the company provides for them.

E _____ I need to be as perceptive as possible to the specific needs of each employee as it relates to his or her job satisfaction and by so doing see if certain elements of their job can be arranged more to their satisfaction in accomplishing the objectives of their job.

5. How Do You Deal With Employee Dissatisfaction?

E _____ I try to see the disagreement through the employee's eyes and make certain that I am not missing an opportunity to positively modify some aspect of their job situation to keep them growing in their work.

A _____ If they don't like their job, they can quit. There are plenty of others in the unemployment lines waiting for their job.

D _____ Employee dissatisfaction is damaging to the whole team effort. I hope that I can counsel with the employee as a friend and see if there isn't a fair solution to the problem.

B _____ I take a two-fold approach; I try to find out first of all what specifically about their job responsibility they feel they don't like and try convincing them of the necessity of those duties or responsibilities and secondly, I emphasize to them the security that is being provided for them by the company.

C _____ I try to put the gleam back in their eyes and the excitement in their lives by painting the "big picture" for them of how accomplishing well in their present position can lead to better pay and higher position in the company.

Creating the Change

6. Describe Your Concept Of The "Ideal" Employee.

D _____ Friendly, always ready to share and encourage others, a member of the team.

A _____ Does his/her work, doesn't give any back-talk.

C _____ An individual with some goals in life -- willing to learn more about their job position and perhaps, if they are really motivated, more about the job just above it.

B _____ One who is punctual, a reliable employee with a high standard of values and an appreciation for the work they do and the security that the company provides.

E _____ An individual willing to look objectively at their job duties and make suggestions on improvement of the job and overall suggestions on how management can give them more freedom and autonomy to do their work in a more productive manner.

The Change

Exercise: At this point each team will have their members one at a time communicate a particular company vision- a goal to another of the team taking the role of one of the personality profiles. The first time around the member of the team playing the personality profile role can tell the other team member which role they have chosen, Chris, Eddie, etc. The second time around they will reverse roles and the person playing the personality role will let the other person determine which personality profile they have chosen by guessing based upon their responses to questions. Refer to the " How Do I Relate To..." page (pg. 249) for suggestions on relating to each personality profile.

HOW DO I RELATE TO...

1. Theorizer (Verbal-Auditory)
    Can I supply all of the relevant information needed to achieve the final outcome?

2. Organizer (Verbal-Written)
    Do I know the rules? Do I have the authority? Can I express the processes needed to achieve what I want?

3. Visualizer (Visual)
    Can I explain what I want in general end-result terms?

4. Emotionalizer (Kinesthetic)
    Do I feel deeply about my needs - Can I convey that?

The Change

ATTRIBUTES OF THE TEAM

Write down two of the biggest problems you currently experience when working in teams....

In a dynamic team there is "disarray" because of constant change and growth. The "stability factor" is created through growth and change. The team that keeps doing the same thing hoping for different results - is disfunctional.

A dynamic team emphasizes individual strengths (personality profiles) of each member as they tie into achieving the total team goal.

Rewards for individual achievement can be given in the form of individual recognition as long as the recognition is tied to the team goal. Money awards are spread out to all in the team based upon total team achievement.

The team respects and encourages its strongest elements (persons) because the whole team benefits from their achievement (back stabbing and politics are short-circuited). Peer pressure begins to encourage team (individual) excellence because everyone benefits when every member does their best using their particular strengths.

Creating the Change

TEAM GROWTH

- The team tries new ideas on a small scale at first.
- Failure is OK as long as we understand and communicate what was learned. We are to be respectful of failing. After all, the end results being worked toward require innovative and changing processes and procedures.
- New successful ideas from individuals in the team are supported by the team because everyone benefits.

ATTRIBUTES OF MANAGEMENT

Management serves as a coach - holding out the vision (goals of the company and specific department) and encouraging the team to develop the processes to achieve the vision. This creates
- A Sense of Responsibility
- Self Esteem
- Excitement
- Commitment
- Team involvement

Directing: Get your report done by 8 in the morning.

Coaching: The team needs your report by 8 in the morning. What kind of scheduling do you think will work best for you to meet that deadline?

The Change

Summary - Five Qualities Of An Effective Manager

1. Old Belief: Work is a chore we must do in order to enjoy the rest of our life.
   New Belief: We can truly fall in love with what we do, if we so chose. If we want to just act and not be totally committed, we should go to Hollywood.

2. Old Belief: The employees' main job is to listen to what management thinks is best and just do it.
   New Belief: Listening is the hardest thing you will ever do, but the most rewarding because it empowers.

3. Old Belief: Different is strange.
   New Belief: Appreciation of differences. No more departments full of clones.

4. Old Belief: When I want my employees to change what they are doing, I want the change now.
   New Belief: People are not machines and you can't adjust a screw and instantly change habits.

5. Old Belief: "Failure" sounds too much like "Business failure" and that's not in my vocabulary.
   New Belief: The challenge is to understand the role of failure in the learning process. Management now needs to be scared to death if employees are not trying new ways of doing things. We want to look past the occurrence of what the employee is doing, to the attitude. Attitude, along with knowledge, is the seed that represents the level of performance other than accidents which are, to an extent, unavoidable.

ATTITUDE

The attitudes of employees in a company in the future is the biggest asset that company has. Far above their equipment, tools and all technology is that one ingredient which cannot be bought: ATTITUDE. It can only be earned by management sincerely and emotionally modeling the performance it desires.

ASSIGNMENT

Listen and look for personality patterns during the work-week. Engage at least two persons in conversation and speak to their personality traits. If they are organized, respond to them in an organized fashion. If they are emotional, be emphatic and intense in your conversation. In a word, enter into their world of perception. Note the results.

FOLLOW-UP SESSION

Group discussion of results from conversation with various personality patterns. How well did they respond when you approached them from their angle of perception? What problems did you encounter? What did you learn? Make certain each manager has a copy of her team secretary's consensus notes on the first two questions from the Management View Assessment. It will be needed during Module Five.

REFERENCES

Maclean, Paul D. "The Paranoid Streak in Man." *Beyond Reductionism*, edited by Arthur Koestler and J.R. Smythies. Boston: Beacon Press, 1969.

Treffert, Darold A. *Extraordinary People*, New York: Harper and Row, 1989.

Penrose, Roger. *The Emperor's New Mind*, New York: Oxford University Press, 1989.

Herrmann, Ned. *The Creative Brain*, Lake Lure, North Carolina: Brain Books, 1989.

NOTE: A most comprehensive hemispheric testing instrument is offered by the Ned Herrmann Group, 2075 Buffalo Creek Road, Lake Lure, North Carolina 28746.

Creating the Change

MODULE THREE - STAFF

NOTE: Much of both the content and context of Staff Modules 3 and 4 are the same as Management - Module 1 and 2. The dynamics are identical in many ways. When the Staff is going through these two one day modules, only the facilitator should be present with them. Management should not be present. The integration and communication of differing viewpoints and workplace challenges of Management/Staff will occur during Module 5.

List Two of Your Expectations for Today's Program

It is important to take a brief period of time to discuss Staff's continuing expectations. What do they expect this program to achieve? Many expectations at this point may be somewhat general. Some may border on the negative. What have they heard through the grapevine? It is important for a facilitator to glean varied expectations in order to get a feel for the audience.

What is Communication? Define it.

Such a simple question! Yet as I have asked that question to a multitude of groups over the years - many of them professional trainers - I have so often received answers such as "It's making sure that I present all the details" or "It's getting my information across" or "It's making sure the other person understands me."

After a number of answers have been proffered, I hasten to suggest that presenting all the details, getting information across and even knowing that the other person understands you will not get the job done. The most effective definition of communication that I can provide is "getting the results we want". When management sets a vision for the company - a customer driven

The Change

vision - all communication must be directed to getting the needed results.

All languages are dirty. They are filled with generalization, deletions and distortions. Unless we not only hurl information at people but get specific feedback - the chances are quite good that we will not get the results we want. Effective methods of communication are the foundation for the entire series of programs. Without effective communication quality cannot exist.

OVERVIEW

- *Historical Perspective of Directive-Driven Culture*
- *Why Management by Directive Is Insufficient For Today's Technological Environment*
- *How Cultural Habits Affect Our Perception Of Work*
- *How Habits Are Formed And How They Can Be Modified*
- *What To Expect In The Process Of Growth And Increased Responsibility Of Self-Managed Teams*

In this section, the information in Chapter One and Two of this book is presented to build a foundation as to what is possible when effective communication and teamwork exist.

Creating the Change

Communication - The Lifeblood Of The Business Organization

Communication - most specifically the transmission of the vision of end results - is the lifeblood of a successful business. You may wish to spend some time creating an analogy - and this could even become an interesting diagram - that a business is not a machine - it's an organism that works in a holistic way, just like the human body. That fact makes moot the question of which is more important - Management or Staff. Making a choice would be as silly as choosing which is most vital in the human body - the heart or the lungs. In an interactive holistic system nothing functions well unless everything functions well.

Employee and management each have a vital role to play and they are dependent upon each other. Communication within an organization is the lifeblood. Just as circulation in the human body must continue for life to be sustained. When communication is not flowing - moving the vision of the company goals deeply and richly within an organization (organism!), the entity is going to get sick.

Throughout the five Modules you will note that many metaphors are used. Stories activate the creative right hemisphere of the brain and can allow us to see new perspectives on old issues. They can allow us to grow not only in knowledge but in understanding of new applications.

Staff View...

1. If you could change any current attitude among management in your department - what would you change?

2. Very frankly, what do you feel is your greatest challenge as an employee as it relates to employee-management communication?

The Change

3. When management has to say "No", how should they do it?

4. Please describe your concept of the "ideal" manager.

At this point, employees fill out the four question staff view. The questions are phrased to reveal attitudinal perspectives. They reveal the viewpoint from which that employee views management. To allow freedom in responding to the assessment the attendees are instructed not to turn in the assessment form. Their comments are for their personal use.

However, once the forms are individually filled out, the focus on the individual assessment form takes an interesting turn. The entire group is asked to break into teams. If there are 40 in the group, we may have 6 teams of 6 or 7 per team. Once in teams, each team is asked to choose a secretary for their team. At that point, each team is instructed to develop a team consensus on each of the four questions they have filled out individually. The chosen secretary will record the team's consensus on each question and at a selected time will report the information to the entire group.

We have discovered that this system seems to free up the attendees' candor in responding to the assessment form. First of all, they seem to be relatively at ease discussing what they have written down among their peers. Secondly, their perception of differing views begins to expand as they hear what others within their team are saying. Even if it is a homogeneous group, there will be some difference of opinion.

Another synergy occurs when the secretary of each team gives his/her consensus presentation to the entire group. There is then a larger incorporation of different perspectives. During each secretary's presentation the facilitator will transfer to a flip chart that team's consensus to each question.

Creating the Change

Many times through this process staff will see other responses to issues they thought were black and white. They will find, to their surprise, that others in the teams, whom they admire and respect, will be coming up with different viewpoints on the same question.

This entire assessment process works so well because attendees are given ownership throughout the process. First, they know that their specific answers are confidential to their team. The team chooses it's own secretary. This personal involvement increases participation in the process. Through this assessment consensus, staff begins to see more clearly their current vision of management performance and changes they feel are needed. Staff expectations of management are brought to the forefront to be discussed.

After the consensus of each team to each of the four questions is transferred to flip chart - then the group as a whole looks for a pattern of the main issues associated with the team responses to each question. The group will then choose one or two major issues that represent the group response to each of the questions. Those main issues will be further addressed in Staff/management Module Five.

Overview of Habits

("Habits" is the "H" in the acronym H-A-T: We must put on our Habits, Attitude, and Timetable in order to control our future.)

At this time we begin to discuss how we all become very easily creatures of our own habits, attitudes and beliefs. Running on "automatic", so to speak, is not a problem as long as our habits are getting us where we want to go. I use a couple of stories that allow the group to laugh with me.

One story relates to a time when the power went off in our home. My wife told me to go get the flashlight. So the first thing I did

The Change

was go into the kitchen and turn on the light switch so I could find the flashlight. How deeply we can be programmed to believe that certain things will happen!

In another example, I changed jobs. That next Monday - I got in my car, had my material in my briefcase to head for my new job, and before I knew it - I was in the parking lot of my old place of employment. How easy it is to run on the same tracks.

Brain researchers have identified the cerebellum as the portion of the brain responsible for reacting to imprinted processes. According to Professor Roger Penrose, University of Oxford, "The cerebellum seems to be much more of an 'automaton' than the cerebrum. Actions under cerebellar control seem almost to take place 'by themselves' without one having to 'think about' them." This "subconscious" portion of our mind runs about 95 percent of our life.

We program a vast array of things into our life and they become automatic. Everything from the tying of shoes to the way we react to buzz words that are religiously or politically charged. It is so easy to continue to be freeflowing in our habits and repeat old actions or thoughts even after we have begun to consciously learn something new. "Intellectual" learning has to filter down to automatic response through either repetition or emotional significance.

What Are The "Triggers" That Activate Our Expectations?

Exercise: Here's an example of how repetition can create responses so powerful that we cannot at first control them. You remember how difficult it may have been in school when you were to study and learn something? Surely the day of judgment would come and the teacher would ask for the material to be recited. Let's turn things around now. I'm going to recite part of something and I

Creating the Change

want you to keep from thinking about the rest of it. Is that fair enough? Can you possibly believe that habits could be so strong that you won't be able to keep from thinking of the rest of it?

Here goes - - *Hickory, Dickory, Dock - the mouse...*

What? You couldn't keep from thinking of the ending?

Let's try again - - *Jack be Nimble, Jack be Quick, Jack jumped...*

"Trigger" Responses

As you can tell from your automatic responses to these ditties which perhaps you have not heard for 20 years, repetition can be a powerful form of programming. The ditties are like "triggers". They set off a programmed response to fill in and complete the "story".

Things which deeply impact us emotionally also can program us to respond a certain way. Repetition and emotional involvement are two powerful systems through which the brain learns. We create what becomes automatic assumptions about people many times through this same process. We assume a person will act the way they have acted in the past or, for some reason, we will have a certain emotional reaction when in the presence of a certain person. Those feelings and assumptions about others come upon us with the speed of light. They can easily control our voice tone and body language as we respond and many times create in the other person the response we assumed would occur. Our habits can control how we react to people unless we step back and ask ourselves:

"Why am I thinking that way about that person?"
"Why do I have the feeling that I'm going to have that kind of experience with that person?"

The Change

Essentially, what I expect of others is what they are most likely to give me. My tone of voice and my body language tell others exactly how I expect to be treated. Those we work with on a daily basis become, in a way, family. If we are not careful, we develop programmed ways of reacting to each other which may not be serving the best communication purposes. We may not be moving where we really want to go with our interpersonal business relationships.

Example: When we are provided information concerning new job procedures. We know that the more we are involved in providing input in the development of changes that will effect our work - the easier it is for us to make the changes. But even then, change can be a challenge.

Trigger Response: I'll make that modification as soon as I can, but don't expect it today.

By stepping back and acting to explore the reasons for certain actions, we create a more effective environment for positive change.

Creative Response: I'll do my very best with this new information. Can I count on you if I need help during this transition?

If the explanation provided by management suggests a confusion about motive or knowledge - ask questions to get more information. Once you feel you understand the changes to your satisfaction but question the feasibility of the time frame given, ask about the time element.

Corrective question: Is there any flexibility in the time frame I am dealing with in making this change?

You are responding in such a manner that feedback is required

Creating the Change

from management. How often in the past have you been left feeling that you did not fully know or understand changes passed on to you? Can you improve on the changes suggested? You should feel free to ask questions and offer improvements.

A trigger that sets off our repetitious or emotional response can be the way a person walks in, his tone of voice. We may assume that he is going to say a certain thing and we're set to react a certain way. Or we assume that we know the motives behind certain actions. It's amazing sometimes the amount of ESP we assume we possess.

We begin to destroy our triggers when we stop and ask ourselves and the other person objective questions about what is happening. It's so easy and yet so incorrect to assume because a person did a certain thing that she has a certain motive. Yet many times we label management with comments, such as, " They really don't care about our personal feelings." or "I'll bet he doesn't treat the customer like he just treated me!"

When we stop and ask objective questions such as "What you (did, said, ask for) is important, let me make sure I understand." we are in the business of exercising emotional discipline. We may consider that as part of our job, although it certainly has deeper personal implications. If we say it sarcastically or defiantly - we continue to signal that we are immediately assigning a motive to the actions. The tone of the question must be sincere. We cannot, should not, ought not, must not assign a label to the motive until we have the facts. Many times the motive of the manager will be sincere. Even though it is perhaps, on occasion, sincere ignorance. Again, interact using the questioning approach to leave plenty of room for feedback and creativity in communication.

It is management's responsibility to provide positive attention and ask objective questions to help minimize any staff activities that are

The Change

created simply to get attention. As we all know, one person may perform an action out of the desire for power, revenge or just to be left alone. Indeed, a person may assume some type of disability in order to be left alone. If management finds itself having to ask the question "Why do you always send your stuff in a certain way when I keep saying it ought to be done another way?" we have already experienced a communication breakdown which hopefully can be remedied. People must be noticed on a daily basis for what they do right. Management must continually project the value of the employee. In a dynamic, growing organization mistakes and errors will occur in the pursuit of the realization of the company vision. Without some error there is no growth.

One of the important dynamics to creating positive expectations involves getting a handle on the fear which can so habitually restrain us from trying new things for fear of making a mistake.

Fear of Failure

The last thing any business person wants to hear about is failure. Intuitively we have geared ourselves to the point where we feel if there is anything in the world we don't want to hear, it's the word "failure" - certainly as in "business failure." Yet we all know, when we stop and think about it, that all processes that improve and create positive change require a zone, a buffer if you will, where creative things can be tried - when limited failure can occur - where the little mistakes that can lead to great ideas come about.

It's only though failure sometimes that we learn the best systems with which to please the customer and maintain ourselves on the cutting edge of the rapidly changing business society in which we find ourselves today. While failure should be "managed" as it relates to amount of capital, time or human resources that are held in potential jeopardy, even "big" mistakes, when handled properly, can become the seeds for growth.

Creating the Change

One consummate marketer once gave me a bit of advice that I have never forgotten. He said, "The road to success is always under construction." It's never finished. If you're going to be fearful because the road isn't finished, you'll never start the journey. You build the road as you go.

Many decades ago, as I recall the story, the CEO of a major company dealing with vacuum tubes - the awakenings of what we now experience as the computer and electronics generation - convened a very important meeting. To be demonstrated was a new generation of test tube. The company's prime clients from all over the country were flown in for this demonstration. At that time, flying was still exotic and quite an expense.

When the group assembled, a young lab assistant entered the room wheeling the test tubes on a cart to the location to hook up for the demonstration. In front of this distinguished audience, the lab assistant found himself helplessly grappling to keep the cart upright when a wheel snagged upon a line running across the tile floor. perhaps you can visualize in slow motion the test tubes made of delicate glass tumbling from the cart and crashing on the tile. Utter devastation. Of course, the demonstration was called off.

The next morning the lab assistant is called to the president's office. As he walks into the room and seats himself, he looks at the president with great contrition and says, " Sir, I know that you are going to fire me..." and at that point the president of the company stands, walks to the assistant, bends down, looks him in the eye and says "Stand up. I want to tell you something. That was a ridiculous statement you just made. How on earth can I fire you? You're too valuable for me to fire. I just gave you a $ 10,000 education yesterday."

Here was one CEO who looked carefully at motive and attitude. Had the assistant's attitude been frivolous, he most likely would

The Change

have fired him. Obviously knowing the young lab assistant was sincerely contrite - the president used the experience to deepen the lad's loyalty, mutual trust and respect toward the president and the company. This being a much told story - one version has the lad becoming in a few years supervisor of the research department - as trusted and dependable a fellow as ever worked in the business. Another version of the story has another CEO many years later finishing the tale and then with a gleam in his eye confiding that he was the lad and that he had worked tirelessly the rest of his life to repay the trust the earlier president had placed in him.

Group Exercise: Ask the group, who in your business or personal life has inspired you? What were her skills or attitudes that make her inspirational to you?

"That's Not My Department"

Programmed triggers or expectations that employees may have when they are not allowed the flexibility to be the eyes and ears for their company's growth create boundaries in Employee/Customer experiences.

One Saturday I drove to a nearby service station market that had newly opened. I normally purchase an early edition of the Sunday paper on Saturday afternoon. So I walked into the mart looking for the paper in a bin as I would find it in several other service station marts in the area. After looking in vain, I asked the attendant about the location of the papers. "Oh," she responded, "the newspapers are in the pay coin boxes out there." "Out there" was 20 feet from the front door of the mart.

As I walked toward the large steel boxes housing the papers, it occurred to me that most of us carry four quarters at all times, right? While walking back into the mart to get change, I decided

Creating the Change

to share with that company a way to keep and increase their business.

Getting the young attendant's attention, I explained "If you will put the newspapers in the store, I and many others will come in to buy them and also get things like milk, soda pop, candy bars and, if our kids are with us, we'll be forced to buy a lot more than we want to. Just the simple incentive created by moving the newspapers into your store can increase your business." I felt I was performing an important customer feedback service to the company until I continued to look into the eyes of the attendant only to discover that the lights were on but nobody was home.

The young lady had no earthly idea what to do with what I had just told her. Her Expectation of her job was to take customers' money and process credit cards. The idea that a customer would provide feedback to help her company grow had apparently never been introduced into the pattern of what she expected during her shift.

Steps To Visioning New Responses

As we begin to vision ourselves providing new responses to circumstances, we begin a process which will allow us to change our programming.

List A Trigger Response You Have Had
In Dealing With Management

Exercise: The attendees should at this Point List a trigger response that they have experienced in the recent past. First, I share my *Assumption Monster* trigger response (the story is in Life-Perceptions, Chapter 3). Then I let those brave souls who will volunteer briefly talk about their trigger responses and how they helped/hindered them.

The Change

Visualize Yourself Stepping Back, Thinking, Then Responding From The Perspective Of Empowerment

They should now take a challenging trigger response they have experienced in the past - one that has not been productive for them - and vision themselves changing that response.

Exercise: Let them write a story illustrating the circumstances in which they were tempted to immediately respond a certain way - but they step back - they consider - and they decide on a different behavior.

What you just said makes me want to shout in your face. but, wait. Let me ask a question, cool down, and deal with the facts of the situation. The way you "speak" to me, the way you walked "arrogantly" into the room - they cause an emotional response. But, wait, I'm assigning motives! Let me step back, visualize myself asking questions to move my expectations into perspective.

As I write the story, I kick in the power of the pre-frontal lobe of the brain (that part which only humans have) and I visualize the end result I desire from my relationship with that person or circumstance.

I see it.
    I feel it.
        I hear it.
            I then feel myself actually living that vision.

I begin to change my expectations as to how I view that individual so that I'm sending out different nonverbal signals to that person. Because the right hemisphere of the brain controls our nonverbal actions (body language, voice tone) the only way I can reshape that nonverbal actions is to vision a new way of reacting. In short, we begin to create the way in which we wish to respond to others

Creating the Change

rather than simply reacting helplessly to triggers that we have been allowing ourselves to become programmed into.

Obviously this process takes visioning, practice and time. We must blend an intellectual desire and emotional commitment to change our triggers. Unless we are committed emotionally to change - we're just playing games.

Setting Priorities

It is amazing how easily business priorities can become based upon the organizational structure of the business as opposed to the customer-driven needs of the business. This leads to "blind spots" in our interactions with our true bosses, the customers.

One associate related his own personal experience of enduring process over customer service. He had taken his auto to a dealership for some service work. He was waiting in a long line of cars to be processed into the service bay. After 30 minutes in this mini-traffic jam, he got out of his car, walked into the service department office and found the manager feverishly filling out forms.

"Did you know your service department driveway is filled with cars waiting to be brought in?" the customer quizzed. "Look," said the manager "I'll be with you all as soon as possible. I have to have these forms filled out before my district director arrives or I'll be in trouble."

The Change

The classical double-bind. The manager is in trouble if the report is not filled out on time and he's also in trouble if he isn't moving the cars through the service department. Companies should never put their people into that kind of trap. Customer service must always come first. Double-binds are great fun in video games but no good in business.

From A Stress Standpoint, How Do You Handle Project Closure? How Many Balls Can You Juggle At The Same Time?

How many balls can you juggle at the same time? Some of us, if we have more than two or three balls in the air - you better not come over and demand my time because I'm going to cut you off short or bite your head off. When your time is taxed with projects and someone in your work team comes to you and says "I've got this problem; I really need to talk to you", how do you respond?

Trigger response: You scream at him and say, "I'm busy right now, can't you see?"

You must be disciplined enough to take 15 seconds, look him right in the eye and say:

Creative response: "You're important to me and what you have to say is important. I want to get with you tomorrow. We'll spend time going over that. When would be the best time for us to get together?"

Actually, I have timed it as taking about 10 seconds to say those words. You positively reinforce the other person's importance. Give your full attention for 15 seconds and you can create a lot of good will - he will be happy to come back tomorrow. However, you must keep your promise. When you and the other person set a time - it must be good as gold.

Creating the Change

What if he says, "This can't wait!" Then you must say to yourself "This must be high priority." Either stop what you are doing or lead him to someone who can help immediately. Sometimes in the heat of battle you must make what I call dirty decisions. "If I stop what I am doing I will cause damage. But If I don't stop what I am doing and see about this other person's problem I will cause damage. Which will cause the greater damage?" Weigh it and make an immediate decision.

As business structure and customer driven needs continue to change the nature of organizations - a rule of thumb for the future is that those crises involving attitude and goodwill had best be taken care of ahead of procedural matters, because attitude and good will both with external customers and internal customers (employees) are the one ingredient that you can't buy and that will set you apart from the competition.

When someone in our work team tries to draw us into her crisis we must keep our expectations open. "Oh no! If I stop and work with her, it will set me back an hour" may not be true. You may get to the core of the issue in five minutes and assure her that you'll have the information needed by noon tomorrow. The less we tense up in fast pace scheduling the more we can stay creative in dealing with interruptions. They will happen, you know.

The Company Meeting

The issue of company meetings should be addressed. As I work with organizations across the country I hear time and time again "I'm sure that communication is important but we've got a tight production schedule. We just don't have room for social time." For many companies meetings become just that - social time. I can sympathize with their complaint. But when we talk about successful employee communication, empowerment or self-managed teams, we are dealing with very focused activities.

The Change

In all meetings and communication there must be a focus on the company vision for customer service and how to achieve it. That focus must come about in conjunction with the emotional and intellectual needs of everyone involved. If I feel a certain way about what is happening in the company, I need to feel free to communicate my feeling without fear. However, I do not need to feel free to talk at length about my uncle and his health. True, that is part of me but it's not relevant to the vision of the company, and in the long term, to my paycheck.

We must have freedom, however, to get personal in our communications about our feelings and our judgments as they relate to our work. In those areas we need to feel that we can unload. We've always done so in the past - but we've communicated with our peers through the grapevine. That took care of our emotional needs but did not help the company.

The company needs the grapevine in the main line of communication. The company however will only earn the right to have the grapevine when each person feels without fear to communicate their feelings and needs as they relate to company issues.

How Committed Are You To The Company Vision?

The company vision means in a nutshell: How we serve the customers' needs. A company exists to fulfill customer needs. Do we always strive to be true and faithful to those needs? Mouthing commitment while speaking otherwise in a different setting eventually can come back to haunt us. It seems there are two extremes among staff as to how they view their job. On one end of the spectrum are those who say, "I work here because I have to. I need the money. I put in my time and try to find enjoyment in other areas of my life. Just tell me what to do, because I don't want to have to think." We do ourselves and the company a disservice when we do not become deeply committed to the vision of the organization.

Emotional commitment and excitement are the keys that unlock our creative potential. If we cannot reevaluate and find areas within our work that create excitement for us - we may be better suited working elsewhere.

On the other end of the spectrum are those who have worked a long time in a particular area and they say, "This is my territory. I know all about the job. You can't tell me anything about it that I don't already know." Well, between being a victim and the "expert" in our work is a middle ground that will allow us to grow personally and in our skills.

The current transformation of many companies from Directive-Driven to team-managed is, in its best form a process. You must be patient with the organization as the process moves ahead. In order to be competitive in a new world marketplace you will have an opportunity for more skill growth and responsibility than ever before.

Attitude

The second part of H.A.T. is Attitude. A nationally known investment banker was on one of my television interview programs several years ago talking about the reasons for his success. We began discussing how attitude is a great measurer of how we treat ourself and what we expect from ourself. He related to me that there was one incident in his life that changed his belief about

The Change

what he could accomplish as an individual.

He was raised on a small dairy farm. He worked long hours from an early age milking cows. When he was about six years of age, he was working near the house when he heard what he thought was the distant sound of his father calling for help. After a moment of listening, he knew it was indeed his father.

Running down into the field, he found his father's upper body caught in a combine. The machine was crushing the life out of his father when he ran to the switch and turned the machine off. At that moment he realized he had value. He knew he was important. He had saved his father's life. Those things which create our attitude tend to shape our future.

Timetable

The final part of H.A.T is Timetable. Habits and Attitudes don't change overnight. Relearning new ways to think and respond requires patience on our part. As organizations begin to change the interaction between management and staff - there will be growing pains. The companies that succeed learn to have a sense of humor and laugh at some of the silly things that happen along the way. No organization can stand non-caring people very long. When individuals and teams within a company are dedicated to what they do - they have the right to enjoy it - to have fun.

If I say that I just want to put in my eight hours, I have a right to do that. However, maybe I should consider that as American business changes, there will be less and less positions for those who just want a "job". Most positions will require continual learning to stay up with the technology needed to work in a factory or office. Just as Chapter Three covered, personal growth is an issue each of us must face and make decisions whether we wish to be a victim or a victor in today's job market.

Creating the Change

Tips on Creating Your Own "Job Security"

If you treat your employers as though they are your clients, amazing things can happen...

There is no job security today. At least not like there was a decade or so ago. With streamlining, cutbacks and constant technological change - as employees - we're swimming in uncharted waters. Your employers are not your benefactors - they are your clients. Use your skills to exceed their expectations and your opportunities with the organization will abound. First, be sure you love what you are doing. That being the case, strive for excellence - always listening carefully to the company's needs. The price for such excellence is not always long hours - many times it is more perceptive thought about what is being done - more effective communication to tie together key people and create a synergy to get the job done. Work smarter as well as harder. Remember: To create your job future, always ask yourself, "If I were the owner of this company- how would I want my employees to channel their energy to build a more profitable organization?"

Advancing in an organization will mean, more and more, helping others cultivate their potential...

In a business with many employees - there is just no way that one person can consistently be the star and best help the company grow - in the long run. Yes, we all want to be stars. Well, here's the best way to do it. Boost the creative potential and effective direction of the energy expended by others in the business. Be a resource, a coach, a cheerleader - support the activities of others in the organization. You won't come up with all the best ideas. You can't. In today's complex business world it's impossible for one person to see all angles for organizational growth. You need the cooperation and perspective of others to see the full picture. Being a star today means you can make things happen as a team. Remember: To

The Change

create your future honor the talents and abilities of others in the organization. Be the one they come to consistently for advice, instruction, and motivation.

If your company does not offer additional skills training - you better go get it somewhere... "Skills coasting" in any company today is not just dangerous - it is usually slow suicide. Skills upgrading and learning new information is the only way to stay employable into and past the year 2000. If your company offers good programs for skills upgrading - be the first in line. Not only to learn - but then to come back and be available to teach and reinforce the new skills to others in the department. Become a champion of skills development - for your personal growth and, of course, for the benefit of the company. If your company is depending only on your current skills and is not offering ongoing training - I hate to tell you, but that is a danger sign for your company's health. Think seriously about the areas you enjoy - then go to a university, vo-tech or other available school - spend your own money if necessary and gain new skills that will better align you to keep your job and advance into a more profitable position. Remember: To create your future - when it comes to job security and training, the old saying "A rolling stone gathers no moss" has never been more true. An employee constantly staying on the cutting edge of skills training gathers fewer pink slips.

What does your company need? You may be in a position to know before they do...What if you discover through the grapevine an important change your company needs to make? What if you stumble upon a new supplier that could save costs and improve quality? Be ready to communicate to your company that which will help the organization grow. The days when we could say, "I just do my job. Other company interests are none of my business" are gone. Anything that affects the company's bottom line is your business. All employees in any company are riding in the same boat. If the boat starts sinking - everyone is in trouble.

Creating the Change

Look for ways to help make your company more profitable. Share those ideas freely with management. Even in the worst case scenario where you end up with no credit for the idea - if it helps keep the company in the black - so much better for your next paycheck. Hopefully, your company has learned to give credit and compensate when possible for productive ideas for business improvement. Remember: To create your future - your company's bottom line is vital to you. Your paycheck comes from those dollars. Think of cost savings, ways to improve productivity, as though you owned the company. For such thinking you will be, if not immediately, then ultimately rewarded in ways that will amaze you.

When all else seems to be failing...remember, no one cares as much about your job future as you do...In the last four programs we have talked about supporting the company you work for - looking for ways to improve profitability. We've discussed constantly upgrading skills. The one thread through all of this...the one ingredient I must emphasize is self-determination to create your own future. If you let someone else create your future for you - you may not like the future you get. Take the initiative.

It's true that fickle weather makes the wind - but it's our hands that can move the direction of the sails. You have the power to determine what you want out of life in the areas of skills, job environment and satisfaction. If things are not right - quit complaining and use that energy to start making changes that will position you to be and do what is most meaningful to you. Remember: To create your employment future - you must make the decisions that will effect your economic and professional circumstances. If you are merely waiting for something to happen. It will. But will you like it?

THE PERSON IN THE MIRROR EACH MORNING IS YOUR TRUE BOSS. YOU ARE YOUR OWN JOB SECURITY

The Change

ASSIGNMENT

During the period of time between this module and the follow-up session become aware of at least two triggers in your daily business experiences. Become aware of two circumstances where you found yourself immediately reacting to someone or something in a programmed manner.

Develop and begin to visualize a new way to cope with those circumstances if the results you have been getting from your reactions are not satisfactory.

FOLLOW-UP SESSION

Employee teams will compare notes on "triggers" they have experienced since the last module. What kind of action plan can begin to change those "triggers"? Elicit examples from those who feel comfortable speaking to their particular experiences.

Remind each team's secretary to keep the notes of the one or two main issues of consensus to the first two questions of Staff View. They will be needed for Module Five.

Creating the Change

MODULE FOUR - STAFF

NOTE: Much of Module Four for Staff will be major sections from Module Two - Management. Facilitators should feel free to expand on the major sections in Module Two.

Facilitator discusses *Constrictive and Expanding Emotions* (pp. 193-195) and goes through the three *Phases of Handling Emotional Responses* (p. 194).

Facilitator will break teams into groups of three for the *Listening Exercise* (p. 201) then the teams will read instructions and do the "Generalizations" Role Playing (pp. 202-207).

Teams will read information relating to the *Role of Representational Systems* and do exercises (pp. 208-211).

Facilitator will explain the *Left/Right Hemisphere Profiles* and administration/scoring of the Word Association Test (pp. 214-220).

It should be emphasized to the attendees that their scores are not to be handed in. These are for their personal evaluation and use. However, those who wish to volunteer can join in a group discussion when the facilitator asks how many scored highest in each area and discusses the strengths of each profile.

Discuss the *Personality Aspects* of the profiles (pp. 225-228). Explain the synergy developed through *interaction of the various profiles* within an organization (pp. 229-236).

Administer the *Perceptive Office Conversation Test* (pp. 238-243). Ask for other examples of comments heard relating to the different profiles.

The Change

Next, administer the *Employee Questionnaire* and have them score it (pp. 281-284, 242-243). Relate those scores to the personality profiles. Discuss the *relationship of attitude to personality* (pg. 242).

The group *Personality Profiles Identification Exercise* (pp. 248-249) will be done at this time.

Summary: Communication means understanding others' differences and allowing those differences to be assets not a reason for division. The individual and the company of the future must be flexible and ready to learn new ways of coping with a fast paced environment.

ASSIGNMENT: Listen and look for personality patterns during the workweek. Engage at least two persons in conversation and speak to their personality traits. If they are organized, respond to them in an organized fashion. If they are emotional, be emphatic and intense in your conversation. In a word, enter into their world of perception. Note the results.

FOLLOW-UP SESSION: Group discussion of results from conversation with various personality patterns. How well did they respond when you approached them from their angle of perception? What problems did you encounter? What did you learn?

Make sure the secretaries of each team have two main items relating to each question on the Staff View (pp. 257-258) ready for discussion during Module Five. Assure staff that the next module will be held in a non-threatening environment. Management has also been through two programs. **They are ready to work with you as a team and to receive input on your perception of change that needs to take place for the company to grow.**

Creating the Change

EMPLOYEE QUESTIONNAIRE

1. My Department Functions Best When:

D _____ Team goals are emphasized.

B _____ When each employee knows the specific information he needs to accomplish his work.

E _____ When my supervisor is visualizing in specific detail the end results that she wishes to achieve with the co-operation of all the employees and when that vision is communicated to us in such a way that we become excited about it.

C _____ When the employees get excited about the "big picture" -- the end results we need to achieve.

A _____ When the supervisor is on top of what everyone is doing so that he can catch anyone who is dragging his feet.

2. If You Were The Supervisor And If You Could Change Any Current Attitude Existing Among The Employees In Your Department -- What Would You Change?

A _____ I would make certain that each employee thoroughly understands that I am the supervisor and that her future with the company hinges on her doing what I tell her to do.

D _____ I would want a stronger emphasis on team effort and fair play so that all employees benefit in their service to the company.

B _____ The specific directions laid down for efficient functioning in the department should be followed more closely.

C _____ Each employee should take a greater responsibility to work toward the overall goals I have set for the department.

E _____ I would first look at the way that I am approaching each

The Change

employee to make certain that he perceives what I want from him and understands in his own terms how he can achieve it.

3. Very Frankly, What Do You Feel Is Your Supervisor's Greatest Weakness?

E ____ Sometimes failing to communicate the overall goals for the department in a way that is really understood by each and every employee.

A ____ Letting employees get away with dragging their feet and trying to "pull a fast one" to get out of doing the work they should be doing.

B ____ Not knowing or not communicating properly the job requirements and specific duties that each employee ought to be performing.

C ____ Sometimes she will get all excited about the goals for the department and that excitement somehow just doesn't catch on with everyone else even when she tries to tell everyone how great the end results will be.

D ____ Sometimes the supervisor will favor one employee over others or spend more time with paperwork when he could be out with the team getting a feel as to whether everything is running OK.

4. What Do You Believe Should Be Done To Reduce Employee Turn-Over In Your Department?

A ____ If an employee will buckle down and do their work and quit trying to slough off - he won't get fired.

D ____ Each individual should gather around the team efforts of the department and feel that he can come to the supervisor for personal help with any problems he may face.

Creating the Change

C _____ If each worker will put forth greater responsibility for her own success she can work her way up the organization.

B _____ Perhaps a better understanding by each employee of the specific duties of his job so that he can perform it better will help make him more satisfied. He really needs also to have as much information as possible about the benefits that the company provides for him.

E _____ The supervisor needs to be as perceptive as possible to the specific needs of each employee as it relates to her job satisfaction and by so doing see if certain elements of her job can be arranged more to their satisfaction in accomplishing the objectives of her job.

5. How Should Employee Dissatisfaction Be Dealt With?

E _____ The supervisor should try to see the disagreement through the employee's eyes and make certain that he is not missing an opportunity to positively modify some aspect of his job situation to keep him growing in his work.

A _____ If they don't like their job, they can quit. There are plenty of others in the unemployment lines waiting for their job.

D _____ Employee dissatisfaction is damaging to the whole team effort. The supervisor should counsel with the employee as a friend and see if there isn't a fair solution to the problem.

B _____ The supervisor should take a two-fold approach; try to find out first of all what specifically about their job responsibility they feel they don't like and try convincing them of the necessity of those duties or responsibilities and secondly, emphasize to them the security that is being provided for them by the company.

C _____ The supervisor should try to put the gleam back in their eyes and the excitement in their life by painting the "big picture" for them of how accomplishing well in their present position can lead to better pay and a higher position in the company.

The Change

6. Please Describe Your Concept Of The "Ideal" Employee.

D _____ Friendly, always ready to share and encourage others, a member of the team.

A _____ Does her work, doesn't give the supervisor any back-talk.

C _____ An individual with some goals in life -- willing to learn more about his job position and perhaps, if he is really motivated, more about the job just above it.

B _____ One who is punctual, a reliable employee with a high standard of values and an appreciation for the work she does and the security that the company provides.

E _____ An individual willing to look objectively at his job duties and make suggestions on improvement of the job and overall suggestions on how management can give him more freedom and autonomy to do his work in a more productive manner.

MODULE FIVE

MANAGEMENT AND STAFF

NOTE: During this Module Management and Staff come together to share what each team's secretary has written as the team's consensus to the first two questions on the Management/Staff View assessment forms.

There will be tables with each employee team and 1 or 2 managers at each table, depending on the employee/management ratio. Before the information begins to be shared, the facilitator re-emphasizes the company as an organism. *Everyone is important. Everyone is vital.*

MANAGEMENT: For them to succeed in the long term, the way these managers, or coaches, are going to be evaluated is not going to be based upon how many bright ideas they come up with. They will be judged by the degree to which they have cultivated ideas and potential within their teams. This will take away that fear of always having to be the bright little boy/girl. Rather, they come to see themselves as the farmer, the nourisher: that person who says to the company CEO "Look what we have done. You gave me these seeds and see how they have grown."

EMPLOYEES: Just as it is management's responsibility to create an environment allowing enjoyment of work - You owe it to yourself to fall in love with what you do. Be free to break away from the old belief that work has to be a drag. When we make a decision to enjoy what we do, our lives becomes so much richer. Those employees who just feel they must put in their "hours" and don't desire to improve their skills and communicative ability will be in less and less demand in the coming years.

The Change

There are seven guidelines to the upcoming sharing of information:

1. LISTEN ACTIVELY: Suspend your inner dialogue until the other person has finished. Reflect back to them what you think they have said. Make sure you understand their view.

2. LOOK FOR POINTS OF AGREEMENT: You will be amazed in how many areas you will be in agreement relating to the needs of the company in order for it to grow and be profitable for everyone.

3. DON'T EXPECT TO SOLVE EVERYTHING: As you get into a number of issues, they may all seem overwhelming. Today, look at the list as resources. You are not going to solve everything immediately. Focus in on one or two areas.

4. EXPECT BEST EFFORTS: Don't expect instant change. When we leave here today change will have begun. Attitudes, perceived opportunities and communication are seeds. Nourish them and give them time to grow.

5. ENJOY THE CHALLENGE: Enjoy the challenge of seeing the issues from the other person's point of view. Exercise your curiosity. You may find this to be a lot of fun.

6. GET TO KNOW ONE ANOTHER BETTER: Here's an opportunity to develop a deeper level of communication with one another.

7. REMEMBER THAT YOU ARE ALL CUSTOMERS: Keep the company mission of service to the customer and to one another in view during all the discussions. Why are we really here today? To serve the customer better. If the customer isn't served, the company won't continue to exist and everyone will have a lot of free time.

Creating the Change

Normally, employees share first with management. I'm a little humorous about this. I'll tell the employees to be gentle because you outnumber management. The secretary of each management team (represented at each table) will read the consensus views on the first two assessment questions. Each one in management has a copy of what the secretary of their team was given as consensus views on the first two questions. They then share their information with the employee team at their table.

Once the information is shared, our goal is to zero in on one or two major issues. The employee team at the table then functions with the management represented at the same table together as a team toward resolving the one or two major issues they as a team will determine are most important and profitable to all involved. Now that the employees at that table and management are considered a total team either a new secretary may be chosen by consensus or, in many cases, the employee secretary will continue in that role for the new management/staff team.

Once the one or two major issues are isolated by each team, the secretary will write down the plan of action as it is developed by the new team. During this process, which will consume most of the day, the facilitator should be walking the room encouraging each team to be as specific in their plan of action as possible. The team's first or second draft of the action plan will still probably not be as specific in time frame and detail as is needed. Remind them that they are developing a road map to create positive change in their work environment.

It's interesting to note some of the main issues within companies that have surfaced in response to the first two questions. These represent a blend of both management and employee responses.

The Change

Assessment Question 1 (pg.257)

- Better communication/people skills
- Willing to take risks
- Willing to change procedures
- Giving credit when it is due
- Getting noticed for our feedback
- Openly listening to others' ideas
- Don't treat employees like children
- Objective awards for employees

Assessment question 2 (pg. 257)

- Being willing to give reasons behind decisions
- Having a clear understanding as to team members' responsibilities
- Taking personality differences into consideration as it relates to performance.
- Trusting and understanding jobs.
- Giving all employees equal ability to communicate within the company.
- Having mutual respect in communication

As you can see, such general considerations must be hammered into specific action plans. For example "Being willing to give reasons behind decisions" as it relates to management, should first be reduced to several specific incidents of how problems relating to that issue have occurred in the past.

Here's one example:

"A new computer program was introduced in our department before we - the employees - were able to give feedback on how that new program would impact our other job functions. As a result, we were frustrated and slowed down by some changes which

Creating the Change

we feel would not have been made in the same way if we had given input. We were not allowed in the change loop. That caused the change to be more awkward and made us feel unimportant."

Discuss the unfavorable consequences of those specific occurrences and then develop an action plan to handle the relaying of decisions in a different, more mutually acceptable manner in the future.

SUMMARY

The formula for coming up with an action plan is:

1) Identify the general issue.

2) Develop specific incidents which embody that issue and discuss how those specific incidents could have been handled differently.

3) Then develop an action plan incorporating a mutually acceptable new way of handling the issue.

ASSIGNMENT

Secretaries have one or two action plans typed out and ready to share with the entire group at the upcoming follow-up session.

The Change

FOLLOW UP-SESSION

Each team will discuss their one or two action plans with the group. How will the action plans make a difference in their work life? What is the time table for the action plan? How will it be implemented, specifically? Is each team willing to really commit to making these changes? If such and such is changed then my attitude, my behavior, my response will change in what way?

We must be specific about the results of the change.

5 Integrating Ethnic Cultures Into the Team Environment

> *Lord, grant that I may not seek so much to be understood as to understand.*
> St. Francis

Rapidly changing world events ensure a multicultural workplace. The crumbling of walls, realignment of borders, the dismantling of apartheid and European Community agreements mean all kinds of workers will climb the corporate ladder in which ever country affords the best opportunity. As we build these diverse groups of people into cohesive work teams there are a few things to consider.

When English Is Second, Third, Fourth...

We are certainly spoiled when it comes to the use of English worldwide. Fortunately for us it is the language of international business, air and sea. We expect internationals to speak English when in the U.S. We also expect them to speak to us in English when we're in their country. Can you think of another cultural group with similar expectations?

Note: This chapter was written by LaJoyce Chatwell Lawton, President Lawton International, International Business Protocol Consultants 5838 Arabian Run, Indianapolis, IN 46208

The Change

Once when while talking with a colleague from Vienna, Austria, he apologized for his English. I replied, "Your English is wonderful, certainly better than my German (non-existent). I realize English is a second language for you." His comment was simply, "Third." One summer in Europe while having lunch, I was seated between an Italian man and woman. Our group was from all over the world and I listened with envy as my two neighbors slipped easily from one language to another. The woman spoke four languages. The man, a thirty-two year old Ph.D., spoke eight languages. My monolingual self slid further and further beneath the table as lunch progressed.

Language is the most obvious difference we encounter when working with internationals. English is their second, third, or fourth language and comprehension levels vary. Use "common" words, those most likely learned during the first few years of language study. My advice is to speak carefully and enunciate clearly. Sometimes speaking at a normal pace means that an international may only understand parts of the sentence. When I first moved to Japan the language sounded like one big blur. I couldn't even "hear" the names of stops on the train the conductor announced. After a while I was able to "hear" the names and no longer had to count stops.

Spelling and Word Meanings

Be aware of alternate spellings for common words. I taught a course in Bermuda and had to get used to seeing "The *organised* businesswoman" in print. Avoid slang - "Raining cats and dogs" can create a vivid mental picture in the minds of international workers. Follow grammar rules more strictly than you ordinarily do in everyday language. What seems obvious to native English speakers may never occur to others. Don't use words that refer to sports or military. Their sports and military experiences are completely different from ours.

Sometimes we make more language mistakes with other people whose native language is also English. When an Englishperson uses the word "vet" he's not referring to an expensive sports car but means to examine critically or appraise. When a worker says she "had intercourse with the taxi driver all the way to Piccadilly", she merely means friendly dialogue. "I'll knock you up in the morning" is just a wake up call to ensure you won't be late to the meeting. These phrases all contain English words but have totally different meanings to us. Because English is so widely spoken, we fail to recognize it's diverse usage.

Rank And Status

Group discussion, often used during U.S. meetings or training sessions, may be totally inappropriate with internationals where rank and status is an issue. In Far and Middle Eastern countries deference is shown to those who have certain rank and status. Lower "ranking" employees may be reluctant to challenge superiors comments or points in a discussion. How's that for inhibiting group process?

Instructors and leaders are typically revered in other cultures and therefore not questioned. When you ask for questions, workers may not say anything out of respect for your position. Because of these "high" positions, professors in other countries may not admit "they don't know" and even go so far as to give wrong answers. International employees are often shocked when leaders reply "I don't know; I'll have to find out and get back to you." They wonder "Why is he/she leading me?"

We are a first name society and many internationals have problems with this egalitarian approach in the work place. Workers in other countries tend to be more formal, using last names until invited to do otherwise. Titles are used much more frequently in other cultures.

The Change

Prolonged eye contact may be considered disrespectful or aggressive. Employees may not look you in the eye because of deference to rank or gender. We consider this shifty eyed, untrustworthy behavior. I had a breakfast meeting with a young man from Saudi Arabia who would not maintain eye contact. It's very disconcerting to have a discussion with someone who continuously breaks eye contact. Also, he was so "late" to the meeting I thought he wasn't coming. I ordered and was eating when he arrived.

Ethics

In our individualistic society, we are expected to work alone. When projects are assigned, the individuals in a group-oriented society will help each other. Is this cheating? When dealing with cultures where Christianity is not the religion, we find that their concept of sin is different from ours. Helping a group member, even with individual work, is not considered cheating. Of course, the ethical view on helping as opposed to cheating may differ from one culture to another so one must always be aware of the local norms.

Non-Verbal Communication

Your title may not be "Trainer" but many managers are responsible for training employees. U.S. professors and trainers can appear to be rather casual to international participants. We may teach with our hands in our pockets, insulting participants from Japan and Germany. Recently, a near riot almost occurred in a classroom at a major university in Oklahoma. When the professor sat in his chair, reared back and crossed his feet on top of the desk, he insulted students from the Middle East. Showing the bottom of your shoes, the dirtiest part of the body, is a grave insult to people from that part of the world.

We often talk without opening our mouths. Take your hand and

Integrating Ethnic Cultures

make the symbol for OK. It's a simple gesture that we use in everyday life meaning everything's fine, perfect, A-OK. In France, it means he's a zero, it's considered obscene in the Mediterranean and it means money in Japan. As expensive as Japan is, I'd be very careful about using any symbol that has to do with money! This symbol and others are constantly used in the workplace but can offend employees, even though the action is unintentional. Their conscious mind tells them meanings are different in the United States, but they find it difficult to pay attention to what your words are saying.

Concept Of Time

What do you do with the employee who constantly comes to work or meetings late? What is "late"? The concept of being on time or late can range from "airport time" to whenever I get there. When I spoke at a conference in Buenos Aires, Argentina, I became aware how much that socializing is an integral part of Latin American business. There was a social on the last evening to close out the event. Cocktails were scheduled for 7:00 p.m. with dinner at 8:00 p.m. The buffet line finally opened at 10:00 p.m. and no apologies were made. The American part of me was screaming with hunger though intellectually I knew that their concept of time differed from mine.

Traditionally, people from Africa, Latin America, and the Caribbean are more concerned with maintaining relationships than keeping track of the time. When meeting or talking with you, it's more important to conclude the conversation than to be "on time" to the next activity. By the same token, when they finally get to the next destination, those individuals are afforded the same undivided attention. The person who came "late" may have completed several agenda items prior to arriving at your meeting. U.S. clocks run, others walk.

The Change

Space

Personal space requirements are different among cultural groups. When you get on the elevator, do you stand close to the other person or do you stand as far away as possible? The next time you get on an elevator, try standing close to someone and note their reaction. Can you get used to someone standing so close to you during a conversation that you can feel his breath on your face? The person does not need Certs but it makes you feel uncomfortable, you begin to back away, thereby offending him. He keeps coming closer and it looks like the two of you are doing some type of dance.

In the U.S., we tend to stand about an arm's length away when conversing. Japanese people tend to stand further away because their typical greeting is a bow, rather than a handshake. Middle Eastern and Latin Americans stand very close and may finger your lapel during conversation. Men standing very close, holding hands or even greetings with kisses have no homosexual connotations. How will you respond when an employee stands closer to you or farther away during conversation than you are accustomed?...Or when you are being touched?

Office space in U.S. companies is often a status symbol. Higher ranking individuals have private offices, corner offices or offices with a view. Japanese managers are typically seated at long tables in large rooms with their employees in descending order of rank. Management can see how the work progresses. International employees may see offices as a barrier between them and management staff.

Businesswomen

How do your international male employees respond to their female manager or supervisor? Are they able to take direction? Tension

Integrating Ethnic Cultures

between these two groups may hinder building an effective team and slow down productivity. In many cultures women are still considered second class citizens and do not have positions of authority. Working women in the U.S. have made considerable progress toward climbing the corporate ladder. Even though we still have a long way to go, other countries look to us for leadership in this area.

Yes, No, And Silence

The Japanese often wonder if we can talk and think at the same time. They need time to reflect over what's been said but we are uncomfortable with silence during meetings or discussions. Yes and no are used differently in other cultures. Heads are nodded opposite to the way we nod to mean yes or no. Saying no verbally may disrupt harmony, so non-verbal ways of saying no are used. Yes merely acknowledges that you are heard, not agreement to purchase your product or service. An international employee may say yes throughout your discussion but not carry out what was discussed. Perhaps he didn't know how to do what you asked, and he wouldn't disrupt harmony by saying no or would not question you because of deference.

Religion

You may feel religion does not belong in the workplace but it can certainly affect productivity among internationals. As was mentioned earlier those who practice religions other than Christianity have a completely different concept of sin and wrong doing. Suppose employees "steal" supplies but feel they are entitled because supplies are abundant in the workplace and they have none.

During Ramadan, Muslim employees may slow their productivity for a month. They don't eat or drink during daylight hours so may

The Change

not have much energy. During the middle of a meeting your Muslim colleague asks for a place to pray or begins praying in your presence. How do you react?

What Will You Do?

In a Copeland and Griggs vignette, a U.S. manager asks a supervisor from India to participate in decision making about the work load. The Indian supervisor feels the manager is paid to make decisions so why do his work for him? The greater the cultural difference, the more chance for miscommunication. Building teamwork among employees is a challenge; add different cultures and the challenge increases. It's impossible to memorize the business protocol of every culture. Fortunately, there are many aids available. Roger Axtell has a series of *Do's and Taboos* books. Brigham Young University publishes *Culturgrams*. Both provide basic information to aid us in successful intercultural communication. Typically when internationals come to the U.S., they have studied our culture and language thoroughly. Knowing the basics of their culture indicates we care and facilitates building cohesive work teams.

Many American companies and institutions have attempted to close communication and social gaps, for example, Baptist Medical Center of Oklahoma City offers English language training to its Vietnamese dietary workers and F&H USA Inc, a Japanese company in Oklahoma, hired a Japanese speaking liaison to ease employee transitions.

Oops!

Whenever I talk about training internationals I always tell on myself first. While living in Japan, I provided business English training to Japanese executives. I went into corporations for conversational English, taught in language schools, and did one-on-

Integrating Ethnic Cultures

one tutoring. Much of what's taught in language schools is taught by rote memory and repetition. Imagine saying "See Dick Run" over and over and over. It was so incredibly boring I had to keep my finger on the spot to keep from losing my place. I stifled many yawns. Thinking back to my methods classes I began to vary the lessons.

I was so proud of myself; I used every method you could imagine. We celebrated Western holidays with appropriate games and activities. (I don't believe in playing games for games' sake; they were all related to topics.) We went to a Western movie, visited my home and ate Western food. The list goes on and on. It was a wonderful class - to me. Imagine my surprise when some evaluations were poor. One comment was "too many games". This was especially surprising when you consider Japanese men are often seen in suits, brief cases on the floor playing away in pachinko parlors after work. Their marathon drinking in hostess bars each night after work is legendary. Play seemed to be the norm, but obviously not in classrooms!

I, Ms Trainer, had not bothered to find out the participants preferred style of learning; instead I imposed my preferences on them. *The Lesson: Know Your Audience.*

The Home Front

I could not complete this chapter without noting that within our own country there are a great number of sub-cultures that deal with Time and Space in ways similar to that of foreign countries and different from what we would consider "Mainstream" American behavior. I have been dismayed at times when I was leading a seminar, to have some people come in late and spend time socializing with friends before settling in to attend to the session. I am sure that they would be surprised that I was dismayed. And... there have been times when everyone was seated waiting for me

The Change

to begin ten minutes before the scheduled time and I was still going over my notes and getting myself in the right psychological mode.

I repeat:

The Lesson: Know Your Audience.

REFERENCES

Axtell, Roger. *Do's and Taboos Around the World,* John Wiley & Sons, New York, 1985.

Axtell, Roger. *Do's and Taboos of Hosting International Visitors,* John Wiley & Sons, New York, 1990.

Axtell, Roger. *Do's and Taboos of International Trade,* John Wiley & Sons, New York, 1989.

Culturgrams, David Kennedy Center for International Studies, Brigham Young University, Provo, Utah.

6 *Technology With An Attitude*

> *In fact, for the past few decades, it is the backlog of unimplemented technological advances, rather than the supply of unused physical resources, that has been the determinant of real growth.*
> Paul Zane Pilzer
> Unlimited Wealth

EDITOR'S NOTE: Attitudes which engender cooperation, trust, and depth of communication make the technological tools we are currently using that much more effective. There must be, in addition to sensitivity to the attitudinal aspects of interpersonal relationships, a childlike awe toward new technical possibilities.

The greatest amount of cooperation and positive attitude in the world will not make the productivity of a shovel brigade equal that of one diesel shovel. Yet attitude spills over into the arena of willingness to explore and invest in new technology: to take a technological risk, in other words. This book would not be complete without highlighting a noted economics researcher's challenge and solution to what seems currently to be a major factor effecting technological stagnation in the United States.

Stephen Paley, Ph.D., Physicist and Economics Researcher, provides in this chapter a comprehensive here-to-fore unpublished economic view of the urgency to create team based learning environments to assure that new technologies are not bypassed and left "on the shelf" when such cutting-edge technologies can significantly impact our

The Change

national economic growth if they are effectively developed and utilized. Dr. Paley's articles "Reasons for and Solutions to the Economic Decline" and "Vital Technologies Go Begging" have appeared in the April, November 1992 editions of Quality Magazine.

The Power of Technology

Is there a most vital factor responsible for creating much of our economic growth? Yes, there is. In 1987, Prof. Robert M. Solow of MIT won the Noble Prize for Economics. He proved that commercializing and effectively using "productivity-increasing" technology, acts as the catalyst for 80-90% of our long term economic growth! (A productivity-increasing technology is one which improves the "efficiency" of a manufacturing process.)

Every manufacturing process has an "input" - (the value of) all the things needed to perform the manufacturing. It also has an "output" - (the value of) the "units" which are manufactured. Consider agriculture our "food manufacturing" process. If viewed on an annual basis, the input to agriculture is a certain amount of land, labor, chemicals, fuel, seeds, machinery, etc. The output is one year's worth of crops. Productivity is defined as "output/input". This definition (as well as our intuition) tells us that productivity is increased if output is increased, or if input is decreased, or if output is increased at the same time that input is decreased.

Usually, the two strongest factors that determine productivity in most of our manufacturing processes are labor costs and technology. Reducing labor costs by reducing salaries or by downsizing - exactly what is happening today - reduces input, which in turn is one way of increasing productivity.

Historically, the main process which resulted in our high standard of living and prosperity, was periodic adoption of new "productivity-increasing" technology into manufacturing. When such technology was introduced into manufacturing, its effect was to greatly decrease input, increase output, or both at the same time.

The increased productivity brought about by each wave of these technologies allowed companies to continue to increase the wages of their employees without causing inflation. With each wage increase, these employees could then buy more goods and services thereby dramatically increasing the size of the economy and "spreading the wealth". Thus, most of the economic growth created by technology lies outside of manufacturing; it doesn't occur however without a strong and healthy manufacturing base at the economy's center.

As we continue to lose more of our industrial base, we are reversing this process of creating and distributing new wealth. As things currently stand, each year the ability to play the "technology game" is diminished in our nation. (1,2)

We have very badly lost the technology and/or manufacturing lead to foreign nations in half of our high tech industries.(2) Another 25% is apparently "up for grabs" and we are not grabbing very hard. In addition, the people who could bring us back are now being systematically eliminated from the work force; over half of the senior engineers in the nation are unemployed with no prospect of being reemployed in engineering.(3)

The Dumbness Of Downsizing

Once the technology/manufacturing lead is lost in an industry, the only apparent way to make up for it (for a while) is by reducing labor costs; this translates into transferring manufacturing overseas, or reducing domestic wages and salaries, or downsizing. But there is an inherent difference between reducing labor costs and using technology to improve productivity.

The Change

The "technology solution", with successive waves of technology, can go on forever. The game of reducing labor costs rapidly comes to an end. For example, a company can only downsize so much before it becomes ineffective. Similarly, reducing wages or transferring manufacturing overseas reduces the size of the domestic U.S. market; for as the average American family earns less, they can purchase fewer goods and services.

If the long-term trend of reduced disposable income per typical family accelerates, it may result in our inability to end recessions. Normally, two-thirds of a recovery is provided by consumer spending. What happens if we reach the point where people are not holding back on spending due to uncertainty? They simply no longer have it to spend.

If the U.S. market is reduced in size, companies may find that their goods and services are in oversupply. But even if some companies can exist on foreign markets, we need to ask ourselves what the economy is about. Is it simply there so that companies can prosper? Or to provide a high standard of living for our own people? Hopefully, the answer is both.

What happened in our nation is this: The loss of part of our technology/ manufacturing base to foreign nations resulted in declining wages and salaries and downsizing. (4,5,6) This occurred not only with high-paying jobs in the industrial sector, but was made worse by a major "multiplier" effect. The service sector is set up to serve the industrial sector. Thus, as the industrial sector loses jobs and downsizes, so must the service sector.

As downsizing became "acceptable", companies that were enjoying large profits also began to downsize. They were usually "rewarded" for downsizing by seeing the value of their stock rise. This is morally inexcusable as well as detrimental to the nation. The fastest way to destroy a nation is to have every person - or in this case every institution - to be only for himself or herself.

Although some U.S. companies were forced by obsolescent technology to seek lower labor costs abroad, we need to recognize that there were others, with no such need, that transferred their manufacturing abroad anyway. Many of these latter companies sought large, excessive profits by dramatically lowering their labor costs without passing any of the savings on to U.S. consumers.

We thus have a problem that is partly driven by technology - or rather by its lack - and partly by opportunism. In the author's opinion, such opportunistic behavior does not represent the workings of an unalterable law of international economics so much as it does unprecedented greed; perhaps the products of such companies should be denied access to U.S. markets?

The vast amount of growth tied to technology has profound implications. All of our eggs are essentially in one basket. It doesn't take models - although we have them - to conclude, that if 80-90% of our long-term growth is lost, our upside is permanent economic stagnation and our downside is economic collapse.

Surviving Global Challenges

Technology is so pervasive that even successful foreign trade depends upon producing manufactured goods which are competitive in world markets; i.e., upon restoring and retaining a technology advantage in manufacturing. Otherwise, we will have little to trade. And opening our markets under these conditions will only enlarge our already monumental trade deficit; for goods will flow primarily one way - into our country.

Because of the "value added" nature of manufacturing, export of raw materials does not begin to generate the economic benefits of

The Change

exporting manufactured goods. Underdeveloped nations export raw materials; developed nations, manufactured goods. The bulk of our exports to Japan however, our largest trading partner, is now raw materials!(7) No stand for or against international free trade is intended here. In the author's view, free trade is like any other issue; whether it is "good" or "bad" for its participants depends upon the details and consequences of any agreements and how they are implemented.

If technology is the foundation of our economy as claimed, then most of the important economic trends - especially the negative ones - should be directly related to our lack-of-technology. This is easily demonstrated.

Everyone "knows", for example, that the Federal deficit is due to Government overspending, however this is not the entire story. By the early 1970s, it was no longer possible to commercialize technologies created by individuals or small companies.(8,9) This effectively eliminated the "engine for economic growth" from our economy. In response, by 1980, our growth rate had plummeted. If this primary source of technology had not been eliminated from the economy - i.e., if our growth rate had not been reduced - the same amount of Government spending since 1980 would not have created this deficit!(10)

Similarly, one can directly relate to our lack-of-technology: our "true" unemployment rate of around 15% (11) - it was 25% at the height of the 1929 Depression; the cancerous long term trend of decreasing disposable income per average family; (4,5,6) the FED'S "forced response" of low interest rates (to end the last recession) and the resulting run-up of stock prices to inflated PE ratios; the nonsustainable productivity - increases brought about by downsizing (rather than technology); our failure to respond with technology to the 6-fold price increase of OPEC oil during the 1970s (representing the largest peace time transfer of wealth in world history); the

S&L collapse, due to the double digit inflation caused by the OPEC oil price increases; etc.

U.S. Economic Renewal

Let's examine what technology can accomplish. Just from the "output over input" definition of productivity, one can show that such technologies, as a class, result simultaneously in: **creation of large quantities of new wealth**; reduction of inflation; significant contribution to positive trade balance; and major reduction in the need for deficit spending (by greatly increasing the size and profitability of the economy, and thus of the tax base). Thus, technology initiates economic renewal.(12)

Now note the limitations of fiscal and monetary policy, which are not capable of renewing the economy.(13,14) Many of the economist's "tools" in both these areas are a consequence, directly or indirectly, of the Keynesian economic model. This model shows how to balance (and regulate) economic growth and how to trade it off against inflation. In particular, it shows how to "turn on" economic growth, when the economy is capable of responding with economic growth. In this sense, it is like a "light switch". It is certainly not the dynamo; e.g., it will not be able to "turn on" much economic growth if our industrial base is lost.

In short, macroeconomic manipulation can "make the patient more comfortable" as he continues to decline long term, but is incapable of reversing the decline.(14)

As the industrial base is lost, real salary, wages and benefits of average Americans tend to decline, as explained. Let's consider now the ability - not the willingness - of employers under these conditions to pay high levels of compensation, so that Americans can continue to enjoy a high standard of living.

The Change

Higher Technology Or Lower Wages

As noted, the primary productivity factors in manufacturing are labor costs and technology. Therefore, in order for U.S. manufacturers to make up for lower foreign labor costs - without reducing the benefits and wages of their U.S. workers - they must either have superior manufacturing technology in old industries, or else produce products, and possess new industries, that foreign nations do not have.

If high wages are to be paid in U.S. manufacturing, we must be significantly ahead in technology and manufacturing; we can't even afford to be on a par with other nations which have lower labor costs than we do! But the very opposite is happening. We have badly lost our technology and manufacturing lead in half of our high tech industries, with apparently more to follow.(1,2)

This situation affects all of us, not just manufacturing workers. The wealth to purchase services comes from the manufacturing sector. As manufacturing jobs and wages decrease, demand for services is reduced. Thus, the volume of services and the rate paid for them will also continue to decline. (The reason we have no inflation today is that demand is down because disposable income of typical American families is down! Yet, even with this, the potential for inflation within the industrial sector still exists. We can now reach production capacity with less production because of the loss of much of our industrial base.)

Unless we rapidly introduce the technologies needed to regain the technology/manufacturing lead in old industries and create new ones, our wages and living standards have no option but to continue their decline toward third world levels!(4,5,6) The restoration of our industrial base is not a take-it-or-leave-it proposition. The benefits derived from its restoration are indispensable. It must therefore be restored, in addition to whatever other national

Technology With An Attitude

agendas are proposed and implemented.

What's Holding Technology Back

Since technology is responsible for initiating 80-90% of our long term growth, we begin by asking a few simple questions:
- What is the "nature" of technologies that are important to the economy?
- Where did most such technologies come from?
- What happened, by the early 1970s, to preferentially prevent commercialization of the technologies that could have done most for the U.S. economy?

Let me first establish the author's expertise for discussing these questions. His background combines science, technology, and innovation with several areas of business and business planning. He is the coinventor of one of the more important technologies to be commercialized over the last few decades, in terms of major benefits for: the national economy; the environment; human health; and resource conservation. He served the company which commercialized this technology as president, has several articles published on technology and the economy, and is completing a book on the subject.

While it was commercial, his technology demonstrated the ability to: dramatically cut the cost of growing crops; increase yields and dramatically increase farmers' profits; save large percentages of irrigation water (and proportionally) the fuel used to pump the water; and, as quoted in *Newsweek,* (15) eliminate the need for 50-70% of the pesticides which are currently required.

This technology is no longer commercial. It's been "sitting on the shelf", so far for a decade, after demonstrating commercially the capabilities listed above. In general, the ability to commercialize most innovative technologies, such as this one, has been non-

The Change

existent, and it's been this way for very many years. As things currently stand, the technologies needed for our economic (and environmental) future have no way of becoming commercial.

With few exceptions most of the technologies important to the U.S. economy were originally innovative.(8,9) That means when they were first made commercial, the concepts upon which they were based represented "seven league advances." (This is in contrast to "incremental" technology - those representing small advances over what is currently commercial.) The more important of these technologies also have a second characteristic. They "make new markets" or "create new industries" which is just one of the ways they initiate major economic growth.

Note that there are two risks for any venture capitalist who might wish to commercialize a new technology. One is the "technology risk"; he needs to know whether the proposed technology is practical, and whether it will "work" in the real world? The other is the "marketing risk".

Both the technology and marketing risks are substantially greater for the technologies that are potentially the most important for the U.S. economy - the ones that are innovative and make new markets. It is much more difficult, for example, to evaluate a technology based on "seven league advances" than an incremental technology. Similarly, the marketing risk of creating a new industry greatly exceeds that of marketing a slight variation of something already commercial.

In terms of where such technologies come from, the U.S. is unique. At least two-thirds of our most important or "pioneering" technologies have been developed by individuals outside of large companies.(8) Today, we have a condition I call the "standoff". Large companies still have capital but most of them have become noninnovative and are no longer capable of developing the technologies that are needed for our economic future.(1,2,12) Individuals, on the other hand, have always produced the majority of the innovative technologies important to the economy.(8,9) Most of them, however, have been denied capital to commercialize their contribution for nearly 20 years.(1,2,8,9,16,17,18,19,20,)

Conclusion: There are very few places left which can both create and then commercialize the innovative technologies needed for our economic future - and now needed for the environment.

Technology And "The Knowledge Barrier" (21,22)

The fundamental problem with technology in our nation is that, unlike Japan and Germany, technology in a broad sense is "administered" here by people who are uneducated in technology. And you can't put novices in charge of something as complex as technology development or manufacturing and expect satisfactory results. Let me illustrate:

In Japan, 70% of the top executives in manufacturing and technology companies are educated not only in business but are also trained and experienced in engineering unto the doctoral level. (The CEO of Toyota, for example, is a world class engine designer.) These people can manage technology properly because they understand it.

The reason hardly anyone wants to bother with technology in our country is a very human one. People deal with what they understand - because that is what makes them comfortable. They avoid what they don't understand, because it is automatically high risk to them, which also makes them uncomfortable when trying to deal with it.

The Change

Another illustration of this knowledge barrier is the circumstance of the U.S. venture capitalist. Since he is generally a "layman" when it comes to technology, he has to "hire an expert" to evaluate for him, the technology risk of a proposed technical venture.

Well, this usually works for incremental technology. But it breaks down completely when it comes to innovative technology. If you ask a dozen experts to evaluate a (new) innovative technology, you will usually get thirteen different opinions.

Consider now what happens to a layman when experts can't agree. If he is going to "play in the game", he is reduced to guessing which dramatically increases his risk. Suppose, on the other hand, that the typical U.S. venture capitalist was trained and experienced in engineering as well as business. To obtain capital for an innovative technology, one would simply find a single venture capitalist who personally judged that the technology was practical (and that the marketing risk was worth taking).

Here is the vast difference between decision-makers who understand the body of knowledge they deal with first-hand, and those who have to "consult an expert" for an opinion.

Conclusion: Because of the "knowledge barrier", the technologies which could have done most for the U.S. economy over the last two decades were the ones least likely to be made commercial.

Since the "agricultural" technology I codeveloped couldn't be recommercialized for many years, I began to wonder if there were other vital technologies suffering the same fate. This question caused me to spend several years (part-time) judging over 300 "shelf-sitting" technologies - 30 of them extensively. Data forces me to the conclusion that much of the technology required for economic renewal is in commercial form, sitting "on the shelf", with no way of becoming commercial due to total lack of venture capital for this purpose!(23)

I have even documented three "superstars"; technologies potentially so powerful, that they could single-handedly make a significant difference to the entire U.S. economy and, in two cases, simultaneously to the environment!(23,24) Such technologies could form the basis of genuine economic renewal in this country, if they could only be made commercial.

Please note that I am not the only one making claims of "shelf-sitting, economy-saving" technologies. Let me quote part of an interview with Gil Hyatt, inventor of the microprocessor, from *The Wall Street Journal:*(25) "...Mr. Hyatt argues that...thousands of 'entrepreneurial engineers' whose inventions are the hope for the U.S. industrial future...are holding back breakthroughs that could transform life on earth and America's competitive posture..."

Most of us "entrepreneurial engineers" are "holding back" only because of the absence of venture capital with which to commercialize our contributions. The idea that our economic (and environmental) futures are unable to "come into existence", and that many of the major answers are "sitting on the shelf", certainly takes some getting used to. But the way they "got on the shelf" is completely logical. And after one has reviewed the nature and origin of our economically important technologies, and the reason for lack-of-capital for innovative technology in this country, it's hard to imagine any other situation. The way things currently stand, our potential for solving major problems of the economy and the environment by introducing the necessary technologies, is sufficiently poor to be courting disaster in both these areas.

A Limited Lifetime For "Shelf-Sitting" Technologies

Before describing how to commercialize these "shelf-sitting"

The Change

technologies, I want to emphasize the need for speed and explain why the situation is "unstable". Although much of the technology needed to revitalize the U.S. economy is "sitting-on-the-shelf", it may not be available too much longer! I can use the 300 "shelf-sitting" technologies which I reviewed as a source of statistical data to show why this is so.

About 2/3 of the technologists who developed these technologies are beyond retirement age. Others are being preferentially cast out of our technical and engineering work force; they are older, senior people, higher on the salary scale, who are nearing retirement, and therefore tempting targets for companies which are downsizing.

As previously indicated, well over half of all U.S. senior engineers are currently unemployed with no likelihood of being reemployed as engineers. (3) Finally, most U.S. companies, at best, are only interested in incremental technology. Under these conditions, they don't need innovators so they have no reason to try to keep them.

It is obvious that, as a group, these innovators are well beyond the age where most of them want to be world-beaters engaged in commercializing a new technology. Some are sick. Others have experienced the reduced strength-and-vigor that comes with age. The question, here, is why does the bias-toward-age exist among most of our nations's innovators. The explanation is simple:

The Demise of U. S. Technical Innovation

The original group of innovators in this country learned how to be innovative by "pulling themselves up by their own bootstraps" over a 20 year period. Prior to the early 1970s, one of them would occasionally take a young engineer under his wing and teach him; this was essentially an apprenticeship process. But in the early 1970s the "organization" of technical development programs changed, and it was no longer possible to carry on the apprenticeship.

Technology With An Attitude

Part of the requirements for training an innovator is teaching him the skills of a technical "generalist". This used to be accomplished by letting just a handful of technical people complete an entire major project. But this changed in the early 1970s, and specialization became the rule.

Specialization was encouraged in Defense for reasons of national security. It ensured that no one knew too much about the overall project, thus making spying more difficult. But it also became the rule in commercial technology-development programs, probably for two reasons. One was misguided concepts of management. The other might have been management's fear that if a few engineers got to know too much, they might form a "break-away" company and become the competition.

So here's where we find ourselves:

We had an original group of technical innovators who learned their skills by "pulling themselves up by their own bootstraps" over a 20 year period. They are now rapidly passing from the scene without (so far) having been permitted to commercialize their technologies, and without having trained many replacements for themselves. If they pass without at least training replacements, the U.S. will no longer have the ability to restore its industrial base or remain an industrial nation!(26,27) And we are talking here about no more than a few thousand surviving innovators! (This is an example of information which will determine our economic destiny that has no place within conventional economic models!)

There is no substitute for our economic and environmental survival except to have talented and knowledgeable technologists and innovators working in an environment in which they are allowed to perform! The solution to U.S. economic decline is to commercialize our "shelf-sitting" technologies, initially on a small or local scale so that they can demonstrate their capabilities.

The Change

As far as dealing with the "age problem" of most of our surviving innovators, I suggest that they become consultants to the companies which commercialize their technologies. That way, the value of their experience may be tapped to some extent without physically exhausting them or taking up all of their time.

A Solution To Funding New Technologies

The following proposal to commercialize these technologies does not solve all problems, but is a reasonable beginning, particularly given the time constraints for solving the problem. This proposal is being made under "emergency conditions" and the author is certainly interested in other people's proposals to commercialize our "shelf-sitting" technologies, including their suggested variations on his own proposal.

Suppose that a nonprofit (charitable) Foundation is set up, to which contributions are tax deductible. The purpose of the Foundation is to provide the "bridge" which will allow major technologies to ultimately become commercial. It will concentrate on technologies which can revitalize old industries, create new ones, and those which offer significant simultaneous advantages to the economy and the environment.

The Foundation will pick up all costs required to demonstrate a major technology to potential customers until they are ready to become actual customers. At this point, the high tech start-up will seek financing to become commercial, if necessary through its own "Reg D" offering. When the company is ready to go commercial, the Foundation will perform one last function. It will turn over to the company its list of contributors (with permission of each contributor).

The company may then wish to seek seed-capital from those who contributed to the Foundation in the demonstration stage. (In fact, this is almost a certainty, since there are no other sources of capital to commercialize these technologies.) Many of the foundation's contributors, in turn, will then have the opportunity to get in on the ground floor of companies with technologies capable of making major contributions to the economy and/or environment.

At the time financing is sought, much of the risk in these high-tech start-ups is gone. No one need worry about the technology; it has already been demonstrated to, and accepted by, potential customers who are ready to become actual customers. And the initial marketing risk is reduced for the same reason; customers are available as soon as the company goes commercial.

We are not talking about much money in the scheme of things to get these technologies commercialized; usually no more than $2-5 million, with most (after the "customer demonstration") closer to the $2 million mark. And demonstrating these technologies to potential customers - the Foundation's mission - will generally be in the $500,000 to $1,000,000 range.

One advantage of the Foundation is that it confers significant credibility upon the demonstration phase. Potential customers are much more likely to take a technology seriously if they are approached by the Foundation as opposed to being directly contacted by the innovators who developed the technology.

Another advantage of the Foundation's activities is that it not only reduces the risk of going commercial, but also lowers the cost of going commercial. It does this in two ways. One is by helping to create paying customers from the very beginning of the commercial phase. This reduces the period of negative cash flow, normally associated with establishing the initial customer base. This, in turn, reduces the capitalization required to reach the point of positive cash flow.

The Change

The Foundation will also make a gift, to the start-up company, of any specialized equipment embodying the proprietary technology which was used in the (nonprofit) demonstration phase. This, again, reduces the required initial capitalization in the commercial phase, as well as gives the start-up company a "working system" as soon as it goes commercial.

The decision of which technologies to demonstrate should be made by a small panel of some of the nation's best technologists; people who have personally created major technology, who also understand how technology "fits" within a commercial context - - perhaps a panel of three. It may also be reasonable to require successful start-ups to give back a small percentage of their profit to the Foundation, so that the Foundation can expand its activities to demonstrate commercially-important technologies.

Today, the funding of the Foundation through tax-deductible contributions is possible. Many people are worried about the future of the U. S. economy, but don't know what they can do about it personally. We can "empower" such people.

The Foundation needs such small amounts of capital in the scheme of things to fulfill its mission, that personal, tax-deductible contributions - used in the manner suggested - can directly affect the nation's economic (and environmental) future. Such contributions could determine whether our economy begins to recover through commercialization of the "proper" technologies, or continues to decline toward Third World status.

Whether or not one believes we are headed for third world status, or considers this to be the best or worst of worlds, there is a single point that is the crux of the matter. Everyone wants to see improvement. And there are technologies sitting on the shelf which can dramatically improve the economy and return good jobs to U.S. workers; solve major environmental problems; and, as stated

Technology With An Attitude

by Gil Hyatt, inventor of the microprocessor, represent "... breakthroughs that could transform life on earth and America's competitive posture..." These potential improvements are sufficient for us to make commercialization of the "shelf-sitting" technologies our #1 priority.

REFERENCES

1. Report of the MIT Commission on Industrial Productivity; MIT Univ. Press; May 2, 1989.
2. Report of the Council on Competitiveness as summarized in "Technology Lags, Report Says", The Daily Oklahoman, p. 18, March 21, 1991.
3. American Engineer, p. 5, Feb. 1992; conclusions based on research by the IEEE-USA Manpower Committee using data from the Engineering Manpower Commission.
4. Uchitelle, L., "Trapped in the Impoverished Middle Class", The New York Times, Section 3, p. 1, Nov. 17, 1991.
5. Malabre, A. L. Jr., "Under Pressure Living Standards Are Slipping and Were Even Before the Recession", The Wall Street Journal, P. 1, Nov. 17, 1991.
6. Uchitelle, L., "U. S. Wages Not Getting Ahead? Better Get Used to It", The New York Times, Week in Review, P. 1, Dec. 16, 1990.
7. Data from the U. S. Department of Commerce; Leading Categories of Goods Traded by the U. S. and Japan for 1993.
8. Testimony before Senate Small Business Committee on Tax Aspects of the Technology Transfer Issue, Congressional Record, Jan. 4, 1978.
9. Harvey, T. W., "Technical Ventures - Catalysts for Economic Growth", Battelle Today, Number 5, Aug. 1977. (This is the in-house publication of Battelle Memorial Institute, Columbus, Ohio, which was one of the most prominent contract research houses in the world. Among other things, Xerography was developed at Battelle.)
10. A simple calculation taking growth rates in the early 1970s, the time when funding essentially vanished for small technology companies and high tech start-ups and projecting them (and associated Federal tax revenues) through the mid 1990s. Annual Federal expenditures in this calculation remain unaltered.
11. Private conversation in March, 1994, with an official of the Bureau of Labor Statistics concerning their methodology for determining the unemployment rate. The most serious flaw is that individuals who use up their unemployment benefits without finding employment are not counted. Also, those who never were eligible for unemployment benefits are not counted. Finally, the Bureau does not distinguish between full- and part-time employment. If we figured the unemployment rate as it is done in Europe and Japan, our rate would be around 15%.
12. Paley, S., "Reasons For and Solutions to the Economic Decline", Quality, pp. 16-20, April 1992. See p. 18, Effects of Productivity-Increasing Technology.

The Change

13. Wanniski, J., "Macroeconomics: The Enemy Within", The New York Times, June 27, 1991. Editorial Comment.
14. Work culminating in the 1987 Nobel Prize for Economics established that the efficient use of productivity-increasing technology is responsible for creating 80-90% of our long term economic growth. Macroeconomics, however deals with optimizing an economy having a <u>fixed</u> technology and resource base. Inability to incorporate technology as a source of economic growth constitutes a fatal flaw in macroeconomics.
15. Schulman, H., "The Comeback of a Crop Doctor", Newsweek, Focus, p. 4, Sept. 20, 1993
16. Gupta, U., "Venture Capital Firms Grow Larger and Larger but Start-Up Companies are Left Out in the Cold", The Wall Street Journal; Sept. 7, 1989.
17. Gupta, U., "For Start-Ups, Funding Squeeze Tightens", The Wall Street Journal, Dec. 28, 1989.
18. Sanger, E., "Invented in the U.S., Spurned in the U.S., A Technology Flourishes in Japan", The New York Times, Section 1, p. 1, Dec. 15, 1990.
19. Henrique, D. B., "Lean Times Ahead in the High Tech Nursery", The New York Times, Jan. 5, 1992.
20. Gupta, U., "Venture Capitalists Find Low Tech Firms Appealing", The Wall Street Journal, p. B2, June 20, 1991.
21. The earliest reference to what I have called the "Knowledge Barrier" appears to have been clearly stated by the British scholar, essayist, and social philosopher, C. P. Snow, about the time of WWII, in his essay, Science and Government."
22. Broder, D. S., "Government Over Its Head; Grappling With Questions of Nature, Leaders Must Act on Scientific Matters Which Bemuse Them", The Washington Post, Apr. 13, 1989.
23. Paley, S., Unpublished study conducted between 1990 and 1993.
24. Paley, S., "Vital Technologies Go Begging", Quality, p. 55, Nov. 1992.
25. Ferguson, T. W., "Liberating Inventors or Shackling Progress With Paperwork?", The Wall Street Journal, March 5, 1991.
26. Arthur D. Little, Inc. News, "Arthur D. Little Announces Finding of Worldwide Innovation Study", Section II, Barriers to (U. S.) Innovation, Dec. 4, 1992.
27. Placek, C., Editorial Comment, "Help Wanted: Skilled Leaders", Quality, p. 8, May, 1992.

OTHER SUGGESTED READINGS

Pilzer, P. Z., "Unlimited Wealth, The Theory and Practice of Economic Alchemy", New York City: Crown Publishers, 1990.
The entire October 19, 1992, issue of Fortune, "Fixing America's Economy".
The entire 1990 bonus issue of Business Week, "Innovation, the Global Race".

7 Overview of Right/Left Brain Research

> *I would go without shirt or shoe,*
> *Friend, tobacco, or bread,*
> *Sooner than lose for a minute the two*
> *Separate sides of my head.*
> Rudyard Kipling,
> *The Two-Sided Man*

For those readers interested in more detailed information on brain hemisphere research, I have included here a brief review of some of the major literature. In addition to the review, there is an analysis leading to what I feel are valid conclusions that learning to utilize both hemispheres in our thinking is the greatest tool toward creativity and quality that we can utilize in today's dynamically changing marketplace.

Today, business and industry in the western world have become locked into left brain closed system thinking (Maslow, 1968). It has been demonstrated that facts alone do not motivate a worker to higher productivity; other nonverbal, emotive elements of the right brain must come into play. These elements are currently not generally understood nor are they being utilized in an organized fashion by business and industry (McGregor, 1960). The costs in loss of productivity and the loss of creativity for the development of a rich socioeconomic climate are enormous.

The Change

There is at this time the need for programs capable of instructing those in business and industry in the use of the non-linear applications of the right brain (The National Center on Education and the Economy, 1990; Hogan, 1991).

Interestingly, throughout history one can find quotes from people such as Benjamin Franklin, Oscar Wilde, Socrates, Albert Einstein, Winston Churchill, and Rudyard Kipling hinting that they were aware that there was a duality in their thinking processes. The ancient Chinese with their dynamic dualistic thought are also to be noted.

Scientific awareness of the isolated functions of the two human brain hemispheres, however, began in 1861 when Paul Broca, surgeon and neuroanatomist, determined the center for articulate language to be in the left hemisphere. His work was followed in 1874 by the work of a German neurologist, Carl Wernicke, who located a second speech center in the left hemisphere (Restak, 1988).

The belief that the left hemisphere of the brain was dominant prevailed almost a hundred years until the research carried out by Roger Sperry (1977) during the 1960's which showed the right hemisphere to be capable of high levels of visual, spatial, and emotional activity independent of the left brain language systems. Through both the separation of the connection hemispheric nerve fibers and EEG techniques, hemispheric specialization was demonstrated (Ornstein, 1972).

The emerging perception among some researchers that the right hemisphere held a non-linear creative potential was assailed by others, particularly behaviorists, touting the exceptional occurrences of the transfer of language capabilities in adults from left to right hemisphere after left brain injury (Skinner, 1957; Corrick, 1983). Another major researcher, Jean Piaget, contended that the mind is always keyed to logical thinking (Hunt, 1982). However, more recent evidence contradicts this and asserts that logical reasoning is a specialized mental activity that has particular value in special circumstances. It is not the mind's natural way of operating (Penrose, 1989).

While Springer (1985) offers compelling views of a brain with unchartered capabilities and Marcel Kinsbourne of the Hospital for Sick Children feels that both hemispheres are used in the imaginative and speculative processes, the hemispheric stimulation research conducted by Wilder Penfield and Phanor Perot confirmed a reception of visual and voice tonality with the absence of language structure as a result of electrical stimulation to the right hemisphere (Penfield, 1963).

Historical Hemispheric Transition

For obvious reasons, little is known about the cogitation of pre-literate humankind. Until language had developed to some extent, there could have been little thinking beyond the range of actual experience (Wells, 1971). If the educated speculations of Julian Jaynes (1973) prove to be correct, the Iliad - now thought to be a document written about 900 B.C. (Desborough, 1964) - creates a disturbing possibility: That the two hemispheres of the human brain functioned as separate conscious units with the actual and experiential being totally divided from the language "narrator". Jaynes is a strong advocate for the evolution of the neurology of consciousness.

The struggles of Greek philosophy to move from the experiential worship of all things to the analysis of all things were not smooth as it continued to attempt to explain phenomena by one universal principle or belief (Thilly, 1914). Plato saw past prevailing belief systems to glimpse the power of knowledge as a potent force which could someday unify emotional efforts.

The Change

When tides of sequential thinking began to wash onto the shores of long cherished tradition and dogma, science was for generations an ill-born child (Beard, 1928): A bittersweet offspring that increased human power but diminished human pride. What was not understood was many times demolished. Witness the destruction of the first known working clock in 1090 A.D. at the hands of the new Chinese Dynasty (Boorstin, 1985).

By the thirteenth century the literary progeny of Aristotle, more worshiped than read, was redefined by Roger Bacon, who threw out dogma and authorities for the sake of experimentation, yet dared to vision a world where knowledge of natural laws would allow humans to soar in the air and travel on land in conveyances powered by machines (Wells, 1971). But vision and emotion continued to rule most often in the form of religious institutions resistant to any social change (Dunlap, 1946). It was not a vision that created a new and better future but which continued to perpetuate the past. That which could not be explained was relegated to the influence of the stars or evil spirits (Restak, 1988).

At the turn of the seventeenth century, even the weight demonstrations by Galileo could not remove the Aristotelian scales from the eyes of the scholars long enough for them to see the iron balls hit the ground simultaneously (Stetson, 1930). With the advent of expanded communication after Gutenberg, more scholars became willing to at least silently entertain the heresy that one could trust one's own reason, explore the reality around him or her, and "dare to know" (Fromm, 1947).

The blind acceptance of the earliest belief systems had kept humankind at a level almost deviceless - subject to the whims of nature (Ward, 1989). Perhaps the raw force of need along with the rare display of power that came from becoming a student of nature as opposed to its worshiper, turned more people toward the desire to know.

Both Einstein and Galton, at an advantageous time to profit from several centuries of scientific questioning, moved back into the non-linear mode of their right brain to discover that when given a pragmatic direction, new concepts and information become available to the conscious without the aid of the language hemisphere (Penrose, 1989).

In the late nineteenth century, the earthy and many times ill-mannered Edison displayed his ability to visualize a new invention before it was yet created and also to forget his own name - all in the same day (DeCamp, 1957). It was that very miracle of wonderment and revelation that had lead researchers closer to understanding how strong visual and emotional brain functioning toward factual objectives lead to paradigm break-throughs and awareness of the significance of information no one else seems to notice (Kuhn, 1962).

With the establishment of Gestalt psychology by Wertheimer, Koffka, and Kohler there came to be an understanding of the extent that humankind can develop open belief systems. Considering Gestalt theory, we can agree that when an expansive belief system is extant, such theory becomes justified. When restrictive belief systems are encountered, the findings proferred through Behaviorism tend to be confirmed. Because the human mind can be restricted to set patterns or flexible to function nonsequentially; both Gestalt and Behaviorism have their place in defining certain structures of thought. The two theories do not conflict. They simply shed light upon the two extremes of which the human mind is capable.

Indeed the fully functioning mind plays as a symphony rhythmically shifting left paradigm-based locus to right open-paradigm awareness, based upon end result visions, to receive the next batch of information needed to move us closer to our goal. The symphony works best when we consciously set our own telemetry.

The Change

Contemporary Reliance upon Fact Based Paradigms In Business and Industry

The long journey from worshipful mythology to inductive reasoning has equipped humankind to become a serious student of phenomena (Fischler, 1987). Now, the stage is set with certain information systems that direct our current business and industrial framework (Calvin, 1989). When something fits, we stop surveying alternatives. Whether it encompasses economics or the social sciences (Bloom, 1987); the helpful information inductive reasoning has borne, fueling our socioeconomic climate, has been transformed into immutable belief systems (Herrman, 1989).

While Drucker (1973) is a hesitant disciple of Theory Y, he expresses a yearning that there is something more, an even more effective way to make the strong and healthy accept the burden of responsibility. Drucker's "Zen approach", which might be rejected out of hand if proffered by a lesser authority, plays right into the right brain learning curve - where there is no fixed and final plateau.

As we move from machines that extend the human muscles, radio and television that extend the human nervous system (Large, 1984) and computers that extend the ratio and speed of information gathering and analysis; a new hero emerges, the creative employee (Toffler, 1990) - the worker who joyfully accepts responsibility and, because she is emotionally committed, looks for creative ways to expand the company - the employee who taps into her deep pool of motivation; "the pleasure of enjoying one's abilities" (Fenichel, 1945), "the autonomous factor in ego development" (Hartman, 1950), "functional autonomy" (Allport, 1937), and the "sense of initiative" (Erickson, 1956).

The left hemisphere: logical, sequential becomes the helmsman - guiding the mental ship to explore new right brain experiential possibilities through the cooperative functioning of both brain hemispheres; nevermore to be starved of knowledge by mythology nor to be locked from innovation through unquestioned factual paradigms (Rokeach, 1960).

BIBLIOGRAPHY

Ackoff, Russell L. *On Purposeful Systems,* New York: Aldine-Atherton, 1972.

Allport, F.H. *Social Psychology,* Cambridge, Mass.: Houghton Mifflin, 1924.

Beard, Charles A. *Whither Mankind--A Panorama of Modern Civilization,* New York: Longmans, Green and Company, 1928.

Bever, T. G. and Chiarello, R. J. "Cerebral Dominance in Musicians and Non-Musicians." *Science,* 1974, 185, 537-39.

Bloom, Allen. *The Closing of the American Mind,* New York: Simon and Schuster, 1987.

Boorstin, Daniel J. *The Discoverers,* New York: Vintage Books, 1985.

Calvin, William H. *The Cerebral Symphony,* New York: Bantam Books, 1989.

Casne, Jill. *Successful Training Strategies,* San Francisco, Cal.: Jossey-Bass Publishers, Ind., 1988.

Corrick, James A. *The Human Brain--Mind and Matter,* New York: Arco Publishing, Ind., 1983.

Covey, Stephen R. *The Seven Habits of Highly Effective People.* New York: Simon and Schuster, 1989.

Csikszentmihalyi, Mihaly. *Flow--The Psychology of Optimal Experience,* New York: Harper and Row Publishers, 1990.

DeCamp, L. Sprague. *The Heroic Age of American Invention,* New York: Doubleday and Company, Inc., 1957.

Desborough, A. *Last Mycenaeans and Their Successors: An Archaeological Survey, c. 1200-1000 B.C.,* Oxford, Clarendon Press, 1964.

Drucker, Peter F. *Management: Tasks, Responsibilities, Practices,* New York: Harper and Row Publishers, Inc., 1973.

Dunlap, Knight. *Religion--Its Functions in Human Life--A Study of Religion from the Point of View of Psychology,* New York: McGraw-Hill Book Company, Inc., 1946.

Durant, Will. *The Study of Philosophy,* New York: Simon and Schuster, 1926.

Eckman P., Levenson, R.W., and Friesen, W.V. "Autonomic nervous system activity distinguishes among emotions." *Science,* 1983, 221, 1208-1210.

Education and The Economy, The National Center on America's Choice: *High Skills or Low Wages,* New York: The National Center of Education and The Economy, 1990.

Eicher, James. *Making the Message Clear,* Santa Cruz, Cal.: Grinder, Delozier and Assoc., Inc., 1987.

Erickson, E.H. "Growth and crises of the healthy personality." In C. Kluckhohn, H.A. Murrau and D.M. Schneider (Eds.), *Personality in nature, society and culture,* New York: Knopf, 1956, pp.185-225.

Erickson, Milton H. *Hypnotic Realities,* New York: Irvington Publishers, Inc., 1976.

Evans, Christopher. *The Micro Millenium,* New York: Simon and Schuster, 1979.

Fenichel, L. *The Psychoanalytic Theory of Neuroses,* New York: Norton, 1945.

Fischler, Martin A. and Firschein, Oscar. *Intelligence: the Eye, the Brain, and the Computer,* Reading, Massachusetts: Addison-Wesley Publishing Company, 1987.

Flowers, Vincent S. and Hughes, Charles L. *Value Systems Analysis: Theory and Management Application,* Dallas, Texas: Center for Values Research, 1978.

Fromm, Erich. *Man for Himself,* New York: Holt, Rinehart and Winston, 1947.

Gazzaniga, M.S. *The Bisected Brain,* New York: Appleton Century-Crofts, 1970.

Gazzaniga, M.S., LeDoux, J.E., Wilson, D.H. "Language, Praxis, and the right hemisphere: clue to some mechanisms of Consciousness." *Neurology,* 1977, 27, 1144-1147.

Haney, William V. *Communication-Patterns and Incidents,* Homewood, Ill.: Richard D. Irwin, Inc., 1960.

Hartman, H. "Comments of the Psychoanalytic theory of the Ego." *Psychoanalytic Studies of Children,* 1950, 5, 74-95.

Herrmann, Ned. *The Creative Brain,* Lake Lure, North Carolina: Brain Books, 1989.

The Change

Hogan, Gypsy "Your Job Skills are Becoming Out of Date." *The Daily Oklahoman,* 30 June 1991, pp.30.

Hunt, Morton. *The Universe Within,* New York: Simon and Schuster, 1982.

Jaynes, Julian. *The Origin of Consciousness in the Breakdown of the Bicameral Mind,* Boston: Houghton Mifflin Co., 1976.

Kuhn, Thomas S. *The Structure of Scientific Revolutions,* Chicago: The University of Chicago, 1962.

Lankton, Stephen R. and Lankton, Carol H. *Tales of Enchantment,* New York: Burnner/Mazel, Inc., 1989.

Large, Peter. *The Micro Revolution Revisited,* Orange, NJ: Rowman and Allenheld Company, 1984.

Lawler, E.E. and Porter, L.W. "The effect of performance on job satisfaction." *Industrial Relations,* 1967, 7, 20-28.

Martin, R.A. and Lefcourt, Herbert M. "Sense of humor as a moderator of the relation between stressors and moods. *Journal of Personality and Social Psychology,* 1983, 45, 1313-1324.

Maslow, Abraham H. *Toward a Psychology of Being,* New York: Litton Educational Publishing, Inc., 1968.

McGregor, Douglas. *The Human Side of Enterprise,* New York: McGraw-Hill Book Company, Inc. 1960.

Naisbitt, John. *Megatrends 2000,* New York: William Morrow and Co., Inc., 1990.

Ornstein, Robert D. *The Psychology of Consciousness,* New York: W.H. Freeman and Company. 1972.

Pelletier, Kenneth. *Toward A Science of Consciousness,* New York: Delta Publishing, 1978.

Penfield, Wilder and Perot, Phanor. "The Brain's Record of Auditory and Visual Experience, A Final Summary and Discussion." *Brain,* 1963, 86, 595-702.

Penrose, Roger. *The Emperor's New Mind,* New York: Oxford University Press, 1989.

Restak, Richard M. *The Mind,* New York: Bantam Books, 1988.

Rokeach, Milton. *The Open and Closed Mind,* New York: Basic Books, Inc., 1960.

Skinner, B.F. *Verbal Behavior,* New York: Appleton Century-Crofts, 1957.

Sperry, R.W. "Bridging Science and Values--A Unifying View of Mind and Brain." *American Psychologist*, 1977, 32, 237-245.

Springer, S.P. and Deutsch, G. *Left Brain, Right Brain,* San Francisco: California, W.,H. Freeman. 1985.

Stetson, Harlan True. *Man and the Stars,* New York: Whittlesey House, 1930.

Thilly, Frank. *A History of Philosophy,* New York: Henry Holt and Company, 1914.

Toffler, Alvin. *Powershift,* New York: Bantam Books, 1990.

Wallace, Anthony F.C. "Revitalization Movements." *American Anthropologist*, 1956, 58 264-281.

Ward, Lester F. *Dynamic Sociology, Vol 1,* New York: D. Appleton and Company, 1898.

Wells, H.G. *The Outline of History, Vol, 1 and 2,* New York: Doubleday and Company, Inc., 1971.

Wigner, E.P. *Symmetries and Reflections, Scientific Essays,* Cambridge, Mass.: M.I.T. Press, 1970.

Wurman, Richard Saul. *Information Anxiety,* New York: Doubleday and Company, Inc., 1989.

APPENDIX

ADDITIONAL TRAINING MATERIALS

As the five Cultural Change Modules found in this book are being implemented, the need arises continually for stories and illustrations that bring important concepts to life.

In this section, there are sixty (60) such stories and illustrations that will allow the trainer to pick and choose in order to aid employees in getting the deeper meaning and application of change in their lives.

As you look through the Topical Index on the following pages, may these selections become the salt and pepper of your training experiences!

TOPICAL INDEX

Page

- 336 The Self-Fulfilling Prophecy
- 337 The Power of Focus
- 338 Paying the Price to Believe in a Dream
- 339 Listening in Sales
- 340 Putting the Customer First
- 341 Ownership of Our Actions
- 342 The Skill of Change
- 343 Management Becoming Coaches
- 344 Attributes for Success
- 345 Time Management
- 346 Patience
- 347 Enjoy Today
- 348 Job Classifications
- 349 Importance of Attitude
- 350 Understanding Habits
- 351 Decision Making
- 352 Emotional Flexibility
- 353 Visioning Our Future
- 354 Business Success
- 355 Quality Begins in the Mind
- 356 Buzzwords
- 357 The Importance of Failure
- 358 The Computer's New Job
- 359 Long Range Planning
- 360 Mental Gravity
- 361 Learning is a Journey
- 362 How We Present Ourselves
- 363 Childhood Lessons
- 364 Satisfaction
- 365 Re-Setting Goals

Page

366 Thinking Employees
367 Encouraging Strengths
368 Perfectionism
369 Mental Creation
370 A New Motion Picture
371 Hard Work is Not Enough
372 Life is Not Fair
373 Use of Mental Focus
374 Dream Breakers
375 Staying on Track
376 Building Resources
377 Effective Optimism
378 Change Takes Time
379 You Get What You Expect
380 Types of Education
381 Love Challenges
382 Peace of Mind
383 Effective Speaking
384 A Sense of Humor
385 The Pain of Learning
386 The Importance of Information
387 The Perfect Exercise
388 Positive Stress
389 Being an Individual
390 Clear Goals
391 Transforming Arguments
392 Self-Promotion
393 Listening Skills
394 Self-Fulfillment
395 Owning Our Vision of the Future

The Self-Fulfilling Prophecy

Herb was doing great at his job until a new manager came on board...

The new manager was just as skilled and understanding as Herb's previous boss - but Herb fell victim to the Self-Fulfilling Prophecy.

After working for ten years with the same supervisor, Herb was introduced to Bill, the new supervisor. Herb began to assume that since this person was new and different there would be problems. Herb immediately said to himself "This guy doesn't shake hands the same." After several days on the job Herb noticed that the new supervisor responded to his requests but did it differently.

We really don't know if Herb adapted to the new supervisor or if Herb's fear of change blocked his ability to continue to enjoy working with the company. A natural process of our mind can be to expect the worst in new situations. Sometimes we've got to step back and realize that quite often new situations can indeed be as good or better than old circumstances.

Remember: To create your future, you owe it to yourself to welcome positive change.

The Power of Focus

Astronomers discovered centuries ago that gazing at the sky with the broad view of the naked eye left a lot unseen. Now we're discovering the same truth about the focusing power of the mind...

Just as a telescope allows an astronomer to focus in on important areas in the far distance, mental focus takes our brain power and directs it like a laser beam toward actions that build our future.

Former bodybuilder, now actor and successful businessman, Arnold Schwarzenegger developed his abilities through focus. One of Arnold's training partners once related he was doing several sets of exercises with Arnold and said to him, "Boy, Arnold, we have 14 sets to go." Arnold's reply to the fellow trainer was, "No. We have only one. The one we are working on right now."

Remember: To create our future, as an individual and as a nation, we can achieve anything we desire, but not everything. We owe it to ourselves to set our priorities and focus all of our energies on them.

Paying the Price to Believe in a Dream

When everyone around you tells you you're stupid for holding onto your dream, you have several choices as to how you can handle it. And for each choice you pay a price...

If you were a fledgling writer just offered $360,000 for a script at a time when you had only a hundred dollars to your name - would you turn it down? Unless he could star in the movie, one writer did.

His power of focus was based upon the strength of his dream. You see, he wanted to be an actor and finally began writing screen plays as a vehicle into acting. He had received hundreds of 'nos' until finally a screenplay was accepted. The studio took the screen play not for $360,000. but on his condition that he would star in the movie - he had to settle for much less but he held onto his dream.

The movie 'Rocky' won many awards and today Sylvester Stallone has reaped the financial benefit of taking the risk to prove his acting as well as his writing ability.

Remember: To create your future, you owe it to yourself to pay a smaller price now for bigger rewards in the future.

Listening in Sales

Perfecting your sales skills should not be just to sell something...

Sales persons are always thought of as selling a good or service. True, that's how they make their living - but it's really not what they do - not the top sales people.

The finest in sales listen, determine the needs of the client and then they propose solutions to the client's needs. The client doesn't need their product. The client needs their own desires fulfilled.

The days of the boisterous salesperson - the backslapping, joke telling, hard line sales pitch person is fading away. No one likes to be pushed into a corner. Yes, we buy emotionally, but we buy emotionally to fulfill our own perceived needs.

All of us are salespeople every day of our lives. Every time we communicate information, we are asking somebody to buy it. Each of us can become a super salesperson in the game of life.

Remember: To create your future, you owe it to yourself to recognize and fulfill the needs of the people who are important to you.

Putting the Customer First

Are you a business owner? Or maybe a shopper? We're all shoppers aren't we? When was the last time you walked into a place of business and were ignored?...

Sometimes, even at the cash register - when you are ready to part with your hard earned cash - the clerk may be on the phone and just happens to notice you after a minute or so. We remember these experiences and sometimes we hold it against the business and we do our shopping elsewhere.

Customer appreciation can't be drummed into the employees by fear or threats. If you are a business owner - or wish you were - and could for a moment face those delinquent employees, what would you say? "Put yourself in my place," you might say. "Consider yourself to be that shopper. What consideration would you expect? Treat me like your boss - because it's my money that keeps your store and your job in existence."

It's true...the sales clerk is the chief salesperson for a store. They sell the store's image - either good or bad.

Remember: To create your future, lavish attention on the customer.

Ownership of Our Actions

Want to accomplish significant things without the pain that usually accompanies "work"?...

How often as adults have we approached an activity requiring discipline with a sense of dread? "This has to, ought to, must be, has got to be done," we say to ourselves and we roll up our sleeves and suffer through it. The act of discipline becomes, at times, tantamount to pain. For us to enjoy what we achieve - it has to be our game. That is, we must be doing it for a reward that is solely ours - not just to please others. I give an acid test during many of my seminars. I ask the question: "How many of you enjoy your work enough that you would continue without financial rewards or peer appreciation?"

Not as many hands go up as should. Life is too short not to find a profession or at least elements of what we do that bring us personally - Joy.

Remember: To create your future, your love of what you do is the final and greatest benefit you will ever receive from your labors in life.

The Skill of Change

If you don't want life to be boring - just stay in the workplace...

Virtually from the beginning of recorded history, people have chosen trades that shaped their worklife from youth to retirement. A person became a blacksmith and, in olden days, that even became a part of his name - Smith. Workplace experts are now saying that the average entrant into today's workplace will change jobs or be involved in major technical upgrades of work skills at least seven times during her work life. The only thing that will be constant now will be change.

No longer will one skill suffice to earn a living - unless you look at that vital skill as the skill of change - learning the process of adapting with the least amount of stress. The human mind is best suited for continuity - not constant upheaval. As humans we're on the verge of having to learn a new way to think of our lives and our work.

Remember: To create your future, you owe it to yourself to look at skills upgrading as one more step toward unlocking your full potential.

Management Becoming Coaches

If employers want commitment from employees - they had better become coaches...

Henry Ford had a great idea. He created the assembly line concept - making people parts of the total mechanism. They became cogs in the big wheel that produced cars and later other products in unprecedented numbers.

Much of Ford's success spurred the idea of scientific management: breaking every job down to its smallest components and training people to be parts of that giant machine known as the factory. No wonder more and more people during this century began to hate their jobs. Persons seek to be a complete system - not a cog in a wheel. To successfully face the future, management can no longer spur employees as though they were winding up and directing the energy of machines. Employees are their equal and must be treated as such.

Remember: To create your future, you owe it to yourself, whether as a manager or as an employee, to work as an equal toward a shared vision.

Attributes for Success

What is the perfect combination for success?...

Becoming successful is a lot like riding a bike. It's holistic. You have to become good at several different activities to succeed. You have to pedal and hold the handlebars and keep your balance.

If you fail at any one of those while riding a bike, it's as good as failing at all of them. Success in life involves a lot more than talent. Many young people start out with talent and no confidence. That's a bad combination. Or they have great confidence but little talent in that particular area.

Still others get it almost right with the confidence and the appropriate talent but with no perseverance. They don't stick with it.

Remember: To create your future, you owe it to yourself to be holistic - to combine appropriate talent, confidence and perseverance. It's a winning combination.

Time Management

Don't worry about trying to manage your time. It's impossible...

We are bombarded by hundreds of offers to help us manage our time better. But the truth is that time ticks along at the same speed regardless of what we do.

We have to concentrate on managing the activities that take place within a given amount of time. Scheduling is the ultimate solution. As long as scheduling doesn't become an end to itself. When we cease being goal oriented we lose our ultimate sense of direction.

Look at time as a highway that can get us to where we want to do - provided we know where we are going. Activities well executed on a day by day basis build a successful future. Time is always there - but our main question should be not "What does the future hold for me?" but "What do my activities hold for the future?"

Remember: To create your future, you owe it to yourself to manage your activities; then time will take care of itself.

Patience

The most powerful tool toward success sometimes isn't energy - it's patience...

I sometimes counsel stressed executives with this illustration: "If you were driving a hundred miles between two cities, going 65 mph and making excellent time - would you be impatient that you were not already there?"

The first answer I usually get is a definite "Of course not." Then after a moment's reflection comes the confession "Well, yes, I would be impatient." When we drive ourselves so hard in life that we don't enjoy the trip - we lose an important edge of success.

Our impatience at not yet arriving that leads to worry and stress is like the race car driver wondering why he isn't making better time while having one foot on the gas and the other partially on the brake.

Remember: To create your future, Put all your energy into what you do but for heaven's sake, have the patience to enjoy the ride.

Enjoy Today

Sometimes you can get a real clear view of what you want by standing face to face with what you don't want...

I have seen so many creative, talented people reach the end of their lives and look back, too late to create the future that they missed. It's more than sad - it's criminal. They robbed themselves of the passion of their lives through their failure to act.

Our life and our time - 24 hours a day - seems to be in such limitless supply that many times we treat it with contempt. The old man facing his last day of life with the pain of knowing that his dreams were never fulfilled is a sad story. But when it is our turn to face this day, whatever our age, we can have armed ourselves with the wisdom to find what we really want. Do it now.

Remember: To create your future, you owe it to yourself to treat every day as the opportunity that it is - and to keep in the back of your mind that life is short - let's face it.

Job Classifications

Unless you like shoeing horses and tanning animal skins, job descriptions may not be for you...

A hundred years ago, job descriptions in our society were obviously quite different from today's. However, they changed slowly over the years with the pace of technology. The speed of technological change is now intensifying and shows no sign of slowing down.

Rigid job descriptions are becoming a burden in today's workplace. More companies are shifting to a flex work approach in which job descriptions are painted with a broad brush that allows the employee to work and learn new skills in a wide area.

Into the year 2000, flexibility is the key. Rote non-thinking jobs are going to third world countries. The employee of the future will be largely self-managed.

Remember: To create your future, you owe it to yourself to become flexible in the skills you offer the workplace. It's good job insurance.

Importance of Attitude

If you want an effective organization - don't pattern it after a machine...

For much of the last four hundred years the human mind, and body for that matter, has been compared by philosophers to a machine. A functioning entity doing certain things in certain ways. Such a manner of thinking about the human condition can bring a comfortable feeling of security - but it's totally wrong.

In the workplace people are complex. It is much more accurate to say that an organization is an organism. The major failure of management has been to lose sight of the ecology of the workplace. There are many ripple effects and ramifications to any action among a group of people.

Attitude is the key - not a command to function in a certain way as you might push a button on a machine. Many times employees understand the attitudinal environment of a specific workplace much better than management. And that causes problems.

Remember: To create your future, you owe it to yourself to take attitudes into consideration when you function in any capacity in the workplace.

Understanding Habits

When you get up in the morning, how do you know that you are you and not someone else?...

Everyday when we awake after a night's sleep, we seem to have this amazing ability to remember who we are and all of our personal history. We take it for granted, but it is amazing just how much we are creatures of habit.

It is our habits and attitudes that form our personality and make us an individual. Do we realize just how little actual thinking we do in a typical day? Aren't we spending most of our waking hours responding, reacting and repeating programmed habits? There's certainly nothing wrong with that scenario - who wants to have to re-learn how to tie their shoes every morning?

Habits and attitudes are great as long as they are taking us where we want to go. Sometimes we need to step back and do some housecleaning - and get rid of habits and attitudes that are standing in the way of our future.

Remember: To create your future, you owe it to yourself to really know who you are. Know your habits and attitudes.

Decision Making

Having choices leads to the toughest part of life...

Rolling up our sleeves and tackling a job takes a lot of energy but, when we commit to it, it certainly can be both fun and challenging. The hardest, most agonizing part of life is usually making the decision as to what to do.

Have you ever noticed how much easier a task seems to be once we have committed to it? It's the making the decision to start that seems to sap the most energy from us. Generally speaking, when you have weighed the pros and cons and find a close to even balance between the two it's best sometimes to just make the choice and be done with it.

Highly successful individuals tend to gather their facts and then make their decisions quickly. They have learned to move past the decision stress factor as soon as possible.

Remember: To create your future, gather the facts but then quickly make your decisions. Being mired in indecision can sometimes be worse than making the wrong decision.

Emotional Flexibility

Did you know that your emotions need to be stretched just like your muscles?...

If you have ever been bed ridden you can remember the difficulty in getting back on your feet and toning long unused muscles. Just as well-toned muscles are essential to the functioning of the body so well-toned emotions create a strong mental balance.

In our society many times as a child we are told not to cry, not to show deep emotional feelings either happy or sad. We need to be little adults, we are told. Well, it seems that if we will look at some of those in society who have broken the mold, moved to the top of their field, we find persons who have deep emotional capacities - all the way from anger directed toward obstacles to deep tearful joy upon achieving a goal.

For an Olympian to cry upon the winner's platform or for a public official to express anger over misused funds are wonderful uses of the power of emotions. We learn to control what we exercise the most.

Remember: To create your future, you owe it to yourself to exercise your emotions.

Visioning Our Future

The past doesn't have to create the future - unless you let it...

If you create a motion picture in your mind's eye of you as a child growing and you speed up this picture, you will see all the events that seemed to shape your life into what it is today.

It does seem upon first glance that the past shapes our future. And it does - when we react to events that happen to us and set no firm vision for our future. If we are incredibly lucky and have a life long string of favorable events occur in our life - then things may be fine.

And yet, not really, because only when we vision the future that we want out of life do we greatly increase the likelihood that at the end of our days we will have achieved it.

We can stop being the victim of our past when we begin to mentally create the future we want. That mental projection allows us to create our future ahead of time.

Remember: To create your future, don't look to the past as your only guide - visualize the future you desire or you are doomed to repeat the past.

Business Success

The most apparently successful persons you see in the business world today may be setting themselves up for a fall...

Over the years I've seen many businesses large and small grow and die. One thing I have noticed is that the businessperson who embarks upon a business venture by renting the executive office suite, leasing the finest Mercedes - had better experience rapid immediate cash flow. Several who moved into a high capital outflow position and then experienced two or three slow months were financially washed out. On the other side of the coin, I have seen small companies - starting as a room in the home - experience slow but steady growth.

By purchasing equipment and supplies as their funds allowed and keeping their debt ratio lean, they saved so that when they were hit by several slow months or times of transition they were able to weather them well.

Remember: To create your future, you owe it to yourself to look past the ego high of having the finest immediately along with a high debt ratio and consider the power of slow and steady economic growth.

Quality Begins in the Mind

Our vast natural resources as a nation will fail us if we forget about quality...

In forty years a small isle with no natural resources has captured the global economic marketplace with quality. The quality Japan has produced came from information applied by team systems stressing individual responsibility.

Unless in our country we can teach commitment to a vision - we will find it hard to produce quality. Our grandchildren will not appreciate living in what could become a third world nation in its infrastructure, economy and quality of goods produced.

In 1989, according to one political economist, affiliates of foreign manufacturers created more jobs in the United States than American-owned manufacturing companies. The key to productivity is quality and the key to quality is emotional commitment - not just natural resources.

Remember: To create your future, you owe it to yourself to see that quality begins with the natural resource of the mind.

Buzzwords

Have you counted the buzzwords in your office? They are all around but are they doing any good?...

All the rage now are posters, signs, decals and even bumper stickers at work filled with buzzwords like "Teamwork Counts/ Quality is #1/Our Pride is Showing" or...well, you can think of others of your own.

No one can deny that there are big changes going on in the workplace, but the truth is that buzzwords and slogans can be an easy way to say that we're doing something when in truth, things are staying pretty much the same. Throughout history words have been tricky. Initially they can have significant - even profound meaning until they are institutionalized into meaningless slogans.

W. Edwards Deming expressed his disdain with such sayings because they can cheapen communication. You owe it to yourself to look at the deeper level of meaning in any slogan your company is using. Look for the real meaning.

Remember: To create your future - if the buzzword is just a word - it's a waste of time.

The Importance of Failure

Failing represents some of the most productive fun many of us have had in life...

How many of you learned to ride a bike when you were little? Most of you, right? Did you jump on the bike and start riding immediately? Or did you go through a learning process by falling off a few times?

I can remember falling off many times. And on a gravel road, I might add. I remember on one of those days, my mother called for me to come in for lunch and I yelled back, "I'm too busy riding my bike". I was actually busy falling off my bike.

My eyes were focused on the end result - the goal of successfully riding the bike. As children we naturally viewed failure as an important part of the learning process. We didn't fear it until we were later taught to fear it. There are no successes in life without failures as a part of the learning process to get us to our goals.

Remember: To create your future, you owe it to yourself to take calculated risks - don't take the failures personally - it's all part of the learning process to get you to your goal.

The Computer's New Job

The fact that computers are taking over a part of our brain isn't really bad news in the long run...

The development of computer systems over the past twenty years is rapidly bringing on line machines that will store, analyze, dissect, and interpret information for us. That used to be the function of the left hemisphere of the human brain: That's the part of our brain where the language system and sequential thought functions originate.

The fact that computers are replacing the need for us to spend countless hours doing sequential tasks will lead to massive retraining, job shuffling, and layoffs in the future. The ultimate result will be societies in which the creative potential of the mind will be highly valued.

A computer can analyze information - but it cannot be creative. That is the eternal providence of the human. As a matter of fact - it's our highest calling.

Remember: To create your future, begin a care and feeding program for your right brain. You will need it more and more in the future.

Long Range Planning

How many big weeds are we having to pull out of our lives because we have neglected to build a master plan?...

On a walk recently I watched a homeowner park his car and walk to an ill kept yard connected to an ill kept house. On the way down the walk the man literally stumbled over a huge weed. In anger the man kicked the weed - pulled it out and went on his way.

It was a rather funny sight to see. I've seen the very same form of activity management in many companies I've counseled. If the homeowner had created a yearly master plan for proper herbicide and fertilizer - the obnoxious weed would have never appeared.

Crisis management is reaction, in most cases, to events that could have been made much easier if planned for in advance. Acting with foresight and avoiding problems can be so much more fun than becoming surrounded with problems that have been growing for some time.

Remember: To create your future, you owe it to yourself to set up housekeeping by planning long range. Develop a system that will minimize the occurrence of emergencies.

Mental Gravity

Once we learn to walk we conquer physical gravity. Now that we're older there is one more gravity to defeat...

Why is it that so many rise to their lowest common denominator? Why are dreams, aspirations and deep desires so quickly smothered by daily routine and mediocrity? How many have you met who started with great hopes and settled for much less?

Just as there is a physical gravity which our muscles must be exercised to overcome, there is a negative mental gravity which we must gear our mental skills to defeat. To keep a dream alive requires falling in love with it and persistently working toward it.

When we let thoughts of defeat crowd into our mind - we begin to succumb to negative mental gravity and we begin to fall.

Remember: To create your future, use your brain as a muscle. Hold your goals constantly in front of you and mentally move past obstacles by developing the strength of determination and persistence.

Learning is a Journey

Did you know that you're in trouble when you know it all? Or, do you already know all about that?...

One of the most educated individuals I have ever known made a statement to me once that bears repeating. He said, "The more I know about any given subject, the more I then realize there is yet to learn."

I would like to engrave that comment and present it as a gift to some in management with whom I have worked over the years. I have seen employees approach them with ideas to be cut off quickly with, "I know all about that" or "That's already been considered."

When we stop and think about it, we realize that in all probability the best ideas haven't even been thought of yet. Saying "I know all about that" is a red flag, a danger signal that we have become inflexible toward new possibilities.

Remember: To create your future, learning is a lifelong journey with no "I finally know it all" destination.

How We Present Ourselves

Only seven percent of what you say has to make any sense...

One noted researcher determined that 55 percent of what we convey during face to face communication is nonverbal - that is, body language, manner of dress, and physical presence. Another 38 percent is voice tone, inflection and speed. Leaving only 7 percent of actual communication involving the words that we speak.

One story tells of a famous actress during the 1930's who came to America to receive an award. She was surrounded at a party by hostesses pleading with her to recite a portion of her lines from a famous play. She finally agreed and recited in her language. As she finished the emotional recital there was not a dry eye in the room.

"How can we thank you?" one hostess gushed. The actress, known for pranks, confessed, "I did a terrible thing. I was just reciting my native alphabet over and over."

Remember: To create your future, think about what you usually don't think about - the way that you present what you are saying.

Childhood Lessons

If all the excitement seems to be gone from life - take a lesson from your childhood...

Remember in our youth how everyday seemed to be a great adventure? And even time seemed to pass more slowly. Learning and experiencing new things was an important part of life.

Today, in modern society, we become confined in a circle of activities that translates into our work and leisure time. Sometimes we find ourselves going through the routine just because the routine is there: and the excitement in life is gone. The solution:

Remember: To create your future, strike out into a new direction in your personal life - and eventually perhaps in your business life. Begin on a small scale doing things that you have always wanted to do. And, most of all, do it for the fun of it. Let the child still in you take you by the hand on an exciting adventure. Excitement will come back into your life.

Satisfaction

If you are satisfied with your life, maybe you shouldn't be...

There is no reason in the world for anyone not being happy with themselves, regardless of their current conditions. Just being alive and having the potential that every human possesses is reason enough to be happy.

Only we can deny ourselves that privilege. But being happy with our potential doesn't mean we should be satisfied with the level at which we are achieving utilizing that potential. Growth is achieved through creative frustration.

One writer summed it up, " Writing is a part of my happiness but it hurts when I do it." Think of the process of achievement as growing pains. No person should ever be satisfied with her life. There is too much to do, too much to achieve and the price of the effort to achieve it is small compared to the feeling of accomplishment.

Remember: To create your future, be happy with who you are, but always reach with creative frustration toward your full potential.

Re-Setting Goals

Unless we know how to deal with it, reaching our goals can be the biggest problem we'll ever have to face...

Perhaps you've heard the story of the athlete who spent years in training, sweating and straining to build the endurance, strength, and capacity to win in the Olympics. His hard work paid off. The medals were won.

Days after the winning, the awards were framed on his wall. A sense of letdown began to creep over him and the question formed: What now?

This athlete had directed all his visions and goals toward the medals and now his future was finished - because he had set no future goals. Some such athletes live the rest of their lives in the hollow glory of the past - never achieving much again. Others who have learned the secret start anew and build fresh challenges that they can fall in love with.

Remember: To create your future, success and learning is a journey not a destination.

Thinking Employees

Until businesses allow their employees to think - they will never get their money's worth...

Real thinking in any human mind goes through four stages. There is a vision, a possibility, we get interested and excited about that possibility - then we develop information to do something about it and finally we achieve something related to that possibility.

In most organizations employees are told what to do and expected to do it. That doesn't require thinking in a real sense. It just requires reacting to the information management has provided.

Some companies are now turning their employees' attitudes around by sharing the company vision with them and asking them to develop the processes to bring the company vision into reality.

When employees are given the full scope of opportunity to think - an avalanche of ideas and enthusiasm happens.

Remember: To create your future, put yourself in a position to think about what you are doing - don't just react.

Encouraging Strengths

Education should help isolate and encourage our strengths, not depress us with our weaknesses...

Many studies highlight the role of self-esteem in effective learning. It all boils down to this: If we believe we can - we can.

From the earliest grades, education can be made to keep its magical adventurous qualities by emphasizing for each student his positive achievements within his greatest areas of strength.

As people are encouraged to build and grow in areas of their greatest potential and interest; it becomes much easier for trained educators to lead the student into uncharted water - into areas that do not come as easily to the student.

When we're winning lots of victories in our fun areas - we're much stronger in attacking new challenges.

Remember: To create your future, nothing encourages achievement better than emphasis on your past successes.

Perfectionism

Seeking perfection is a quick way to become unhappy...

How many times have you heard someone say, "I'll sure be happy when that is over" or "Once that promotion comes through I'll sure be happy." If you turn those statements around it's as though the person is saying, "I've decided to refrain from being happy until such and such happens."

It's enough to make you think that we seem to want to ration our happiness, as though it were a limited commodity. If you wait for the perfect time, the perfect place, the perfect circumstances to be happy. Forget it. Happiness will never come.

Perfection isn't possible. It's an elusive rainbow you'll never reach. Life isn't perfect. Only one thing is for certain, as one nineteenth century philosopher said, "Most people are about as happy as they make up their minds to be."

Remember: To create your future, live up to your highest potential - but don't make life a search for perfection.

Mental Creation

Everything is created twice - first in our minds and then in our lives...

The pre-frontal lobe of the human brain is a marvelous piece of matter. We are the only creatures in the world with as large a frontal cap on our brain.

It allows us to visualize possibilities ahead of time. It makes it possible for us to plan our life in advance and then develop processes to bring those plans into reality. It's really amazing when we think about it. That is, when we think.

If we go through life buying into other's beliefs and expectations about us - we are simply reacting to life. Others are in essence planning our future for us. I guess in that case we really don't need a prefrontal lobe. We can just live life day to day and see what happens.

We only need that marvelous part of our brain if we wish to set our own visions and dreams for the future. When we don't set a planned course for the future of our life - it is as though we had no prefrontal lobe. We diminish ourselves to the level of a nonthinking creature.

Remember: To create your future, you owe it to yourself to plan your future for yourself.

A New Motion Picture

We all have a motion picture theater in our heads. Seen any good movies lately?...

How often after making a mistake or getting a negative response do we find ourselves playing back that mistake or negative response over and over in the theater of our mind?

As we play this negative thing back we feel again the hurt, the embarrassment of that moment. It is as though we are getting a perverse kick out of emphasizing a negative situation.

We are now discovering that by putting a new motion picture in the place of the mistake or negative response we can program ourselves to avoid repeating the old negative behaviors.

We can just as easily run a motion picture in our mind of us responding successfully to that situation in which we flopped. We can go ahead and feel the joy and self esteem that comes from knowing we have the confidence and power to do things well.

Remember: To create your future, you owe it to yourself to select the motion picture you want to run in the theater of your mind.

Hard Work Is Not Enough

For those times when even hard work doesn't seem to get you anywhere, there is a solution...

When all the hard work and effort we put into something important in our lives seems to have about the same effect as butting our head against a brick wall - it's time to change our actions.

One definition of insanity that we all fall victim to from time to time is in continuing to do the same actions expecting different results. When what we are doing isn't getting us where we want to go - it's not that we are imperfect, it's not that we are dumb, it's not that other people are out to get us - it's just that we need to change what we are doing and move on to a new set of actions.

That's not always easy when the old set of actions have become habitual. Breaking habits takes time and it takes thinking - thinking about what we are doing and why we're doing it.

Remember: To create your future, the best way out of an impasse is to do things differently - and see what happens.

Life is Not Fair

Sometimes the hardest pill to swallow is that life isn't perfect...

My five year old is constantly reminding me that life isn't fair and what am I going to do about it. Somebody does something that he doesn't like and he screams, "That's not fair." "You're right," I reply, "life isn't fair. But that's the way it happens to be." He doesn't like that answer. But if life were always fair - there would be no growth and development.

Controlled conflict inside society and within ourselves is what brings deeper growth and insight. The founders of our country studied what other societies had done for thousands of years to deal with the fact that life isn't fair. Our constitution is based upon division of powers - it's based upon controlled conflict.

When everyone agrees on everything growth stops, or, I should say, it's suppressed because as long as humans will be humans the best we can hope for is controlled conflict.

Remember: To create your future, take the time to learn from differences and disputes.

Use of Mental Focus

Focusing on the immediate can either build us or leave us empty...

In setting long range goals, I believe that everyone would agree that they have to be developed one day at a time. The concentration that we place on such activities leading toward a final accomplishment is a natural ability of the mind.

We can use it in two different ways. If we form a visual and emotional picture of something we wish to achieve and then break down the activities that must be accomplished to bring that future into reality, we have ripe fodder for the power of focus.

For too many people, their daily focus is based upon diversions that are not linked to a future goal. It's like daily focus occurring at random, by accident- based upon whatever seems interesting that day, e.g., a TV program.

Random use of focus is a long term waste. Sometimes we don't really comprehend the immensity of the waste until the latter years of our life.

Remember: To create your future, focus a part of your energy every day on your long term goals.

Dream Breakers

Do you listen to Dream Breakers? If you do, stop it...

"I know you really want to do that," someone will say, "but don't be too disappointed if it doesn't turn out, after all," they will say, "very few people have accomplished it."

Yes, very few people have accomplished it - very few people have accomplished anything that takes dedicated effort, discipline, and persistence if they listen to the Dream Breakers. Dream Breakers are all around you. They work along-side you, they visit you on the week ends and maybe, just maybe, they sleep with you at night.

These are not bad people or people who wish you harm. On the contrary, they are well intentioned people who just don't really believe that things above a certain level of accomplishment can really be achieved - at least not by them or by you.

The Dream Breakers - you can love them, care for them, even pity them - just don't listen to them.

Remember: To create your future, listen to the DreamMakers in your own head, not the Dream-Breakers standing beside you.

Staying on Track

To accomplish long term tasks we need lots of feedback...

If you were shooting a cannon over a high hill to hit a target not seen by you, you might just fire and fire and fire until you thought you hit it. Not a good idea, Right? Next would be to have a spotter at the top of the hill to yell to you. "Pretty good shot. You almost hit it." Still not a great idea, right?

What if your spotter said " A little to the left - you're getting close." Much better information, right?

A young lady some years ago who lost the use of her arms due to brain injury utilized a neuroelectronic monitor to see the tiniest electrical signals being sent from her muscles and using that feedback she literally grew new neural circuits in her brain to bypass injured areas. She regained the use of her arms.

Remember: To create your future, seek the most specific feedback possible as you work toward a long term goal. It's vital information for staying on track.

Building Resources

The best reason for buying a book may not be to sit down and read it all...

Years ago I visited a friend who seemed quite knowledgeable in many areas. I looked over his library and asked. "You've read all these books?" "No, they are for reference. When I need information on just about anything, I can find it," he said as he gestured toward the bookcase that filled one side of his study. "It began as a habit of buying at least a book a month either by mail or from a local book store"

I saw the result of his habit - 2,000 books on subjects from outer space to psychology. He explained that after buying a book he would scan the book - read some high points and become familiar enough with the book to have it always available as a reference.

He also made one comment that has always stuck with me. "It isn't how much you know that matters - it's knowing what you need to know. And when I need to know something I know where to find it."

Remember: To create your future, build a reference library to stay up with what you need to know from the current information avalanche.

Effective Optimism

Just being optimistic about the light at the end of the tunnel doesn't mean you won't get smashed by the train...

There are two components to what I call effective optimism. We have all run into people who are all excited about this or that business venture. Rose color glasses they have on. Everything is wonderful. Nothing bad can happen.

They are in seventh heaven until the challenging specifics of the business reality set in. Then you see them six months later - once again excited about another idea that just can't fail. They have enthusiasm, but they don't have enough facts.

Effective optimism is based upon gathering the necessary information to determine that your dream has a possibility for success and building ahead of time a detailed plan to achieve that dream. Effective optimism is the belief that a well prepared plan can succeed. It isn't overplanning - it is the balance between reasonable planning and rushing headlong toward the rainbow.

Remember: To create your future, do enough research to give power to your optimism.

Change Takes Time

Change is fun to talk about - but have you ever tried doing it?...

The coming change in business to self-managed teams is emotionally upsetting at first to both workers and management. If you are a worker having always been told what to do - how do you respond when someone begins giving you responsibility to determine how you do your job?

Sounds great - but it takes some time to get used to. If you are management - how do you begin to feel comfortable becoming a coach instead of a giver of specific directions? How do you overcome the deep seated desire to look over the workers' shoulders and continue to direct them to do the work the way you would want it done - even if their self-managed approach takes care of the work just as well or better?

Remember: To create our future, as employee or manager, change takes a process to happen. And team management is essential for quality in a global marketplace.

You Get What You Expect

Watch out for what you expect - you probably will get it...

I was watching a TV sitcom recently - two business partners in the series were arguing and one exclaimed, "What do you mean - how dare I contradict you? I haven't even said anything about that!" and the other partner replied, "No, but you were about to."

Research has shown that our attitude shapes our expectations in the workplace. The power of that shaping is done through body language and voice tone. While few people will come up to you and say, "I'm depressed and I expect this to be a lousy day"; they will nonetheless tell you the same even more powerfully through their actions. Others will usually react to them according to their expectations.

The person, on the other hand, with strong positive expectations can control a group or department by acting in a way that encourages others to live up to their highest potential.

Remember: To create your future, you don't get what you want out of life - you get what you expect.

Types of Education

There are three types of educated people - Which one are you?...

Among any people who have been exposed to education - that's basically all of us - there are, first, the Undereducated. This is the person who knows there is a lot more to be learned about virtually everything and that he or she will never have learned it all by the end of their life. The search for knowledge is an endless journey. The Undereducated person asks a lot of questions.

The second category is the Ignorant. They have learned enough to get by and they have stopped asking questions. Life is a circle - get up go to work, watch TV, go to bed, get up go to work - well, you get the idea. They are good hardworking people who have stopped asking questions. They can join the ranks of the Undereducated if they choose.

Finally there are Stupid people. Many times they are highly educated. They know everything. They never ask questions, because they already know all the answers.

Remember: To create your future, ask a lot of questions - education is a journey not a destination.

Love Challenges

When the mama bird throws the baby bird out of the nest - it's time to fly...

Isn't it amazing how creative and innovative we can become when our back is against the wall - when circumstances demand action. When it's time to jump out of the nest and fly - somehow we find the wings.

The creative aspect of our mind, numbed by daily rituals of habit and routine, is brought back to life in times of crisis - when we lose our job, when a loved one dies, when someone we care about is in trouble. It's in times of great challenge when we learn how far we can reach - how much we can grow.

William James equated the normal use of the mind to the wiggling of the little finger while keeping the rest of the enormous physical potential of the body in reserve. Our best mental resources are seldom called upon except in times of crisis.

Remember: To create your future, don't hate challenges. Use them as weights to grow mentally stronger.

Peace of Mind

When greeting others - why do we always say "Hello" or "How are you?"...

In one yet underdeveloped part of the world there are clans of nomadic tribesmen who greet one another with this question "Do you have peace of mind?" That is the closest their phrase will translate into English.

They don't look at the neighbor's BMW, the way she keeps her grass cut, the prestige of her job. This nomadic tribe asks a simple question that cuts through all the nonsense and goes to the heart of our existence: "Do you have peace of mind?" They don't ask, "How's the size of your bank account?" or "Did your daughter make it to the best college?"

Instead they are on a journey through life that is valued based upon peace of mind, which, researchers have now discovered, pays us with a premium that is rather priceless - a longer healthier life.

Remember: To create your future, choose peace of mind first, then add the toys.

Effective Speaking

When was the last time a friend visited with you and pulled out notes to read his or her comments...

When we speak one on one, we speak what we feel. When we speak in front of a group, a metamorphosis occurs - we believe that we will forget everything we know - so we take a script or copious notes with us. We become a different person in front of an audience.

As master of ceremonies I have visited during lunch with many an animated speaker - full of wit and fun only to experience a totally different person on the podium reading a speech with no personality.

Audiences hunger to hear from people who will converse with them. They long to be entertained as a witty conversation entertains. As an audience we want to see, feel, and enjoy a person's real personality.

When you enjoy speaking, we enjoy listening to you - when you do that we won't remember your mistakes - we'll remember your message.

Remember: To create your future, when you speak to an audience, relax and speak to each of us as friends.

A Sense of Humor

Having a sense of humor is a serious matter...

It took a Norman Cousins to show us that laughter can be not only fun but lifesaving. Each of us can discover in our own individual way that a sense of humor can help us keep life's challenges in perspective.

When we visit with persons who seem to grow through challenges - who seem to be stronger for the experience of tribulations - we find in those people a sense of humor about their past disasters and disappointments.

When we are around those who have become bitter with life - we find no sense of humor or growth toward greater visions. A sense of humor is really a sense of the power that each of us has to bring order to our lives, to determine for ourselves how we will feel about what life deals us.

The most successful people who have come back from the depths of failure can laugh about it.

Remember: To create your future, cultivate your sense of humor about life - it's a great power.

The Pain of Learning

The pain of learning has a good side - think about it...

There is something called the Learning Curve. As we move away from an old habit and old way of doing something; there can be pain. Have you ever experienced learning a new software package for your computer? More of us will as time goes by.

The Learning Curve is rough at first because our mind is constantly trying to tie all the new things we are learning to our old ways of doing them. The end result? Initial confusion, frustration, and sometimes the question, "Am I ever going to learn this?"

Something amazing happens after a period of time and the learning begins to make sense - the pain is eased and the excitement of beginning mastery comes over us.

Remember: To create your future, as you learn new things you will always face the Learning Curve. There is a period of confusion and frustration, that's the price of learning. In the long run, it's a small price to pay.

The Importance of Information

Life and sailing are a lot more fun when we know what is going to be in front of us...

Actually, I mentioned sailing because nobody who sails want to crash into the rocks due to poor planning. Many careers end up crashing on unexpected shores for lack of information about that particular career.

There was a very famous writer who, before he sent out his early manuscripts, read book after book about the trials and tribulations of successful writers. He gleaned a panoramic view of what lay ahead of him in that great chasm that separates the novice writer from the well compensated professional.

First of all he loved writing, but he then knew that he would get a lot of rejection slips - and he did. But he knew that other great writers had also.

Remember: To create your future, it makes the path toward a successful career much easier when you have the information that enables you to know the areas of frustrations and disappointment that have greeted others pursuing the same goals. If they can make it; so can you.

The Perfect Exercise

If you have time to think - you have time for the perfect exercise...

We would all be amazed if we really knew how many decisions were made, ideas hatched and problems solved while the thinker was engaged in the act of walking. Walking, from a medical view, is the nearly perfect exercise. It brings all the body into play.

It is aerobic - it strengthens the heart without undue punishment on the ligaments and bones. In addition many dedicated walkers will swear by the fact that their best ideas come to them during their walks. Does the blood flow better to the brain? Does the rhythmic motion of the body stimulate thought?

Something happens - and ideas flow. Two miles a day at a brisk pace - that's a 30 minute walk - 5 days a week and your doctor will smile at you. I have a suspicion that you'll come up with some new, exciting and possibly profitable ideas during your 2 and a half hours per week doing this perfect exercise.

Remember: To create your future, walk toward it.

Positive Stress

Have you had any real excitement in your life recently? Remember, your body needs it...

Moving toward a goal that we have set - striving toward a challenge stimulates the body and mind - provided that we have made the decision that what we are doing is important to us. There must be an ownership of the challenge. There is a stress to achieving challenges - but it is a positive stress. Research is beginning to reveal that without this wonderful thing known as positive stress - our body and mind do not grow to their full potential.

We certainly want to avoid negative stress - that's being a victim and having no control over our outcomes. Negative stress, when we feel trapped, is devastating to the physical body. Positive stress is setting a goal, developing a plan to reach it, and focusing our physical and mental energies toward the area of achievement we desire.

Remember: To create your future, enjoy the excitement of positive stress.

Being an Individual

How can one become more of the individual one wants to be? It has a lot to do with goals...

We have many opportunities to react to the multitude of standards and expectations engendered by society. Many of these are good and very helpful - such as driving on the right side of the road and stopping at stop signs. However, for each of us to become our individual selves and not just a reflection of current opinions - we have to accept the opportunity to create unique visions of our own goals and expectations in life.

Each time we bring one of those visions into reality through our own efforts we become more of a unique individual. While accepting all the values and expectations around us can be safe and comfortable - it allows little individual creative growth.

Our personal identity and self confidence grow stronger when we invest our energy in the goals we have chosen to pursue just for the joy of it.

Remember: To create your future, you owe it to yourself to be more than the sum total of society's expectations - you owe it to yourself to be your own creation.

Clear Goals

It's time to make your goals come alive...

When was the last time you hopped into the car, maybe put your dog in the back seat along with packed suitcases, and headed off on a trip without having the slightest idea as to where you were going?

Never? You mean you always took a map along or you relied on a mental picture of the way to your destination in order to get there? Well, how accurate did the map have to be to get you to your travel goal? It had to show the road and highway numbers?

What if the map had been faded because something had been spilled on it? You could barely make out the highway marker and numbers, so you had to guess.

If we have a poor map or hazy memory of our destination, we may not reach it.

Remember: To create your future, you must paint mental stroke by mental stroke, with the paint brush of your thoughts and desires, a clear, crisp mental picture of your goals in life.

Transforming Argument

In your personal or business life - do you want an argument or a solution?...

Here's some great argument material: "If you are going to be as unreasonable as you were last time we discussed this - then let's skip it." or "Since my problem is trivial, I'd rather not take up your time."

Almost any emotional response to those statements will lead to problems unless we come back with a question - such as "Help me understand. How have I been unreasonable?" or "Help me understand. How is your problem trivial?"

Your tone of voice when asking the question must, of course, be sincere. Sincere questions, rather than retorts, kill arguments and begin to create understanding.

Remember: To create your future, by asking someone who wishes to argue to further explain their needs - you take the wind out of their sails. You move from the problem to a search for solutions.

Self-Promotion

If you don't sell yourself - nobody else will...

I've seen many on a career path continue their learning processes - stay current with technical expertise in their field - and yet not grow in the company. They had the goods but they were not marketing themselves to their employer.

The company must be kept continually aware of new skills you have developed. You must toot your own horn and do it in the right way, such as volunteering for new tasks and assignments or being the first to take the time to learn the new software package the company has purchased.

Being aggressive in demonstrating your increased usefulness to the company will be even more critical in the years of significant change that face all of us. As long as you can back up your words with action - make the people key to your growth in the company aware not only of your expertise but your desire and active involvement in learning more.

Remember: To create your future, you must market yourself within your company as though the company were your client.

Listening Skills

Is the running commentary in your head keeping you from understanding others?...

A manager in the depth of confusion contacted me. Her employees had given feedback that she did not listen to their needs and problems. "I'll have to start having more meetings," she told me. "How often do you sit down and listen to employees?" I asked. "I currently have weekly meetings - I can make it twice a week," she said. "That's not what I asked," I replied. "I asked how often do you listen to your employees?"

She was confused at first about my question. I learned that when she had an employee in her office, she would be listening to her own judgments about that person as he talked. She didn't hear what the person was saying.

She responded with what she thought the person needed. The employee's talking to her could have been eliminated and the results would have been the same. She didn't realize what she was doing.

Remember: To create your future, listening means we focus on what is being said. Then we can communicate to them with understanding.

Self-Fulfillment

When was the last time that you visited that special place where you really live?...

Perhaps it's a song from the long past that reminds you of a special time. Maybe it's an award - reminding you of a past accomplishment. It may be your child or another loved one being close to you - and away you go to that special place.

There is deep within each of us a room where our most intense feelings live. When we are in that special room we know what wonderful things we are capable of. We know how much we can love, how much we can care, how much we can achieve.

Through most of our daily life the door to that room is closed and we are on the outside. To live - to really live - we need to be in that room as much as possible.

Remember: To create your future, you cannot afford to lock yourself out of that special room where your deepest thoughts, feelings and desires live. Your real future is in that room.

Owning Our Vision of the Future

What do you really own? Are you sure?...

When natural disasters cause devastation, the electronic media brings the ones suffering loss right into our homes. We see the fate suffered by those who lost everything due to a major hurricane. In the eyes of some victims we see total loss. Complete emptiness. Yet in the eyes of others there is a twinkle, a power.

What do we really own? All can be swept away, but the power we have to create a vision of our future and bring it into reality can never be taken away from us unless we give it away.

How many of us envision deeply and meditate emotionally upon OUR vision of the future? Or are we just reacting daily to whatever happens to us?

When we just react we give up OUR power to create. Life is not perfect and it's not fair - but we stack the cards in our favor when we plan our own future.

Remember: To create your future, create a detailed vision of that future and emotionally move toward it. That is the only power that is ours and ours alone.

-NOTES-

-NOTES-

-NOTES-

-NOTES-

-NOTES-